.G

ROYAL HISTORICAL SOCIETY
STUDIES IN HISTORY 51

THE TERRITORIAL ARMY
1906 – 1940

THE TERRITORIAL ARMY
1906 – 1940

Peter Dennis

THE ROYAL HISTORICAL SOCIETY
THE BOYDELL PRESS

© Peter Dennis 1987

First published 1987

Published for the Royal Historical Society by
The Boydell Press
an imprint of Boydell & Brewer Ltd
PO Box 9   Woodbridge   Suffolk IP12 3DF
and Wolfeboro, New Hampshire 03894-2069, USA

ISBN 0 86193 208 0

British Library Cataloguing in Publication Data
Dennis, Peter, *1945-*
The territorial army, 1906-1940. — (Royal
Historical Society studies in history series,
ISSN 0269-2244 ; no. 51)
1. Great Britain. *Army. Territorial Army* —
History
I. Title   II. Royal Historical Society
III. Series
355.3'7'0941   UA661
ISBN 0-86193-208-0

Library of Congress Cataloging-in-Publication Data applied for

Printed and bound in Great Britain
by Short Run Press Ltd, Exeter

Contents

The Society records its gratitude to the following whose generosity made possible the initiation of this series: The British Academy; The Pilgrim Trust; The Twenty-Seven Foundation; The United States Embassy's Bicentennial funds; The Wolfson Trust; several private donors.

Acknowledgements

I wish to thank the directors and staffs of the libraries and archives that I visited in the course of my research, especially the Public Record Office, the Scottish Record Office, the Imperial War Museum, the many County Record Offices listed in the bibliography, and the Massey Library, RMC Kingston. I am especially grateful to the Council of Territorial and Volunteer Reserve Associations, the East Anglia TA&VR Association, the North of England TA&VR Association, and the Lowlands TA&VR Association, which allowed me to examine the Territorial Army records in their possession and to quote from them as I have wished, and whose respective Secretaries were so accommodating to my requests. The interpretation of this material, and indeed of the other records I have consulted, is mine alone. I am also grateful to the following for permission to use the records that they control: the Earl of Derby, the Earl of Scarbrough, the Trustees of the Liddell Hart Centre for Military Archives, and Major C. J. Wilson. Quotations from Crown copyright records appear by permission of the Controller of HM Stationery Office. An earlier version of chapter 4 was published in the *Journal of Contemporary History* (October 1981), and I thank the editors for allowing me to draw on it here.

A number of former Territorials wrote to me at length about their experiences, and I wish to acknowledge their assistance: Mr P. Beaton, Mr H. R. Black, Mr F. L. Howard, Colonel G. W. Noakes, OBE, TD, JP, DL, and Major G. W. H. Woods.

I am most grateful to The Royal Military College of Canada for granting me leave in which to carry out the research for this book, and to the Social Sciences and Humanities Research Council of Canada and the RMC Arts Division Research Fund for their generous financial support.

Many friends and colleagues have given me the benefit of their advice: George Betts, Brian Bond, A. M. J. Hyatt, John McCarthy, Adrian Preston, Richard Preston, John Robertson, Theodore Ropp, Donald Schurman, and Neville Thompson. I am indebted to them all. Without the encouragement of Christine Linehan, executive editor of this series, this book would not have been published.

My greatest debt is to my most generous critic, my wife Iréna.

Peter Dennis
1984

Canberra

Note on Sources

Unless otherwise stated (e.g., 'Middlesex Territorial Association, Recruiting Committee') all references to the records of County Territorial Associations are to the general meetings of the particular Association. The papers of some of the County Associations are now held by the respective TA&VR Associations (see bibliography), and these are generally not catalogued, hence only a date is given in the reference.

Introduction

The Territorial Army in Britain has had a chequered history. Apart from a short period immediately after its establishment, it suffered from periodic indifference and neglect, and occasional hostility, both at the hands of the government and from the public. Its place in the all-important order of defence spending priorities and hence, to a large extent, its fortunes, reflected the wider considerations that shaped British defence policy. It is therefore in a national context that the Territorial Army must first be studied.

But the Territorial Army was also a local organisation, subject to local conditions and community support that varied throughout the country. The founding principle laid down by Haldane, namely the division of control between the War Office and the County Territorial Associations, both helped and hindered the Territorials. It enabled them to adapt recruiting practices more readily to local circumstances, and thus to weather the worst periods of the late 1920s and 1930s more effectively than a highly centralised organisation could have done. On the other hand it gave to the County Associations a degree of power that they did not always use wisely.

The place of the Territorial Army in Britain's defence structure and the problems of raising a national body of part-time soldiers on a local basis are the two main concerns of this study. Some experts shudder when the question is asked: 'What is the Army for?' but in the political world in particular there has always been pressure on whatever government is in power to justify expenditure on all or part of the defence system. It was a misfortune of history that the Territorial Army was born out of a political concern for economy in government spending as much as for any appreciation of strategic circumstances, and subsequently had to live for two decades in a tightly restrictive budgetary climate. Its second misfortune was that instead of being able to emerge from the First World War with an unchallengeable record with which to confront its

1

critics and to cement its place in the central military organisation of the nation, it was pushed aside and prevented from fulfilling the very task for which it had been established.

Political pressures had prevented Haldane from articulating as clearly and as forcefully as he would have liked the true purpose of the Territorial Army, namely to provide reinforcements in complete units for the Regular divisions of the Expeditionary Force. That reluctance to make absolutely clear the functions of the Territorial Army, and Haldane's consequent inability to impose a foreign service liability on pre-war Territorials, was a powerful handicap to their acceptance by the country as an essential part of the defence forces. The second handicap was one that the Territorials imposed on themselves. After the war they were understandably bitter and angry at the treatment they had received from Kitchener and the War Office, and they were determined to ensure that in any revived Territorial scheme they would not expose themselves to such abuse again. In the process of protecting what they saw as their legitimate rights, they so surrounded their conditions of service with restrictive qualifications that they tended to alienate the War Office. Instead of working with the War Office and the Regular Army, the Territorial Associations all too often tended to become prickly and obsessive, intent on finding 'breaches of faith' where none existed or 'slights and pinpricks' where wider defence cuts had in all fairness to include the Territorials as well.

This study is not in any sense a unit history or a battle history. The colourful stories of the famous and the less well-known Territorial units have been told in many cases by their unit historians. My focus is the broader one, which has been all but neglected, especially the peacetime history of the Territorial Army. I have concentrated on the peacetime problems of the Territorials because it was then that they faced their most difficult and unique challenges. The ability to survive and to maintain a military organization of over one hundred thousand men in the face of savage reductions in expenditure and of government and public apathy was in some ways just as much a test of the Territorial spirit as the ordeal of battle.

In any case, in both wars, and especially in the second, the scale of Britain's military participation meant that the Territorials could not maintain their monopoly as the sole means of expanding the nation's forces. The introduction of conscription in 1939 and the Territorials' harnessing to that policy, together with the creation of a vast National Army on the outbreak of war, submerged the special qualities of the peacetime Territorial units. Their achievements during the war have rightly been given the highest praise, but the Territorial units that fought in North Africa, Italy or north-west Europe bore little relation, save in name, to the units of the inter-war period. The Territorial Army of the 1920s and the 1930s kept alive a tradition of part-time soldiering, and they maintained a base on which the great expansion of the Second World War could partly rest. When that expansion did come they too became part of an enormous national army. To that extent, and perhaps to that extent alone, they fulfilled the wider hopes of their founder.

Comparatively little has been written on the Territorial Army, but sources for its study are abundant. Nearly every County Territorial Association's papers have survived, most of them now held in County Record Offices. Few have been used extensively, most not at all. Yet they are a rich source for the local historian, who may find in this study some generalizations on which to base a more detailed examination of the Territorial Army in a particular area.

1

The Birth of the Territorials

The formation of a Liberal government under Sir Henry Campbell-Bannerman in 1905 brought to the War Office the most remarkable Secretary of State for War that Britain has had in the twentieth century. Passed over for the post he most coveted, that of Lord Chancellor, Richard Burdon Haldane took the War Office in order to persuade Edward Grey to join the Cabinet as Foreign Secretary. It was a risky move on Haldane's part. The Liberals had come to office on a platform of 'Peace, Retrenchment, and Reform', and the War Office was hardly the place for an ambitious politician to attract attention, unless it was by cutting back expenditure on the Army to please the radical wing of the Liberal Party. When asked who had shown any interest in going to the War Office, Campbell-Bannerman had told Haldane: 'Nobody will touch it with a barge pole'. 'Then give it to me', Haldane said with a touch of self-sacrifice. This, at least, was the version Haldane gave in his posthumously published autobiography.[1] This self-serving explanation must be set against the fact that having been involved in an earlier and unsuccessful attempt to overthrow Campbell-Bannerman, Haldane could expect little sympathy from the new Prime Minister, who took some satisfaction in sending his erstwhile opponent to a department which had recently been the downfall of two Conservative Secretaries of State for War.

Haldane brought to the War Office a powerful array of intellectual gifts. An eminent lawyer by profession, he had a deep interest in philosophy which spurred him to go back to first principles when approaching any problem. It was partly this willingness to question all assumptions that enabled him to undertake a radical restructuring of the Army. Again in his autobiography Haldane claimed that

[1] R. B. Haldane, *Richard Burdon Haldane: an Autobiography* (London, 1929), p. 173. For a detailed examination of Haldane's claims on his own behalf, see Edward M. Spiers, *Haldane: an Army Reformer* (Edinburgh, 1980), chapter 1.

he came to the War Office as a 'young and blushing virgin', without knowledge of or ideas about Army reform.[2] No doubt this admission helped disarm his potential critics in the War Office, especially the members of the Army Council who had done so much to thwart the proposals of his predecessor, but it was not exactly true. While Haldane had never taken a passionate interest in the Army, he had been a member of a 1900 committee on smokeless propellants and had spoken in his own constituency about the need for Army reform. Furthermore no senior Liberal member of parliament could have watched the efforts of the Conservative Secretary of State for War to come to grips with the question of Army reform and remain ignorant for long of the basic problems.

That reform was necessary was generally recognized. The traumatic experience of the South African war and the abysmal performance of the British Army there had exposed weaknesses that could no longer be ignored. In addition, rising tensions within Europe, centreing on the emergence of Germany as a great naval as well as a military power, made reform an urgent necessity. After the South African war some steps had been taken to place military policy on a sounder and more professional basis. The creation of the Committee of Imperial Defence in 1902, with Sir George Clarke as its secretary, and of the General Staff, provided the structure within which policy could be studied and formulated. Cooperation between the Army and the Royal Navy, however, was virtually non-existent. The First Sea Lord, Admiral Sir John Fisher, dismissed the usefulness of a Naval Staff, and saw the CID as a dangerous challenge to the Navy's authority. In one sense, though, the CID had proved very useful to the Navy, for in 1903 a special subcommittee had examined and finally dismissed the proposition that Britain was vulnerable to invasion and that large land forces had, as a consequence, to be stationed in Britain itself.[3] This endorsement of the 'blue water' strategy temporarily, at least, confounded the 'bolt from the blue' advocates.

When Haldane told the Army Council, no doubt to their intense bewilderment, that he wanted to create 'a Hegelian Army', he was suggesting that his task lay in reconciling the military needs of defence with the political need for economy, and to do this in a way that would not irrevocably alienate vital political support. It was a task fraught with danger: differing views of the nature of the problem and its solution ran up against well-entrenched and

2 Haldane, *An Autobiography*, p. 183.
3 John Gooch, 'Haldane and the ''National Army'' ', in John Gooch and I. F. W. Beckett (eds.), *Politicians and Defence* (Manchester, 1981), p. 73.

powerful interest groups within the Army, while proposals to effect any sort of reform brought the question into the wider political arena where the pressures of party politics distorted genuine differences over the defence issue. For a Liberal Secretary of State for War the dangers were two-fold: there was no guarantee at all that work in the War Office would attract the necessary support within the Liberal party unless substantial savings could be made on the Army vote, and there was every possibility that he might be personally engulfed by the controversy surrounding the question of Army reform.[4]

Haldane had several advantages that his hapless predecessors had not enjoyed. The first was that he was not saddled with the need to provide for the home defence of Britain against invasion. The CID's dismissal of that threat enormously simplified Haldane's task. The second advantage was that he came to the War Office unencumbered by party commitments, except for the general agreement to reduce expenditure on the Army. In the parliamentary debates on the reform schemes of his Conservative predecessors, Haldane had not identified himself with any particular group, nor had the Liberal party as a whole carefully defined its position. The circumstances were such, therefore, that Haldane had a much freer hand than either Brodrick or Arnold-Forster had been able to apply to the task.

He did not waste time. In December and January he went to Cloan, his home in Scotland, to ponder the complexities of Army reform. Assisted by his Military Secretary, Colonel G. F. Ellison, he examined in detail every aspect of the Army establishment in an attempt to combine economy with efficiency. It was during this period of study and discussion, when his lawyer's training undoubtedly helped him in mastering the difficulties of the problem, that he fixed upon the question of the Army's ability to send a striking force to the continent. In later life, desperate to defend himself against the vicious wartime attacks that had brought his political career to an early end, Haldane would claim that he had virtually foreseen the developments of future events and had modelled his reforms around the need to provide a sufficiently strong expeditionary force to assist France in a war against Germany.[5] Added impetus to this line of thinking was provided by Sir Edward Grey's inquiry in January about British plans to aid France if, as the French thought, they were likely to be attacked by Germany that summer.[6]

[4] See Albert Tucker, 'The Issue of Army Reform in the Unionist Government, 1903 – 5', *The Historical Journal*, IX (1966), 90 – 100.
[5] R. B. Haldane, *Before the War* (London, 1920), pp. 29 – 33; *An Autobiography*, p. 187.
[6] Haldane, *An Autobiography*, pp. 189 – 90.

There can be no doubt that this turn of events had a powerful influence on Haldane's thinking. He immediately returned to London, and won Campbell-Bannerman's approval for continuing the secret staff talks with the French that had been initiated the previous year. Yet, as with his protestations of military ignorance, Haldane's claims in this regard must be treated with some scepticism. One of the earliest reports to come to him on assuming office was from the Director of Military Operations, stressing the varied nature of the calls that might be made on the Army, ranging from massive commitments to the defence of India to major interventions in Europe. For several years before this, there had been emerging in the War Office a growing body of opinion that emphasized the need for military flexibility in place of the long-standing acceptance that India should automatically consume the bulk of Britain's strength. Grey's question to Haldane therefore brought into sharp focus a War Office concern that preceded Haldane's study of the needs of the Army, while a subsequent test of mobilisation procedures showed how poorly prepared the Army was.[7]

Haldane's contribution should be seen not so much in terms of the originality that he later claimed for his reforms, but in that circumstances were such that it was a propitious moment to combine reform with economy. Haldane made sure that, unlike Arnold-Forster, he kept his military advisers informed and where possible carried them with him. At the same time he made a determined effort to reduce the Army vote, thus securing parliamentary support from his Liberal colleagues. In the absence of any firmly agreed Liberal policy on the nature of Army reform, Haldane was able to stake out well-prepared positions following his 'retreat' at Cloan. By emphasizing the continuity of his policy with that of the declared position of Balfour, former Conservative Prime Minister and founder of the CID, he undercut much of the opposition's potential criticism, while his promises of substantial reductions in manpower and expenditure swung Liberal support solidly behind him.

Nor were these promises empty ones. In his first Army Estimates Haldane was able to effect some savings on the previous Conservative budget, not enough to satisfy his own supporters but at least sufficient to give notice that economy and efficiency were the twin pillars on which his Army policy rested. Within months of his first Estimates, he had announced his proposed changes in the Army. The home Army would prepare itself to fight overseas, and an

<hr />

[7] Gooch, 'Haldane and the "National Army" ', pp. 74–5.

Expeditionary Force would be formed from sixty-one home battalions of the Line complemented by six Guards battalions, four brigades of cavalry and full artillery support. Since he was determined to retain the Cardwellian system of linked battalions, and since he also refused to alter the size of the garrison in India, both the size of his Expeditionary Force and his scope for economies were contingent upon achieving cuts elsewhere. Consultations with the Admiralty and the Colonial Office enabled him to make reductions in some colonial garrisons. With the size of the Expeditionary Force thus prescribed by the military system that he had largely inherited (rather than dictated, as he subsequently claimed, by his appreciation of the threat to France), Haldane was able to make substantial reductions. He proposed to disband two of the Guards battalions not ear-marked for the Expeditionary Force, and to dispense with some 3,850 artillerymen, whose services would not be needed since the change in policy on coastal defences had released 10,000 Militia garrison gunners for service with the Expeditionary Force. In all Haldane estimated that he could reduce the Army by 20,000, with commensurate savings in expenditure.[8]

The ensuing Parliamentary uproar was easily weathered. Haldane had produced a comprehensive and rational scheme that could withstand the attacks of special interest groups, while the vast majority of his own party were mollified by the projected savings of £2.6 millions, which brought the Estimates for 1907 – 8 below the ceiling of £28 millions. Furthermore the attacks of his critics on his proposals for the Regular Army were overshadowed by the reaction to his schemes for the 'second line' of the Army. His greatest struggles were to come not over the role of the Regular Army, but on the question of the reserve forces — the Militia, the Yeomanry, and the Volunteers.

Between them, these forces constituted a large body of reserves, but one that was poorly organised and coordinated and inadequately equipped and trained. The Militia, the old 'Constitutional Force', existed as little more than a recruiting vehicle for the Regular Army, into whose ranks some 35 per cent of its members passed each year (although 20 per cent deserted and a further 25 per cent were discharged before completing their term of service).[9] The Cardwell reforms of 1872 had brought Militia units much closer to

[8] Parl. Debs. (Commons), 4th series, vol. 160, cols. 1088 – 98 (12 July 1906).
[9] J. K. Dunlop, The Development of the British Army, 1899 – 1914 (London, 1938), p. 18.

Regular battalions, and in practice the Militia virtually ceased to have any independent existence, even though the illusion of separate units, able to fight in their own right, continued to win strong support from Militia commanding officers. The Yeomanry had its origins in the mounted landowners and farmers raised during the Napoleonic invasion scare at the beginning of the nineteenth century, and was subsequently used throughout the century to keep the peace in various civil disturbances.

By the early twentieth century, the Volunteers were the most numerous of the second line forces. Although some traced their lineage back to the 'trained bands' that had been raised in the sixteenth century, the vast majority of Volunteer units dated from the more recent French invasion scares between 1859 and 1861. The Volunteers were, in the words of one recent historian, 'the military expression of the spirit of self-help, Victorian capitalism in arms'.[10] Originally established as private — and exclusive — military clubs, membership of which entailed the payment of entrance and annual fees, they had at first been almost entirely self-sufficient, the War Office providing only the barest essentials in equipment. This independence was gradually whittled away as state support increased, until by 1902 the Volunteers were receiving over one million pounds annually in government grants.

The composition of the force changed too. From its beginnings as a middle class movement it became a 'recreation enjoyed by the working class, and acceptable to the middle class, for it took place under their control, and was stamped with the seals of patriotism and respectability'.[11] Quite apart from the question of the status that the Volunteers enjoyed — by the end of the nineteenth century they had become as much as anything figures of mild ridicule, their military value was open to serious question. Training was often minimal and, more important, was for the most part localised, so that standards varied widely. Even the War Office's annual subsidy did not give it much control over the Volunteers. Service could be terminated at two weeks' notice so that, as *The Times* Military Correspondent noted, 'if a commanding officer is given an order, he may allege that his funds [often provided out of his own pocket] do not permit him to carry it out, or that if he does his men will leave'.[12] The Volunteers were raised for the purpose of home

---

[10] Hugh Cunningham, *The Volunteer Force: A Social and Political History 1859 – 1908* (London, 1975), p. 1.

[11] *Ibid.*, p. 155.

[12] *The Times*, 2 February 1907.

defence, yet neither their training, equipment, organisation or administration fitted them to undertake that role in the absence of the Regular Army overseas. As a second line for the Regular Army, they had not shown themselves in a particularly good light during the Boer War, when only 13,000 out of a total of 230,000 had offered to serve overseas.

To this array of forces Haldane was determined to apply the same principles that helped direct his approach to the Regular Army: what purpose did they serve in war that justified the expenditure of public funds upon them, and how did they fit into the overall military scheme to provide for the nation's defence needs? The answer to the first question was not reassuring. In the face of a continental enemy such as Germany, the combination of Militia, Yeomanry and Volunteers was hardly an adequate substitute for a highly trained second line. Nor were these forces in any real sense integrated into Britain's wartime military system. Yet in another way they held the key to this part of Haldane's reforms. He wanted to apply to the continental concept of the Nation-in-Arms a peculiarly British twist: a system operating on voluntary instead of compulsory service, working through local institutions rather than the Regular Army. The Yeomanry and the Volunteers, for all their obvious imperfections, at least embodied some of this ideal, which itself was as much a recognition of political reality as it was the product of any philosophical investigation.

In April 1906 Haldane wrote:

> The problem, as it presents itself to my mind, is how to reorganise the military forces of this country in such a fashion as to give the whole nation what is really a National Army, not separated from itself by artificial barriers of caste and class, but regarded by the people as something that is their very own. It is the essence of such a conception that an army fulfilling these requirements should have its roots within the people them- selves, and should be developed at its summit into that perfection of organization which can only come to be regarded as an organic whole, existing for the whole purpose of protecting British interests, no matter where in the world those interests are threatened.[13]

Haldane envisaged a 'Territorial Army', raised and administered locally but under central training control, which would become a

---

[13] Haldane, Fourth Memorandum, 25 April 1906, Haldane Papers, MS 5918, ff. 44 – 5.

military school for the nation, manned by young men successively indoctrinated in the military ethos by a new curriculum at school and by experience in a local cadet corps. (The official title, 'Territorial Force', was not changed to 'Territorial Army' until 1921, but the two terms were virtually interchangeable from the first.)

In March, when presenting his first Army Estimates to parliament, Haldane had outlined his scheme in general terms. Special interest groups were not yet aware of the full implications of his proposals, and his gesture towards a reduction in expenditure won him the backing of his own party. It was, he wrote to his mother, 'the greatest success I have ever had . . .. It is a relief from our uncertainty'. He was only too well aware of what had happened to previous attempts at reform and knew full well that the entrenched interests of the Militia, Yeomanry and Volunteers would fight vigorously to protect their positions. As he explained to his mother: 'I intend to go with great deliberation — testing the ground before each step.'[14]

To this end he appointed a large committee representing the Militia, Yeomanry and Volunteers, and various other interested parties, to examine his scheme and if possible to reach agreement on it. The chairman of the committee, which became known as the 'Duma' (after Russia's experiment with an advisory council), was Lord Esher, who had been one of the most fervent supporters of the cause of Army reform, and who had the complete confidence of the King. The latter was especially important. There had been a furious royal response to Haldane's proposal to disband two Guards battalions and he therefore realised that it was essential to have the King's support if his scheme was to succeed. Indeed, one of Esher's first acts as chairman was to reassure the King that the committee over which he presided was not about to foist on the Army radical changes that would undermine traditional authority. The committee, he told the King,

> is composed of men who by political conviction, birth, station and education are opposed to the Government now in Office, and whose predilection may be assumed to be . . . opposed absolutely to anything in the shape of what is generally understood by the term 'citizen army'.[15]

---

[14] Haldane to his mother, 9 March 1906, Haldane Papers, MS 5918, ff. 105 – 6.

[15] M. V. Brett (ed.), *Letters and Journals of Reginald Viscount Esher* (London, 1934), II, pp. 167 – 8.

The strongest resistance to Haldane's proposals came from the Militia. Offered the choice between drawing closer to the Regular Army and formalising what had long been the reality of its position and function, or joining Haldane's new Territorial Army scheme with the Volunteers and the Yeomanry and retaining their seniority, the Militia representatives flatly rejected both. The committee was unable to reach any agreement on the future of the Militia, and several meetings between Haldane, his advisers and senior Militia representatives failed to resolve the issue. Faced with total Militia intransigence Haldane, with Esher's firm backing, dropped his conciliatory approach and announced that since the Militia had failed to adapt to his new scheme it would be abolished. At the suggestion of the Director of Military Operations, Major General Spencer Ewart, it was resurrected as a Special Reserve, its depots being retained as reserve battalion cadres which would produce drafts for the Regular Army in time of war.[16] The problem of how to produce drafts for the Regular Army had been the one question that Haldane's original proposals had failed to address. To that extent the uncompromising attitude of the Militia representatives turned out to be a blessing in disguise.

There were also objections raised by the Volunteer representatives, this time to the most original proposal in Haldane's scheme. Haldane planned to establish a Territorial Association in each county, charged with raising and administering the Territorial units within its borders. This threatened to deprive Volunteer commanding officers of their cherished autonomy and to bring them under increasingly close War Office supervision. When bitter opposition arose among the Volunteers, Haldane lost his nerve and seemed ready to compromise or abandon what Esher thought was the 'only *constructive* policy he has to his credit'. Haldane's fault, Esher complained, 'lies in his wish to be all things to all people'.[17] As the opposition mounted and Haldane's resolve seemed to wobble, Esher suggested that the county associations be made more palatable to the Volunteers (and to the Yeomanry who did not wish to come under the Associations' control) by minimising their elective nature (with local political, union and educational interests represented) and increasing the number of coopted military members. 'What is wanted', Esher urged Haldane, 'is a plan which

---

[16] Spiers, *Haldane*, chapter 5; Gooch, 'Haldane and the "National Army" ', pp. 77 – 80; Dunlop, *The Development of the British Army*, pp. 268 – 78.

[17] Brett (ed.), *Letters and Journals*, II, p. 174.

seizes hold of the imagination of the public: which induces them to say, we will give this plan a trial.'[18] Yet the plan that Esher proposed, and the change that Haldane was subsequently forced to accept, involved the drastic reduction of the elected membership of the Associations, that is, the downgrading of the public's role in the affairs of the Territorial Army. As the price of minimising Volunteer intransigence, a key element of Haldane's concept of the National Army was sacrificed before the Territorials were even born.

There were other compromises forced on Haldane. Although when announcing his proposals to the House in February he had stressed that the Territorials would be raised for overseas service in support of the Regular Army, he dropped this commitment eight days later when introducing his Territorial and Reserve Forces Act. The role of the Territorials, he emphasized several times, was home defence. Since the invasion threat had been dismissed as unlikely by the CID several years before, and the whole thrust of Haldane's reforms had been to restructure the second line to provide support of an Expeditionary Force, his insistence on a home defence role went against the very purpose of his wider scheme. The change was a tactical one. Haldane had always intended to use the Territorial Army overseas, and indeed his promise that on the outbreak of war the Territorials would receive six months' training made sense only in that context, but the Volunteers had objected strenuously to having an overseas obligation as an integral part of Territorial conditions of service. Haldane was forced to back down again and to rely on the good voluntary intentions of the Territorials. In a memorandum written in November 1906 he had expressed the hope that 'from one-sixth to one-fourth of the force' would voluntarily undertake an overseas obligation, or, as he put it to the House:

> our belief is that at the end of . . . [six months' training] not only would they be enormously more efficient than the Volunteers or Yeomanry forces at this present time, but that they would be ready, finding themselves in their units, to say, 'We wish to go abroad and take our part in the theatre of war, to fight in the interests of the nation and for the defence of the Empire.'[19]

His stress on the home defence role of the Territorials was designed

[18] *Ibid.*, 195–6.
[19] *Parl. Debs.* (Commons), 4th series, vol. 169, col. 1301 (25 February 1907). See also Spiers, *Haldane*, pp. 108–13.

not so much to allay Volunteer fears as to persuade them to join the Territorials, and to calm radical critics disturbed by talk of the Expeditionary Force. In the short term Haldane probably succeeded in these aims but the cost was high. Many of the subsequent troubles that the Territorial Army encountered, both before and after the test of war, arose out of the confusion surrounding the birth of the Territorials, designed to support the Regular Expeditionary Force yet referred to as a force raised for home defence. It was a telling comment on the perceived strength of the opposition to his proposals that the central purpose of the reorganisation of the second line forces of the country was so distorted and misrepresented, not least by Haldane himself.

Despite all the controversy surrounding Haldane's proposals, and in view of the fate of previous attempts at reform, there was surprisingly little sustained Parliamentary opposition to Haldane's bill. Those who represented special interests naturally protested that they were being unfairly treated, none more so than the Militia lobby in the Lords. The supporters of the Militia, however, won little sympathy: their opposition was so unyielding and their position so hopeless that most of the debates centred on securing the best possible terms for the Yeomanry and Volunteers. After the final reading of the bill in June, Haldane's victory was unexpectedly easy: by a vote of 286 to 63 (with most of the Unionists abstaining) the Commons voted to establish the Territorial Force. The resistance that had been feared in the Lords crumbled away, and apart from a few minor amendments the bill passed unscathed.

Haldane then announced that 1 April 1908 would be the formal inauguration date for the Territorial Force. In the intervening eight months the machinery for the raising and administration of the Territorials had to be established. His approach in setting up the County Associations, which had been the object of such distrust and opposition among the Volunteer officers, in particular, was to win over the 'natural leaders' in each county, in the hope that their support and participation would in time bring in wider support at the local level. Apart from his own efforts in speaking frequently at Volunteer gatherings throughout the country, Haldane relied heavily on the intervention of the King, who summoned the Lords Lieutenant of the counties to Buckingham Palace on 26 October 1907, and impressed on them that the establishment and success of the Territorial Army depended on their response to his appeal. It was this identification of the King with the new force that made the Territorials, despite their origins and the taint that they had in some quarters of being a 'citizen army', socially acceptable and that

14

indeed impelled the social elite of the counties to throw their weight behind them, as Haldane had hoped. After the meeting at Buckingham Palace, he remarked: 'The King's intervention has produced the requisite steam for the engine, and I am working day and night to take full advantage of the moment.'[20]

When recruiting formally began on 1 April 1908 the signs were encouraging. At the end of the first week Haldane wrote to his mother that 'the Volunteers are pouring in and it is not too much to hope that the critical point is now passed, and that the new Army is going to be a real success'.[21] As later events were to show that was much too sanguine a view. In fact the birth of the Territorial Army proved to be much easier than expected, whereas its subsequent trials were greater than anyone had foreseen.

[20] Haldane to his sister, 1 November 1907, Haldane Papers, MS 6011, f. 36.
[21] Haldane to his mother, 7 April 1908, Haldane Papers, MS 5979, f. 154.

2

Tests and Trials

The initial response to Haldane's call for recruits was encouraging. Despite the misgivings of many Volunteer and Yeomanry representatives, the transition to the Territorial Force was remarkably smooth, helped no doubt by the attractive terms that Haldane had offered and also by the promise, which had never been held out to the Volunteers, that Territorial units would be formed into brigades and divisions, thus creating a self-contained Army that would deserve to be taken seriously. The swelling numbers, however, did not silence Haldane's critics. The Labour Party and the trade unions refused to be associated with the new citizens' army, fearing that it would eventually be turned against the working class to maintain an essentially conservative society by intervening in strikes and industrial action on behalf of the civil authority. Conservatives scorned the Territorial Force as a 'Radical nostrum', while paying tribute to the patriotism of those who joined it, and insisted that it would be incapable of fulfilling its allotted role. Many Radicals were either hostile or indifferent, and even among the ranks of leading Territorial supporters there were many who doubted the wisdom of Haldane's approach. Haldane responded to these doubts and criticisms with a punishing round of public appearances, encouraging, persuading, and berating the country as if his single-handed efforts would decide the fate of his scheme.

As long as recruiting went well, Haldane could parry the attacks of critics with relative ease. With the strong support of the War Office, he could reply forcefully, if not always convincingly, to criticism of the training and capability of the Territorial artillery, a controversy which caused a worried Edward VII to express the wish that Haldane would bow to 'expert' military opinion. But Haldane could just as easily produce his own experts, and this particular dispute soon faded away, even though his critics had by no means been persuaded by his arguments.[1]

[1] Spiers, *Haldane*, pp. 166 – 7.

Other circumstances that helped create a favourable recruiting atmosphere were seized upon and exploited by Haldane. The opening in January 1909 of Guy du Maurier's play, *An Englishman's Home*, rekindled long-standing popular fears about Britain's vulnerability to invasion. The play was an immediate success, and to his delight Haldane found that recruiting for the Territorial Force, which in his heavy schedule of speeches he had been extolling as the nation's security against invasion, picked up significantly. In a gesture worthy of Hore-Belisha, the publicity-conscious Secretary of State for War in the Chamberlain government, he had a recruiting booth set up in the theatre foyer. Whatever might have been said about the propriety of these methods, Haldane could point with some satisfaction to a net increase of over 30,000 recruits in the first seven weeks of 1909.[2]

Within a year of its birth, the Territorial Force had reached a strength of 9,313 officers and 259,463 other ranks. This achievement was acknowledged in a ceremony at Windsor Castle, where the King presented colours to 108 Territorial units. Haldane, who was present, felt that his 'great reform of the Army is now complete & an accomplished fact'.[3] This was much too premature a judgment. Within six months the rate of recruiting had declined significantly, and the critics of the Territorial Force, temporarily quietened but not silenced by the encouraging early response, were soon on the offensive again.

The strongest and most sustained attack came from the National Service League, which had been founded in 1902 when the strategic argument between the 'blue water' and 'bolt from the blue' schools was at its height. The League utterly rejected what it regarded as the complacency inherent in the 'blue water' approach to home defence, namely that Britain was protected against invasion by the Royal Navy, and that there were more than enough troops at home to take care of any small raids that might be able to slip through the net. In particular the League attacked the Territorial Force concept as inadequate to meet the needs of Britain's home defence. Once the expected numbers failed to enlist, and the Territorials showed no signs of reaching their establishment, the League unleashed a barrage of criticism, attacking the Territorial Force and those who continued to put their faith in it, even when its failure was, according to the League, all too evident.

[2] *Ibid.*, pp. 170 – 1.
[3] Haldane to his mother, 23 June 1909, Haldane Papers, MS 5981, f. 257.

The League indicated its own preferred remedy: compulsory national service. Members of the League, Conservative and Unionist almost to a man, believed that the imposition of national service on the youth of Britain would have an invaluable moral and social influence upon them, as well as providing the numbers that the protection of Britain's security at home demanded. 'Conscription' was a word they abhorred: it had 'continental' overtones, and what distinguished their proposal from the model of compulsory military service that existed widely in Europe was their suggestion that national service was for home defence only and that it would be carried out through a reorganised Territorial Force. This would be military service on behalf of national defence rather than the continental sort of conscription that was the basis of national aggression.

In one sense the National Service League came remarkably close to supporting one of Haldane's most striking concepts, that the Army should be a vehicle for social and moral influence, that a 'Nation-in-Arms' should be created with the Army as a 'school for the Nation'. Whereas Haldane had stressed that this concept had to be adapted to the British character and genius, and hence be based on the voluntary system operating through local organisations representing the entire social spectrum, the National Service League rejected the voluntary approach, arguing that it could not produce the required numbers and that it allowed the shirker and the coward to escape his national duty. As with almost all modern proponents of conscription (who have also shied away from the term, preferring the more palatable 'national service'), they saw it in much wider terms than merely the means of building an Army, to whatever end. Compulsory military service had an almost mystical attraction for them. It was the standard against which the virility and staying-power of the nation was to be measured. The Army, in which all would serve under equal conditions, would bind the nation together, putting its welfare ahead of party, class and sectarian interests. Britain's willingness to accept national service would be the test of its sense of purpose, and demonstrate to the rest of the world, and especially to the powers in Europe, that democracy had not weakened its moral fibre or lessened its ability to defend itself.

Another of Haldane's ideas, and one which political realities had compelled him to drop, was to use the school system to inculcate basic military habits and skills in the youth of the nation. Many members of the National Service League supported that plan, but also argued that it was a poor substitute for real military training at

18

a mature age. The concept of compulsory cadet training, along the lines adopted by Australia and New Zealand,[4] was heartily endorsed by another pressure group, the National Defence Association. It too attacked the Government's approach to military planning and preparation as utterly inadequate and misconceived, and if its public appeals never matched the shrillness of the League's it was nevertheless another source of criticism that the Government had to meet.

The Territorial Force was the target of many of these attacks, but the debate was a much wider one, and inevitably perhaps, the Territorials were often unfairly criticised. The National Service League, for example, insisted that the Territorials as Haldane had created them were incapable of safeguarding the nation against invasion, and that only a much larger home army, raised on the basis of compulsion, would provide the necessary degree of security. But Haldane had never thought of the Territorials as a force raised basically for home defence. For him the Territorials were the second line behind the Regular Army component of the Expeditionary Force. Political pressures from the Volunteer and Yeomanry representatives and from his own Liberal colleagues, forced him to abandon his plan to make the Territorials liable to service overseas, an obligation that was fundamental to his concept of their proper role. Instead he had to rely upon the hope that they would voluntarily accept the imperial service obligation, and that if the occasion arose they would not shrink from the call. The result was that the final scheme that Haldane unveiled in 1907 was a compromise that concealed Haldane's true intentions while misleading those who supported the Territorials. Although there was no foreign service obligation and although most of the publicity given to the new force centred on its home defence role, Haldane's eyes were fixed firmly on the possibility of war overseas, probably in Europe, and not on the dangers of invasion. The dismissal of the invasion threat in 1903, which had been confirmed by another official enquiry in October 1908,[5] as well as Haldane's own acceptance of the 'blue water' arguments, had been one of the starting points in the evolution of his scheme of reform.

The two sides in this great debate were talking about quite different things. The National Service League and its supporters

---

4   See John Barrett, *Falling In: Australians and 'Boy Conscription' 1911 – 1915* (Sydney, 1979). Barrett shows that conscriptionists in Australia obtained much of their supporting literature from the National Service League.

5   Gooch, 'Haldane and the "National Army" ', p. 81.

demanded compulsory military service to remedy the perceived deficiencies in Britain's home defence; those who supported Haldane's concept of the Territorial Force based on voluntary enlistment emphasized its role as part of the Expeditionary Force, the second and subsequent contingents that would follow the Regular Army after a period of six months' full-time training (a period which, of course, made no sense at all within the context of the home defence argument). This debate might have remained a purely academic if acrimonious one had it not been for the ability of the League to launch a brilliant campaign to awaken the British public to the dangers facing it. In 1905, the aged Field Marshal Lord Roberts of Kandahar accepted the presidency of the League, and began to attack the Government's stand on defence and especially the Territorial Force with a vigour that belied his advanced years. Here was a critic, fearless and outspoken, who could not easily be ignored or dismissed as a party hack, a man who could claim with some truth to stand above partisan interests and whose own example of distinguished military service lent weight to his denunciations of Haldane and those who advised him.

As the recruiting figures for 1910 showed an unmistakable decline in Territorial enlistments, the League grew bolder in its attacks. Feeling himself to be under growing pressure to defend the Territorials and to answer the arguments of the League, Haldane authorised the publication of *Compulsory Service*, a vigorous defence of the Territorial scheme by Sir Ian Hamilton, Adjutant-General until 1 August 1910.[6] Since Hamilton was a serving officer, it was at best a questionable tactic, and one that brought Haldane a great deal of criticism. This he rejected, refusing to concede that he had erred by publishing Hamilton's tract and by introducing it at length himself.[7]

Hamilton's argument was that the special circumstances of Britain's position were such that Britain had unique military needs. Home defence rested primarily on the ability of the Navy to maintain command of the sea. With that assured the Army could be used overseas in an offensive role, while a second line of home defence would rest upon forces retained in Britain of sufficient strength to defeat a raiding party or to compel a would-be invader to send so large a force that it could not slip past the Navy. In this overall context, Hamilton insisted, the National Service League's

6 General Sir Ian Hamilton, *Compulsory Service: A Study of the Question in the Light of Experience* (London, 1910).
7 Spiers, *Haldane*, pp. 176–81.

call for compulsory military service was unnecessary and extravagant. The overseas force could not be recruited on a compulsory basis, and the home defence role did not require the numbers that conscription would produce.

The following year the League responded with *Fallacies and Facts: An Answer to 'Compulsory Service'*. Roberts noted with some glee that Hamilton, who now proclaimed himself the champion of the voluntary system, had previously, and on frequent occasions, spoken out in favour of a compulsory military service as the only means by which trained soldiers in sufficient numbers could be produced. A more serious criticism was that both Hamilton and Haldane, while rejecting the League's proposal for compulsory military service, had nevertheless left the door open to compulsion under certain circumstances. Haldane had written of the possibility of creating an Expeditionary Force of more than six divisions of infantry and one of cavalry: 'This larger force would be prepared after the Continental model and compulsorily recruited, with the minimum of two years' training that would be requisite.'[8] Hamilton had concluded that the nation needed a triple line of defence, with the third line — behind the Regular Army, the Reserve and the Territorials — being recruited on a compulsory basis.[9] 'Was ever a stronger or more unexpected backing given to the advocates of compulsory military service', charged Roberts.[10]

Once again the two sides were arguing at cross purposes. The League pressed for compulsion as one answer to what they saw as the main problem facing the country, the inadequacy of the system of home defence. Haldane and his supporters dismissed this argument, and could point to several official enquiries which had judged the forces allotted to home defence adequate to meet the threat of invasion. Nevertheless Haldane did not completely rule out a degree of compulsion for overseas military operations in certain circumstances, a course which was rendered hypothetical by the political realities of the day. So long as the League maintained that its prime concern was home defence, Haldane could resist its attacks, and the voluntary system could remain unharmed. Once the focus of the argument shifted to continental military operations, however, as happened shortly after the war broke out, then the proponents of compulsion had a much stronger case. But by

[8] Hamilton, *Compulsory Service*, p. 40 (Haldane's Introduction).
[9] *Ibid.*, pp. 145 – 6.
[10] Field Marshal Earl Roberts, *Fallacies and Facts: An Answer to 'Compulsory Service'* (London, 1911), pp. 42 – 3.

then the nature of the argument had changed, or as their critics might have said, the new conditions of warfare had flushed the compulsionists out into the open.

A series of tours throughout Britain, with huge public meetings in key cities, enabled the National Service League to spread its views and gather growing support. The opponents of compulsion were no less vigorous in propounding their beliefs, and the pages of Hansard and the press are replete with arid debates and endless correspondence on the virtues of the two systems. The Territoriàl Force was affected in two ways. Its supporters argued that the constant denigration of the Force by the National Service League and other critics adversely cut into recruiting, with the result that the Force began to decline from its peak strength in 1910, a strength which critics delighted in pointing out had never been more than 81 per cent of the authorised establishment. Since 1910 there had been a steady drop in numbers, from 272,000 in 1910 to 261,000 in 1912.[11] The 'mere existence' of the League discouraged enlistment, wrote one critic to The Times.[12] The Under-Secretary of State for Foreign Affairs, F. D. Acland, accused the League of doing 'incalculable harm' to the Force: 'They did lip service to it in public, but in private they went around among employers of labour doing all they could to discourage service in that force.'[13] These charges, which implied a lack of patriotism on the part of Territorial critics, were forcefully denied by Roberts and his followers, but not entirely convincingly. They argued that of course they wanted to see the Territorial Force succeed, but that it had not and that fact had to be faced.[14] It was a disingenuous reply, for the whole case for national service rested on the undesirability of the voluntary system, whether or not it could produce the requisite numbers. Only compulsion could ensure that the entire manhood of the nation undertook military service, and hence was exposed to the benefits of military training while fulfilling one of the obligations of citizenship. As Roberts put it in a letter to The Times, 'discipline alone can confront discipline on the field of battle'.[15]

Whether or not the attacks of the National Service League directly affected recruiting is difficult to determine, but it is clear that increasingly the League asserted itself within the Territorial

---

[11] See appendix.
[12] Robert A. Johnson, letter to The Times, 1 January 1912.
[13] Speech at Rochdale, 25 November 1912.
[14] The Times, leader, 25 February 1913.
[15] The Times, 8 January 1912.

movement. Roberts claimed that 'nearly a quarter of the members of County Associations' belonged to the League;[16] Lord Newton spoke of the 'eloquent fact that nearly every officer of the Territorial Force is in favour of the National Service League'.[17] Even allowing for an understandable degree of exaggeration, the support of many of those most prominently associated with the Territorial Force was by no means unconditional.

For some like Esher, it was 'the last chance which . . . will be given to the voluntary system'. Before the Force was established he told the King's Private Secretary: 'As you know I am a firm believer in compulsion', but added that the voluntary experiment of relying upon the youth of the country (i.e. the 18 – 24 age group) to provide sufficient numbers had to be allowed to fail first.[18] The Earl of Derby, who maintained close connections with the Territorial movement for more than forty years, both as Secretary of State for War (1916 – 18 and 1922 – 4) and as President of the West Lancashire Territorial Association, admitted in 1913 that while he was a strong supporter of the Territorial Force, he also believed in the policy that 'every body in the country should be trained for the purpose of using his right arm in the defence of our shores'.[19] The Earl of Scarbrough, who was Director-General of the Territorial Army from 1917 to 1921 and Chairman of the West Riding Territorial Association throughout the interwar period, was an enthusiastic member of the National Defence Association, and a prime mover behind the sending of a memorandum to the Prime Minister in 1913. The Association emphasized the inadequacy of the training of the Territorials, the poor attendance for the full duration of the annual camp, and the inability of the Force to protect the country against attack. Scarbrough stressed to Seely, Haldane's successor as Secretary of State in 1912, that while the Association was pressing for the introduction of universal military training for the youth of the nation, that did not mean that it supported calls for compulsory adult training. Its sole object was to prepare the Territorial Force for active service, and to bring its strength up to the 'proper level'. Scarbrough insisted that this did not imply a willingness to resort to conscription, but it was not a convincing denial, and when Roberts asked him to sit on the platform at a public meeting

[16] *Ibid.*
[17] *Parl. Debs.* (Lords), 5th series, vol. 13, col. 958 (10 February 1913).
[18] Brett, *Letters and Journals*, II, pp. 186, 190 – 1.
[19] *The Times*, 17 March 1913.

of the National Service League in Leeds in 1913, Scarbrough accepted.[20]

A growing inclination to accept the National Service League's argument was evident not only in individuals but also in the County Associations. In February 1913 the West Riding Territorial Association unanimously adopted a motion proposed by Scarbrough to call attention to the failure of the voluntary system — 'even after five years' vigorous recruiting' — to produce the necessary numbers of men. As one member reluctantly put it, the figures quoted by Scarbrough 'showed conclusively that the Territorial Force had not been a success, and he could not conceal from himself that they had come to the parting of the ways'. The County of London Association (of which Esher was the Chairman) resolved that 'some system should be adopted which would provide a Territorial Force adequate in numbers for the defence of the country', and both the Middlesex and the City of Aberdeen Associations passed similar motions at the urging of the Council of County Territorial Associations.[21]

What had gone wrong? Supporters and critics alike agreed on a number of failings, apart from the obvious inability of the Force to attract its full establishment of officers and men. Many were alarmed by the undue proportion of young men in the Force. In 1909, for example, 98,000 NCOs and men out of a total of 260,000 were under twenty years of age; this excessive number of the 'physically immature' could not but detract from the military effectiveness of the Force, wrote one *Times* correspondent, a view that was shared by the Inspector-General of Home Forces in 1913.[22] Another factor that diminished the efficiency of the Force was its inability to retain men after their initial term of service. Even though the number of recruits rose steadily after 1910 (although it never reached the peak figure of 110,000 that was achieved in 1909), barely half those whose engagement had expired in 1912 sought to re-engage. Thus the Force was constantly plagued by inexperience and youth,

[20] Scarbrough to Seely, 14 March 1913; Roberts to Scarbrough, 20 March 1913: Scarbrough Papers. The text of the National Defence Association's memorandum to the Prime Minister was published in *The Times* on 28 February 1913.

[21] West Riding Territorial Association, 3 February 1913, Acc. 1469/2; County of London Territorial Association, 17 April 1913, A/TA/1; Middlesex Territorial Association, 24 February 1913, Acc. 994/2; City of Aberdeen Territorial Association, 25 February 1913, MD 4/2.

[22] Cd. 5212, *Parl. Papers* (1910), LX; *The Times*, 15 August 1913; 'Annual Report by the Inspector-General of Home Forces for 1913', WO 163/20.

neither of which could be compensated for by the enthusiasm which young recruits brought to their Territorial service.[23]

Haldane's original Territorial scheme had partly been based on the response of the 'natural leaders' of the counties to the Government's call. The King had been prevailed upon to appeal to the Lords Lieutenant in the hope that they would be able to use their influence to attract sufficient men of the right stamp and calibre to fill the establishment of officers. Those hopes were never realized. Before the war the Territorials consistently lacked almost 20 per cent of their officer establishment, even though, as Sir John French, Inspector-General of the Forces, noted in a report in 1909, this was 'often due to the desire of officers to obtain the best class they can'. The importance of the careful selection of officers was also stressed by the Commanding Officer of the 2nd Battalion, the Oxfordshire and Buckinghamshire Light Infantry, who warned that 'they must be gentlemen. If a bad class is introduced in a regiment it will be difficult to get the best class to join. Besides the wrong class will eventually work to the top and the parents will object to their sons joining the unit.'[24]

A much more telling criticism of the Territorial officer corps was made on the basis of their professionalism. While most of the Territorial Divisional Commanders (Regular officers) commended their Territorial officers for their enthusiasm and general intelligence, they noted that the officers were unable to spend sufficient time studying the details of the military profession or attending specialised courses. Haldane had recognised this inherent deficiency in part-time soldiers, but had hoped that the secondment of Regular staff to Territorial units would go some way towards remedying the problem. That, according to a War Office committee appointed to examine the role of the permanent staff in Territorial units, had not happened: the permanent staff were not given the same entitlement that they enjoyed when working with a Regular unit; there was wide disparity between units in the conditions under which they served; and time spent with Territorial units was not considered professionally advantageous.[25]

One of the most vigorous objections to Haldane's scheme had been raised over his proposal to make the Territorial Force a

---

[23] Cd. 6505, *Parl. Papers* (1912), LI.

[24] Cd. 4611, Appendix E, *Parl. Papers* (1909), LI; GOC-in-C, Eastern Command, to War Office, 23 October 1911, Appendix D, WO 32/9192.

[25] See the reports from Divisional Commanders in WO 32/9192; 'Report of the Committee on Emoluments of the Permanent Staff of the Territorial Force', 9 August 1910, WO 32/11273.

completely self-contained army, equipped with its full complement of artillery. This suggestion had been greeted with scorn by the Regular soldiers, who reminded him that the artillery was the most scientific and demanding of all the arms, and hardly one that amateur soldiers, however well-meaning, could master in several hours of practice each week. Roberts used this supposed weakness as another argument against the efficacy of the Territorials, and there were indications that the King was sufficiently perturbed by the criticisms of Regular soldiers to demand that Haldane change this part of his plan. Eventually, with Esher's help, Haldane convinced the King that the Territorial Artillery could perform at an acceptable standard, as Douglas Haig earlier had advised.[26] Opposition died hard, however. In 1911 the GOC-in-C of the West Riding Division reported to the War Office that the Territorial Artillery 'might be of use against an enemy not provided with artillery, but I cannot conceive that they will be fit to combat trained artillery without at least six to nine months' embodied training'.[27] That provision, as Haldane had patiently explained to the King, was one of the key elements of his plan.

Much had also been made of the scanty training that the Territorials undertook. Weekly drills, an occasional weekend's training, and a maximum of fifteen days' annual camp hardly added up to a rigorous requirement. Yet even that seemed beyond the reach of many Territorials. The National Service League pointed to the fact that in 1910, for example, over one third of the Territorial Force failed to pass the musketry test, which had been criticised as being excessively lenient.[28] It was generally agreed by supporters and critics alike that serious military training could be undertaken only during the annual camp, but in 1912 only 155,000 out of 252,000 NCOs and men attended camp for the full fifteen days, while more than 6,000 were absent without leave.[29]

There are various explanations for this. Many Territorials did not find it easy to take fifteen days' leave from their jobs. Even if

[26] Spiers, *Haldane*, pp. 166 – 7.

[27] Lt-General G. M. Bullock to War Office, 9 September 1911, WO 32/9192.

[28] Roberts, *Fallacies and Facts*, p. 99. As a former Director of Military Training noted in 1914, a man who failed to qualify in the musketry test, which consisted of firing 23 rounds annually, could subsequently pass simply by firing an additional 50 rounds within a year. 'Report of the Committee on Musketry Training for the Territorial Force', Appendix 1, April 1914, WO 32/5451.

[29] Cd. 6505.

they could afford to go without pay for a week, some employers would not grant the extra leave or, if they did, the foreman and supervisors made it difficult for those who claimed it.[30] A partial solution had been the institution of separation (or marriage) allowance for all married men and NCOs, but that alone could not bring the significant improvement that was necessary. As the numbers in the Force began to decline slowly but steadily, there was a growing demand for some sort of payment to be made to Territorials, on top of the reimbursement for travel to drills that they received. (The latter had been another issue that threatened to bring the King's displeasure down on Haldane and his advisers. Having agreed to present regimental colours to Territorial units in 1909, the King was angered by the War Office's initial refusal to pay the travelling expenses of those Territorials involved in the ceremonies.[31])

The strongest pressures for the establishment of a bounty came from Scotland. The City of Glasgow Association sent a deputation to the Secretary of State for War in April 1913, asking that a bonus should be instituted so that 'no man should lose by joining'.[32] There was considerable opposition to the very idea of 'paying' Territorials. The ideal solution, Sir George McCrae advised Seely on the basis of his Edinburgh experience, was to offer the potential recruit an attractive inducement without saddling the War Office with excessive costs and without diverging too much from the voluntary concept.[33] With the apparent failure of the middle class to come forward, the Territorials were increasingly having to rely upon the working class to maintain their numbers; but as the annual returns clearly showed even there the Force was losing ground. Those who did enlist found that all too often they were out of pocket, especially if they attended the full fifteen days' camp, for they normally had to take the second week off from their jobs without pay. That was surely asking too much of the patriotic working man.

Matters came to a head in November 1913, when a CCTA deputation put the question to the Prime Minister, the Secretary of State for War, and the Director-General of the Territorial Force. The CCTA called for a comprehensive package of concessions, both to

---

[30] Sir George McCrae to Seely, 16 November 1913, WO 32/11242. For a discussion of similar problems in the inter-war Territorial Army, see chapter 8.

[31] Lord Knollys to Haldane, 7 May 1909, Haldane Papers, MS 5908, ff. 105 – 6.

[32] City of Glasgow Association, 17 March 1913; *The Times*, 2 April 1913.

[33] McCrae to Seely, 16 November 1913, WO 32/11242.

27

individual Territorials and to those patriotic employers who supported them. They recommended that direct allowances be paid to officers, that a bonus be paid to all men in the Force, that the marriage allowance be increased and that the state pay the insurance contributions of all Territorials. As for employers, it asked that they be granted a tax-free allowance of £30 for each Territorial in their employ.[34] This, thought McCrae, was going much too far. Nothing so lavish was needed: perhaps a shilling per day for the first eight days in camp, with two shillings per day for the remaining seven days, thus encouraging men to stay for the full duration of the camp without forcing them to be unduly put upon.[35] The Director-General of the Territorial Force, General Sir Edward Bethune, was not happy with the idea. He admitted that the payment of marriage allowance had brought about an increase in the number of those who went to camp for fifteen days (one estimate had put the increase as high as twenty per cent), but still he felt that there would be no appreciable increase in recruiting. Or rather, those recruits who did come in as a result of a bounty would not be of the 'right class':

> My own opinion is that the more money we pay out in doles to the Territorial the more we get away from the voluntary system and the more we begin to tap the class of man who really cannot afford to do voluntary soldiering.[36]

'Surely', he added shortly afterwards, 'the apathetic man is not to set the tune for the whole country.'[37] 'If we have seriously to bribe people to go into the Force', he concluded gloomily, 'my opinion is that it is time to take up some form of training that will bear evenly on all sections of the population.'[38]

That was more than the Government was prepared to consider. The payment of a small bonus might well bring about a recruiting improvement, just as the marriage allowance had done with regard to attendance at camp. In 1914, therefore, the War Office announced that henceforth Territorials who made themselves efficient by attending the full fifteen days at camp would be paid a bounty of

[34] *The Times*, 27 November 1913.
[35] McCrae to Seely, 16 and 28 November 1913, WO 32/11242.
[36] Bethune to Parliamentary Secretary to Secretary of State, 27 November 1913, WO 32/11243.
[37] Same to same, 6 December 1913, WO 32/11243.
[38] Same to same, 27 November 1913, WO 32/11243.

£1.[39] Whether or not the institution of the bounty would have improved recruiting in the pre-war years cannot be determined, and the evidence of the post-war period does not lead to a firm conclusion. But for the Associations it became and remained a symbol of the niggardly and unrealistic approach of the War Office to Territorial affairs.

As well as pushing for a more sympathetic attitude from the central authorities, the Associations tried desperately to point out the attraction of Territorial soldiering, in the hope that more men would enlist. Their efforts were largely unsuccessful, and simply brought sneers from those who were implacably opposed to the Force. Lord Newton was typical of many who despaired of the voluntary system when he lashed out at one recruiting effort that emphasised the social facilities that Territorials enjoyed: they were 'contemptible and miserable expedients'; could anything have a 'more humiliating and despicable effect on foreign opinion than the fact that we should be reduced to these shifts and devices'?[40] These 'expedients', however, had been for the Volunteers, were for the Territorials, and remain for their successors, an integral part of volunteer soldiering, for, as one historian has written: 'If the British were to be educated to arms in peacetime at all, perhaps it could be through the medium which they had developed and made so peculiarly their own: the club.'[41]

For all the attacks upon it by the National Service League and other critics, and notwithstanding its inability to reach its establishment, the Territorial Force was by 1914 beginning to take shape along the lines that Haldane had laid down. But one flaw remained: the lack of a foreign service obligation. In order to bypass what was politically impossible to impose, the War Office called on Territorials to undertake that commitment voluntarily. The response was not impressive, and merely added weight to the arguments of those who claimed that the voluntary system could not provide for Britain's military needs. In 1913 out of a total strength of 251,000, only 1,152 officers and 18,903 NCOs and men had taken the imperial service obligation.[42] This was the greatest single weakness of

---

[39] *Parl. Debs.* (Commons), 5th series, vol. 59, col. 1090 (10 March 1914).

[40] *Parl. Debs.* (Lords), 5th series, vol. 13, col. 960 (10 February 1913).

[41] Michael Howard, *Lord Haldane and the Territorial Army* (London, 1967), p. 15. For a fuller discussion of these problems, see chapter 8 below.

[42] Cd. 6613, *Parl. Papers* (1913), LI.

the Territorial Force as Haldane had conceived it: with less than 10 per cent of its strength available for overseas service it could hardly be considered a viable second line for the Regular Army. Yet to impose a foreign service obligation on the Territorials would have been seen as grossly unfair, and brought the Government dangerously close to opening the door to a wider form of compulsion. Without that obligation, however, the Territorial Force could not fulfil what in Haldane's mind had been its most important function, to expand the Regular Expeditionary Force and to provide the machinery for the expansion fo the nation's military power in time of war.

In any case the turn of events in August 1914 brought to the War Office a man who had nothing but contempt for the entire concept of the Territorial Force. In response to pressures from many quarters, Asquith relinquished the War Office which he had been occupying since March in addition to being Prime Minister, and appointed Field Marshal Earl Kitchener of Khartoum as Secretary of State for War. A national hero to much of the British public, Kitchener brought to the War Office the drive and determination that the gravity of the crisis demanded. But he was also woefully ignorant of Britain's military forces and the changes that had taken place in the Haldane era. In particular he distrusted the Territorial Force, and had done so since he first heard of Haldane's attempts to bring together the Militia, Volunteers and Yeomanry.[43] He disliked the County Associations because they were dominated by civilians (the Territorials, he remarked, were administered by mayors in their parlours[44]), and because he saw in them a source of unwelcome pressure for military patronage. He dismissed the training that the Territorials had in peacetime as being of no account, and insisted that well-meaning amateurs (a Town Clerk's Army, he once called them[45]) could never replace fully-trained soldiers. His previous experience and professional studies simply reinforced his aversion to the Territorial Force and what it stood for. He was unable to accept any plan or body that did not carry his own personal stamp, and for him, as for many others in the tense weeks of August 1914, the Territorials were all too obviously the brain-child of the

---

[43] Kitchener to Lady Salisbury, 7 June 1906, quoted in Philip Magnus, *Kitchener: Portrait of an Imperialist* (London, 1958), p. 233.

[44] David French, *British Economic and Strategic Planning 1905 – 1915* (London, 1982), p. 126.

[45] Viscount Grey of Fallodon, *Twenty-five Years, 1892 – 1916* (London, 1925), II, p. 68.

philosophical and allegedly pro-German Haldane. Rather than entrust the expansion of the nation's forces to this organisation, which he held in utter contempt, Kitchener decided to bypass the Territorial Army and create his own 'New Armies' on a scale commensurate with the massive struggle that he foresaw.[46] Neither Haldane's pleas with him not to cast away the machinery that had been so carefully and painfully built up,[47] nor the immediate response of the Territorials to appeals for overseas volunteers could shake his resolve.

On August 8, two days after taking office, Kitchener issued his first appeal for 100,000 volunteers. The County Associations were forbidden to recruit in excess of the Territorial Force's establishment ← until Kitchener had reached his target. Thereafter the New Armies 'enjoyed a monopoly of official favour', with the result that although recruiting remained open for either the Territorials or the New Armies, the latter were far more popular. The County Associations continued to recruit and administer their units, while the New Armies were handled through the Adjutant General's department at the War Office. Protests that this arrangement caused a great deal of unnecessary duplication failed to move Kitchener, for, as one critic has written, 'his dislike of . . . the Territorial Army was instinctive and inveterate, so that argument was useless'.[48]

Nevertheless Kitchener was quickly compelled by circumstances to recognize that for all their apparent shortcomings the Territorials could not be ignored, if for no other reason than that they could help to hold the line while his own New Armies were being raised and trained. Within two weeks of Kitchener deciding that he would accept the offer of any Territorial unit that volunteered for overseas service, more than seventy units had met his conditions. Thereafter, over the next four months, the Territorials were encouraged to expand, first by forming second line units in September, and then in November by raising third line units.

Overall, 318 Territorial battalions undertook foreign service during the war, compared with 404 battalions of the New Armies. Kitchener's initial inclination to bypass the Territorials entirely did not long survive, but whether the 'statistical evidence alone gives lie to the criticisms that Kitchener neglected the Territorial force'[49]

[46] George H. Cassar, *Kitchener: Architect of Victory* (London, 1977), pp. 197–202.

[47] Haldane, *An Autobiography*, pp. 278–9.

[48] Magnus, *Kitchener*, p. 290.

[49] Peter Simkins, 'Kitchener and the Expansion of the Army', in Gooch and Beckett, *Politicians and Defence*, p. 99. This is the most succinct

is a moot point. Apart from his prejudice against amateur soldiers, Kitchener had doubted that the County Associations would be capable of handling the mass of recruits that he expected to attract. In reality, it was the Adjutant-General's department of the War Office that proved inadequate to the task. The County Associations performed invaluable service, and did so in the face of a War Office attitude of disdain bordering on open contempt that persisted throughout the war. It was this attitude, or at least the conviction among Territorials that it pervaded the War Office from Kitchener down, that created so much ill feeling both during and after the war. The waste and inefficiency that the dual system of recruiting involved could hardly be laid at the Associations' door: they were not responsible for the side-stepping of Haldane's scheme nor for the makeshift, not to say eccentric, methods of administration that Kitchener brought to the War Office. What the raw statistics do not reveal is the bitterness that Kitchener's policies created. The Territorials were not treated on the same basis as the New Armies, either in terms of material support or of official favour and publicity. While some Territorial grievances were undoubtedly exaggerated, they did have a basis in fact, and the War Office's continuing refusal to acknowledge them was to have unfortunate consequences in the post-war reconstruction period.

The work of the County Associations was largely of a mundane but essential nature. Each Association had to feed, clothe and equip its troops, and to draw upon local resources wherever possible to do it. The competition for scarce supplies that this involved was offset by the fact that the Associations had a much better idea of local conditions, and could more readily adapt their purchasing and hiring programmes than the War Office, with its highly centralised bureaucratic structure. But again Kitchener's influence undermined the attempts of the Associations to ready their troops for action. Northumberland, for example, was twice overruled when its contracts for boots were cancelled on the orders of the War Office, which commandeered the entire supply for the New Armies.[50] When the Regular and Territorial Armies were mobilised on August 5, the Regular staff attached to Territorial units for training purposes were removed and sent back to their Regular units. The great majority of Regular staff that subsequently became

account of the recruiting policies in the first two years of the war, and forms the basis of my remarks in this and the preceding paragraph.

[50] 'History of the Territorial Force Association of the County of Northumberland', Appendix I of Northumberland Territorial Association, 12 December 1919, NRO 408/6.

available for training new recruits were attached to New Army units, the Territorials by and large being left to fend for themselves. Equipment was in appallingly short supply. In mid-December 1914 there were only 240,000 rifles available out of 400,000 required for the Territorial Force, and the provision of artillery for the Territorials was markedly inferior to that of the Regular Army.[51]

The most onerous task that the Associations had to perform was to administer separation and dependants' allowances. Originally it had been decided that Associations would be responsible only for married men embodied and serving at home, but in 1915 this was expanded to include all Territorials. The system of calculating allowances for wives, children and dependants was a complicated one, and each Association had to build up its own administration, competing for clerical staff that became increasingly scarce. By 1917 the Northumberland Association had a staff of 64 clerks (50 of them women) to handle the allowances of more than 24,000 soldiers, a sum that amounted to almost one million pounds per year.[52] The work that was done in this area, as well as the recruiting record of the Associations during the war, when they worked under all manner of handicaps resulting from the prevailing attitude in the War Office, was a powerful answer to Kitchener's conviction that the machinery Haldane had established was incapable of being used to expand the nation's forces.

An even more compelling argument in favour of the Territorials was their performance in battle. Orders for mobilisation came on 5 August, while many units were in summer camp. In September the London Scottish became the first Territorial unit to land in France, and by the end of the year there were twenty-three Territorial infantry battalions, seven yeomanry regiments, and six Territorial field companies of the Royal Engineers in France. These early arrivals, drawn mainly from the North Midland, South Midland and Second London Divisions,[53] served with Regular brigades. Not

---

[51] J. E. Edmonds, *Military Operations: France and Belgium, 1915*, vol. 1 (London, 1927), p. 57; vol. 2 (London, 1928), p. 6.

[52] 'History of the Territorial Force Association of the County of Northumberland'.

[53] In May 1915 the Territorial Divisions, which hitherto had gone by their area designation only, were numbered in sequence after Regular and Reserve Divisions. Hence the North Midland Division became the 46th, the South Midland the 48th, and the Second London Division the 47th. In a sense, this inclusion of the Territorial Divisions in the formal order of battle was a long overdue recognition of the place that the Territorials held in the military system, Kitchener's hostility notwithstanding:

until March 1915 did the first complete Territorial Division, the North Midland (46th), go to France, and by the end of April it had been joined by a further five Territorial Divisions. All these forces needed additional training, but few had the six months that had originally been laid down by Haldane in 1906. The London Scottish and the Oxfordshire Hussars went into action on 1 November, and the British Commander-in-Chief in France, Sir John French, later wrote that 'without the assistance which the Territorials afforded between October, 1914, and June, 1915, it would have been impossible to have held the line in France and Belgium'.[54]

As the fighting intensified French pressed for more and more troops to be sent to France. The New Armies were still months away from being ready to take the field, and the result was that Territorial units were dispatched 'as they were considered fit, and even earlier'.[55] In April 1915, in the fighting for Hill 60, Second Lieutenant G. H. Wodley of the 9th London Regiment (Queen Victoria's Rifles) became the first Territorial officer to win the Victoria Cross. The following month, Lance-Sergeant D. W. Belcher of the London Rifle Brigade won the second Territorial VC at Frezenberg Ridge. In April at St Julien, the Northumberland Brigade, consisting of the 4th, 6th and 7th Northumberland Fusiliers, became the first Territorial brigade to go into action as a brigade. It suffered crippling losses, with over two-thirds of its strength becoming casualties. Recruiting for the New Armies was given priority in Britain, and Territorial units were not allowed to draw replacements until home defence units had reached their establishment. By May the position in the Territorial units in France was so desperate, with few reinforcements to make good the staggering losses, that three of the weakest units, the London Rifle Brigade, the Rangers, and the Kensington Regiment, had to be withdrawn from the line, the latter so depleted that it was amalgamated with several other deficient units.[56]

The growing number of casualties, and the rate at which they were sustained, raised one of the most difficult problems that the War Office encountered with the Territorial Force. Haldane had always stressed that the Territorials were to be considered as a self-contained second line army, and not merely as a collection of units that could be raided to make good the wastage suffered by Regular units. The Territorials were never intended to act as a draft-finding

---

[54] Field Marshal Viscount French of Ypres, *1914* (London, 1919), p. 204.
[55] Edmonds, *France and Belgium, 1915*, vol. 1, p. 155.
[56] *Ibid.*, p. 340; vol. 2, pp. 261 – 2.

body in the way that the old Militia had been, but that was all too often forgotten under the pressures of war. The Welsh Division (the 53rd) suffered most. At the beginning of the war it was virtually broken up, its units parcelled out among Regular divisions in France and India 'as though it had been a casual pool of battalions for reinforcement'.[57] As the scale of fighting heightened, the War Office became increasingly anxious to make use as it saw fit of those Territorial units (and even individuals within them) that were passably capable of going into action. There was, however, a major obstacle: the undertaking given to all Territorials who had enlisted before embodiment which stated that members of the Territorial Force could only be posted to units within their own corps. In the case of those who had taken the foreign service obligation, the 'pledge', as it subsequently became known, was even more restrictive, for it prohibited the posting of individuals away from their original unit without their consent. A strong regimental spirit in Territorial units and the fact that many recruits joined because of the influence of their friends, made it seem unlikely that many Territorials would volunteer to be transferred to other units.

To the War Office this undertaking was a serious anomaly in time of war. It prevented it from using all available man-power where and how it wanted, and gave to those Territorials who had joined before the Force was embodied in August 1914 a status and privilege enjoyed by no other body of soldiers. Kitchener was determined to do away with these restrictions, and to put the old Territorials on the same footing as the Regular Army (and as the post-mobilisation Territorials).[58] A bill was therefore drawn up in 1915 to amend the Territorial Force Act to bring the Territorial terms of enlistment into line with those of all other forces, but it ran into unexpected opposition. The Director-General of the Territorial Force advised against it, arguing that the need for such a drastic step was far from proven, and that it would create enormous resentment among the Territorials and interfere with recruiting. If there was a case for the War Office having powers to transfer men to other units, he was sure that the Territorials would respond when it was put to them, just as they had answered the call to volunteer for overseas service.[59] Asquith hesitated, recognizing that

---

[57] C. H. Dudley Ward, *History of the 53rd (Welsh) Division (T.F.) 1914 – 1918* (Cardiff, 1927), p. 12.

[58] Minute by Adjutant-General, 19 February 1915, WO 32/5452.

[59] DGTF to Adjutant-General, 26 February 1915; to DPS, 11 March 1915: WO 32/5452.

the changing of the conditions of service, 'in flat defiance of this undertaking', would justify a charge of breach of faith. As Sir John Simon, the Home Secretary, concluded: 'The whole basis of recruiting for Territorial Battalions would disappear; opposition from the Territorial Associations is inevitable, and I fear it would be said that no appeals for recruits based upon War Office promises can be made henceforward'.[60] The War Office backed down, but required that future recruits sign an undertaking that they would consent to transfer to a different corps if necessary. This new procedure, Derby told the War Office when pleading for its cancellation, was 'simply murdering recruiting for the Territorial Force'.[61] Again the War Office withdrew under pressure, but the following year it tried once more. By then the need for posting flexibility was paramount, and the War Office had learned something from its attempt the year before. This time it tried to arm itself with the powers that it required while not wholly destroying the concept of the integrity of units that was so dear to many Territorials. The compromise it proposed, and one which received the endorsement of the Director-General of the Territorial Force, allowed it to change the county basis of Territorial corps and to juggle corps boundaries, and more important, it made it possible to transfer a Territorial to a Regular unit so long as it was within his own corps. This was a reasonable solution to the problem, and remained the basis of Territorial service for the rest of the war.[62]

Not all Territorial units served in France and Belgium. Many, including whole units that had volunteered for service overseas, were kept at home, either as defence against the invasion that never came, or to train new Territorial units. Others, including much of the 53rd (Welsh) Division, were sent to India at the beginning of the war so that Regular units on garrison duty there could be relieved and sent directly into action in France. Of all the grievances that the Territorials had during and after the war, none were greater than those of the Territorials in India. Their services there were forgotten, and they were denied any of the honours and medals that would have been their due, and which they were specifically promised. Although they had also fought in Mesopotamia and the Near East, they later faced accusations that they had 'saved their skins'. Despite being some of the first volunteers for overseas

---

[60] Simon to Kitchener, 29 April 1915, WO 32/5452.
[61] Derby to Adjutant-General, 2 July 1915, WO 32/5452.
[62] Assistant Adjutant-General to Adjutant-General, 4 March 1916; DGTF to Adjutant-General, 4 April 1916: WO 32/5452.

service, they were among the last to return to England, in some cases more than four years after leaving. (This point will be developed further in chapter three).

They were treated shabbily, but in many ways not very differently from the majority of Territorials. Taken for granted, looked upon with contempt or amused indifference, bypassed in favour of Kitchener's New Armies, the Territorials had lived up to Haldane's expectations as far as circumstances allowed. Their record was a magnificent one. Seventy-one Territorials won the Victoria Cross. Territorials fought in all the major areas of battle, and won praise from every quarter. Long before Kitchener's New Armies were ready for action units of the Territorial Force had been into battle, often at frightful cost. There is no reason to believe that if Kitchener had followed Haldane's plan and thrown his enormous prestige behind the Territorial Force it would not have been able to recruit and administer the forces needed for the scale of the struggle. True, Haldane had never envisaged raising the numbers of troops that Britain did eventually put into the field, but the machinery he created for the Territorial Army would surely have been a better basis on which to establish a national army than the makeshift organisation that Kitchener set up.

Equally certainly, by its performance, particularly in 1914 and the first half of 1915, the Territorial Force upheld the spirit of Haldane's reforms. When the scale of war grew beyond what almost anyone had foreseen, it was perhaps inevitable that the special qualities of the Territorials should have been submerged in the mobilisation of the entire nation's resources. So too, it was tragic that after the war it was mainly the problems and shortcomings of the Territorial scheme, rather than its achievements, that should have been remembered.

3

The Reconstitution of the Force

At the end of the war the future of the Territorial Force posed a considerable problem to the Government and to the War Office in particular. In view of their fighting record and sterling example of voluntary military service, especially in the early months of the war in support of the British Expeditionary Force and, shortly afterwards, in relief of the Regular garrison in India, the Territorials felt they were entitled to a fair consideration in post-war military planning, and not simply to be cast away or relegated to the status of a tolerated but not much encouraged force. The Government and the War Office were not unsympathetic to this modest claim, but to move beyond this recognition to defining a useful and realistic role for the Territorial Force was an exacting task.

Part of the difficulty lay in the fact that the Territorials could no longer be considered in any way central to the defence needs of the country, most of all in the short term. A primary role for the Territorials as home defence troops seemed to be ruled out by post-war conditions. The defeat of the German Army and the scuttling of the German fleet at Scapa Flow laid to rest the invasion scares that had swept Britain before the war. Now it hardly seemed necessary to maintain an army at home to guard against invasion forces that eluded the Royal Navy and threatened a country devoid of Regular troops. A 'bolt from the blue' was all but impossible, and remained so in the authorities' eyes until well into the 1930s, when air power made the problem of a system of home defence independent of the protection of the Navy a question of paramount importance.

Nor was there much point in thinking of a garrison role for the Territorials. Some Territorial troops had been sent to India during the war, but it was highly doubtful whether the conditions that had pertained in the early stages of the war would apply in future contingencies. It had been possible to replace Regular garrisons in India with Territorials because the likelihood of serious trouble there was small. The sub-continent seemed relatively quiet, and Britain's long-standing rival, Russia, was now an ally. By 1919, however, the situation was very different. The nationalist movement in India was agitating for far-reaching political concessions, and the massacre at Amritsar seemed but the first round of the violence that was bound to come. The new Bolshevik government in the Soviet Union swung the focus of Britain's military concern away from Western Europe and once more to the east. Throughout the 1920s it was the Russian threat to Britain's imperial interests that loomed most menacingly in the eyes of British planners. Not until 1933 did the Committee of Imperial Defence shift its emphasis back to Europe and warn of the dangers of the resurgence of German power. In the post-war world the Territorial Army, with its partially trained forces, could not be relied upon to provide immediate relief for Regular garrison troops and to release them for more important duties elsewhere. It was equally difficult to use Territorials as peacetime garrison troops. That entailed long tours of duty that were inappropriate for part-time volunteers, even if the government of the day was willing to risk the political storm that would arise if it tried to send the Territorial Army out of the country before a national emergency was declared and general military service introduced.

Haldane's idea of the Territorial Army as the basis for the expansion of the military power of the nation, the means by which the Regular Expeditionary Force was to be supported in the field, appeared to have no immediate relevance in 1919. The German Army was crushed, and while the peace settlement had not yet been finalised, there seemed to be little likelihood that a major expeditionary force requiring massive reinforcements would be needed for some time, if at all. The Empire, including the newly won, and shortly thereafter mandated, territories, threatened to be a source of continual strife for years to come. But the potential enemies there, Russia excepted, were classed as 'undeveloped' aggressors: against them the Regular Army would be capable of holding its own.

The problems confronting the War Office were much closer to home. The Regular Army was being dragged into a bitter campaign in Ireland as the single most intractable problem that the United Kingdom ever faced moved into an increasingly violent phase. In the wake of a great national war the Irish troubles were an exasperating diversion from the readjustments that had to be made in post-war Britain. The War Office had to deal with the demobilisation of the millions of men who had been conscripted during the war. Their release from military service and their orderly return to civilian life was a much more immediate problem than the future of the Territorial Force. Indeed, at the end of the 'war to end war', with the Government preparing to embark on an ambitious programme of social reconstruction, there was something almost bizarre about the Territorial movement pressing its claims for an early decision as to its future. After four years of horrifying involvement in a war whose total cost was only beginning to become apparent, at a time when military values and considerations were being discarded along with khaki uniforms, it was hardly to be expected that the Territorials would find an eager audience to listen to their pleas.

The Territorials, however, were not without their supporters, and as with the Volunteers, their political influence was considerable. This made the Force a body whose opinions could not easily be swept aside. In the House of Commons a sizeable number of MPs had Territorial connections, and even those who had no official involvement with the Territorial Force through the County Associations, had to pay some attention to local feelings of pride over the wartime achievements of the Territorial units within their constituencies. In the House of Lords the Territorials found a natural well of sympathy in the peers who played such an active part in their local Associations. In this sense, and in this sense alone, the Territorials were strongly placed to bring pressure on the Government to reach a favourable decision as to their future. The political influence of the Territorials after the war derived from their numbers rather than from any realisation that they had been indispensable in the disarray of the early years of the war. There was little support for the idea that Britain had to make ready for another great war, and for once perhaps, the War Office was not anxious to make its plans for the next war on the basis of the last. It was this cautious appraisal of the lessons of the war rather than any hostility as such to the Territorial Army that made the War Office proceed slowly. In its scheme of things, with the need to protect the Regular Army against spending cuts its first priority, the future of the Territorial Army was not a prime concern and could not be until the major issues had been settled. For the country at large, tired of the dominating influence of military considerations after four years of continental war, the claims of the Territorials were a tiresome demonstration of what it hoped could at last be laid aside.

The working-out of the reconstitution proposals in 1919 and 1920 must be placed in the context of this general lack of interest, the claims and grievances of the Territorials, and the greater priorities pressing on the War Office. With the impending demise of the Military Service Act, voluntary service again became the only means of expanding the Regular Army, but since it was unlikely that the Army would be involved in a major war in the foreseeable future, the inherent deficiencies of the Territorials as a genuine second line dominated discussions. The resolution of these difficulties was inevitably a compromise, and owed as much to expediency as to carefully considered judgment. It was to create further difficulties in the later 1920s and the 1930s when the political and economic climate was much less sympathetic to problems bearing on defence.

In February 1919 the Director-General of the Territorial Force, the Earl of Scarbrough, submitted proposals to the Army Council for the reconstitution of the Territorials. Favourable conditions existed, he suggested, for laying the foundations of a part-time second line at the same time as a volunteer first line was being established. There was a large pool of trained man-power which had either just completed or was about to complete its engagement, and which might well be prepared to undertake further service if sufficiently attractive terms were announced. The general feeling of comradeship that had developed in the course of the war could be channelled by the War Office into a new Territorial Force appropriately remodelled along the lines of Britain's post-war requirements. Once the essential conditions of service — the pay and the obligations that went with it — had been settled, recruiting could begin. This should be done quickly before the interest in part-time soldiering faded away among the trained man-power that was most useful to the War Office. Even if a speedy agreement was found to be impossible, he still thought it wise to set up the essential framework and to take applicants' names, with the necessary safeguards and guarantees in case the final conditions did not satisfy those who had initially indicated their willingness to serve.[1]

While this proposal was being studied within the War Office, Winston Churchill, Secretary of State for War, was coming under pressure in the House of Commons to provide specific details regarding the reconstitution of the Territorial Force, the acceptance of which in principle he had already made known. He was warned that any undue delay in announcing his scheme would result in a serious setback, for once the initial interest had been lost and men

---

[1] 'Reconstruction of the Territorial Force', 24 February 1919, WO 32/11246.

41

had settled back into civilian life it would be very difficult to revive it.[2] This criticism was frequently levelled against the War Office in the following months, as Parliament and the Territorials awaited the Government's plans. But as Churchill replied to his critics, the reconstitution of the Territorials had to be carried out within a much wider context than simply that of the future of the second line. Until the overall problems of Britain's political and military adjustment to the conditions of the post-war world had been studied, no steps could be taken that might later prove to be of a mere stop-gap nature.[3]

The General Staff quickly made known its reservations about the Territorials. It was unanimously agreed that there was no case for reconstituting the Territorial Force except on the basis of a foreign service obligation that would require the Territorials to serve overseas in the event of a 'national emergency'. But to define a 'national emergency' was difficult. In a major crisis it was understood that general conscription would be imposed; the grey area covered the 'moderate' wars in the Empire and on its fringes that appeared all too possible. It was doubtful if the ranks of the Territorial Force could be filled if there was an obligation to serve in imperial wars that did not warrant general conscription, especially since in such circumstances the primary requirements of the Regular Army would be for drafts to maintain the strength of Regular units rather than for whole Territorial units to serve as a genuine second line.[4]

One of the strongest fears of the Territorials had always been that the Regular Army and the War Office would ignore the integrity of its units and merely draw on them for draft-finding purposes. Scarbrough suggested that the imperial service pill might be sweetened by linking it with a guarantee that if the Territorial Force was embodied for overseas service, it would proceed and operate in its original units, with compulsory transfers being permitted only in extraordinary circumstances and then only as a temporary measure.

While this might have calmed the worst fears of the Territorials,

---

[2]   Sir Samuel Scott, Conservative MP, *Parl. Debs.* (Commons), 5th series, vol. 113, col. 104 (3 March 1919). Scott had served for some years in the Royal West Kent Yeomanry.

[3]   *Ibid.*, col. 78.

[4]   Minutes by the Adjutant-General (1 and 24 March 1919), the Deputy Director of Military Operations [Walter Kirk, Director-General of the Territorial Army 1936 – 39] (12 March 1919), and the Deputy Chief of the General Staff (21 March 1919): WO 32/11246.

it created serious problems for the War Office (see chapter 7). If it promised to maintain the integrity of Territorial units, the usefulness of the Territorial Force as a means of supporting the Regular Army in a moderate war would be severely circumscribed if not destroyed. And in the extreme case of a national emergency such a pledge would undercut the efficiency of a wider mobilisation scheme under general conscription by creating a special class of soldiers. Without such a pledge, however, recruiting might be so impeded that the new Territorial Force would be still-born. The problem appeared insoluble, especially since there was a common feeling among those who studied Scarbrough's proposals that no commitments should be entered into that would subsequently tie the hands of the War Office. If that entailed a delay in reaching a final decision, with the risk that the current interest in the Territorials might have waned by the time the conditions were established, that was regrettable, but unavoidable.

There was, however, general agreement that the Force should be reconstituted. A sub-committee of the War Office, chaired by the Adjutant-General, Sir George Milne, submitted its proposals at the end of March.[5] It recommended the reconstruction of the Force on the pre-war basis of fourteen infantry divisions and fourteen mounted brigades, raised and administered by the County Associations that were the hallmark of Haldane's original scheme. While recognizing that the precise terms of service would not be formulated for some time, it pressed for the immediate appointment of divisional and brigade staffs so that application for enlistment (as opposed to enlistment itself, or attestation) could begin as soon as possible.

The thorny problem of conditions of service was to be resolved by an uneasy compromise. Territorials would be liable for overseas service once — and not before — general conscription had been introduced. When that situation arose they would proceed overseas with their own units but would then be available for service as the War Office saw fit. No pledge would be given to maintain the integrity of units subsequent to embarkation, although every effort would be made to do so.

The compensation for these burdens lay in the liberal pay scales and concessions that the sub-committee proposed, namely that while in camp Territorials would receive the same pay and allowances as the corresponding ranks in the Regular Army, and that a legal obligation would be imposed on employers to allow their

---

[5] Adjutant-General to Secretary of State, 31 March 1919, WO 32/11246. ✓

employees any additional leave necessary to enable them to attend the annual fifteen days' camp. These were expensive and not entirely satisfactory proposals. If adopted they would commit the War Office to maintaining a well-paid force that would not fit easily into the military requirements of the country.

On the basis of Milne's report, Churchill addressed a meeting of Territorial representatives on 1 April 1919. His position was not an easy one, for in summoning the representatives to meet him when he had only the most general proposals to lay before them, he opened the door to an airing of all the grievances, real or imaginary, that the Territorials felt they had suffered. If that happened and an atmosphere of recrimination developed, the cooperation that was necessary for the successful reconstitution of the Force would be destroyed. He was therefore generous in his praise of the Territorials' achievement during the war, quick to acknowledge the error that Kitchener and the Government had made in by-passing Haldane's scheme for using the Territorials to expand Britain's military power in time of emergency, and open in admitting that the international situation did not yet permit a final decision to be reached on the precise terms of the reconstitution.

Delivered in that vein, his remarks were well received and most of his critics were temporarily disarmed. He proposed that the pre-war organization of fourteen infantry and fourteen mounted brigades be adhered to, and that immediate steps be taken to begin appointing divisional and brigade staffs. Suitably qualified Territorial officers would be eligible for commands at the brigade level, thus settling one of the strongest Territorial grievances. Haldane's undertaking that Territorials would be considered for senior commands had never been honoured in spirit: though they may have been considered, very few were ever appointed. (Though Churchill was willing to change that, little was done until well into the 1930s. The War Office consistently opposed the appointment of Territorials to senior commands on the grounds that it would deprive Regular officers of the positions.) Enlistment in the ranks was for the moment to be restricted to men who had already served in the Regular or the Territorial Army. Once accepted for service in the new Territorial Force they would be paid while in training at the same rates as the Regular Army. These proposals were well calculated to appeal to the Territorials' wish to be taken seriously as a military force, and to be treated in the same way as the Regulars. In return Churchill made it clear that the new terms of service would involve a major departure from the pre-war system. Firstly, men would be enlisted under a foreign service obligation which would not be put into effect until a general service act had been passed and conscription imposed on the nation as a whole. Secondly, while promising to do everything possible to keep units intact when they were sent overseas, he warned that the War Office would be unable to give a firm guarantee to preserve the integrity of Territorial units. He concluded by suggesting a further meeting in the near future when the exact terms had been finalised and after the Territorial Associations had been able to sound out local opinion.[6]

A month later Churchill again met the Territorial representatives. He was still unable to give them the promised details, yet urged the need for a speedy revival of the Territorial movement. The latter was hardly a novel suggestion to his listeners, but they were concerned at his emphasis on the ability of the Territorial Force, in the absence of the Special Reserve that provided drafts, to 'secure the Regular Military Forces of the country that amphibious and world-wide mobility on which the security of our Empire depends'.[7] This implied a role for the Territorials not as a genuine self-contained second line but as a body providing reinforcements for Regular units. The April promise to maintain the integrity of Territorial units as far as possible seemed to have been pushed aside.

In fact, as the War Office worked on the pamphlet describing the conditions of service, reservations about the scheme that Churchill had outlined grew. Again, as with Scarbrough's original proposals in February, there was a unanimous opinion against giving any pledge on the integrity of units, since the primary need of the Regular Army was for drafts over and above what the Regular Reserve could provide. By now it was accepted (at least for the moment) that enlistment in the new Territorial Force had to be on the basis of a foreign service commitment. For its part, the War Office wanted that to be the only commitment. It was reluctant to be encumbered by obligations that would restrict its ability to use the Territorials when, how, and where it saw fit. Shackling the Force with pledges that could not be kept under wartime conditions was no way to justify the revival of the Territorials. Until that contentious issue could be settled, there was little point in talking about the commencement of recruiting. Notwithstanding the mounting criticism over the delay in publishing its precise proposals, the military members of the War Office felt

[6] *The Times*, 3 April 1919.
[7] *Ibid.*, 3 May 1919.

that the scheme was being drawn up with undue haste.[8]

The tension between Churchill's public commitment to reconstitute the Territorial Force and the reservations of his professional military advisers came to a head in August 1919, when the Cabinet imposed stringent limits on defence expenditure and laid down that future service estimates were to be based on the assumption that no major war would occur within ten years and that no expeditionary force would be needed.[9] The Chief of the Imperial General Staff, Field Marshal Sir Henry Wilson, explained to Churchill that Britain's military requirements were for peace garrisons in the Empire and the means to reinforce those garrisons. What was not needed was any power of great expansion or troops allotted purely to home defence. The conclusion was unmistakable: the Territorials had no role to play in Britain's post-war circumstances, and any money spent on them would divert funds that were in short supply from the pressing needs of the Regular Army.[10]

Churchill insisted that it was politically 'absolutely necessary' to go ahead with the public undertakings to rebuild the Territorials, but Wilson replied that it was wrong to consider the case of the Territorials before the needs of the Regular Army had been satisfied. This was especially so when a reconstituted Territorial Force would not fulfil the draft-finding requirements of the Regular Army in a 'moderate war', i.e. one that did not warrant the introduction of general conscription. He warned:

> Remember that it may be politically wise, politically expedient, even politically necessary to re-create the old Territorial Force, on this subject I express no opinion except that in our present financial state such a course may conceivably cause the loss of a portion of our Empire. If with all the facts before them, the Cabinet decide on this course I have absolutely nothing further to say.[11]

Churchill could not leave it there. As he reminded Wilson:

> it was on your advice, with your full agreement and in the presence of the whole Army Council that more than six months

---

[8] Minutes by the Quartermaster-General (10 June 1919), the Director of Organization (13 June 1919), and the Director-General of Mobilization (17 June 1919): WO 32/11246.

[9] War Cabinet 616, 15 August 1919, CAB 32/12.

[10] 'The Future of the Army', 7 August 1919, GT 8039, CAB 24/87.

[11] Wilson, diary entry, 26 September 1919; Wilson to Churchill, 6 October 1919, Wilson Papers, Correspondence Files 18 B/17.

ago I announced in public conference . . . that the Territorial Force would be reconstituted. . . . Every step has been taken with your full agreement and on your advice.

In these circumstances it is somewhat disconcerting that the General Staff should now, apparently, not want the Territorial Force at all and calmly come forward with the suggestion to abolish it . . ..

I am quite certain that neither the Government nor Parliament, nor, I may add, the Public will accept the abolition of the Territorial Force and they would think it astonishing that an Army Council which had so cordially endorsed all previous declarations on this subject should now stultify themselves by a complete reversal of policy. The course of events would not be altered, but we should be completely discredited.[12]

Churchill's publicly announced deadline of 1 October as the date by which the final proposals were to be unveiled had passed, and still no agreement had been reached.

In an attempt to reconcile Wilson's basic objections with Churchill's pressing need to arrive at some final decisions, Scarbrough produced an unwieldy compromise. Given the military situation and the Cabinet pronouncement on defence expenditure, it would be an unjustified 'extravagance' to establish a Territorial Force solely for home defence. If the Territorials wished to be taken seriously as a military force, it could only be on the basis of a foreign service obligation, which most seemed willing to accept. Then the Force would be a genuine second line. The wide-spread fear among Territorials that the general service obligation might be too suddenly implemented could be put to rest by the creation of a 'special class' of Territorials. These would be men who accepted an obligation similar to that of the Regular Army Reserve in that they could be called out on the proclamation of an emergency and used as drafts for Regular units. In return for undertaking this obligation they would receive an additional bounty. This 'special class', Scarbrough suggested, would act as a 'visible buffer' between the Regular Army and the main body of the Territorials, and would add weight to the Government's undertaking, in lieu of a firm pledge, that transfers from Territorial units would only be made as a temporary measure.[13]

12 Churchill to Wilson, 2 October 1919, Wilson Papers, Correspondence Files 18 B3/17.
13 'Organization of the Territorial Force', 21 November 1919, WO 32/2681.

Scarbrough claimed — on what basis it is difficult to say — that this would replace a costly and inefficient system of reserves with a 'single, simple and inexpensive organization closely assimilated to that of the Regular Forces'. In fact the two-tier system would divide Territorial units into those who had pledged and those who had not, for although the 'special class' would be supernumerary to the establishment of each unit, training would be undertaken in common and an unhealthy rivalry would probably develop. As for the claim that the new organization would be inexpensive, the cost of the reconstitution scheme as a whole had been one of the main sticking points. The Financial Secretary of the War Office, Sir Charles Harris, was strongly critical of the level of inducements that it was proposed to offer recruits. Not only was the cost too great in general terms, but it seemed foolish to attract large numbers of soldiers in this way if funds to train them would not be available after the imposition of financial restrictions in August.[14] The 'special class' simply added to the cost. It was estimated that a recruit would cost £44 per annum as opposed to £19 for a member of the Army Reserve. In effect the War Office would be competing with itself through higher bounties for the same men, at least in the short term. Until Regular soldiers completed their engagements and moved into the Regular Reserve, there would be a shortage of man-power on which to draw for the Reserve, the 'special class' of the Territorial Force, and the Territorial Force itself.[15] This was hardly a 'single, simple and inexpensive organization'.

Although the scheme was by no means ideal it did satisfy the main objections of both Churchill and his military advisers. Even though Wilson still hesitated, he had at least been able to secure the means of supplying the Regular Army with reinforcements — at an apparently exorbitant cost, while Churchill was at last approaching long-overdue agreement on the terms that had been promised by the end of September. On 1st December he wrote to the Cabinet, emphasizing the need to reach a swift decision, and sought permission to publish a pamphlet outlining the War Office's proposals. This was despite the fact that many in the War Office still felt that no preliminary announcements should be made until the Government itself had agreed on the precise nature of the terms of reconstitution.

[14] Harris to Under-Secretary of State, 20 October 1919, WO 32/11247. These criticisms of the pay scales were echoed by the Master-General of the Ordnance, who said that Wilson agreed with him. 1 December 1919, WO 32/2681.

[15] Scarbrough to Churchill, 6 January 1920; Adjutant-General to Churchill, 7 January 1920: WO 32/2681.

Churchill admitted that he had reservations about imposing a foreign service obligation, but added that his advisers had assured him that the attractive pay and bounties would more than offset any injury the new burden might do to recruiting. In any case, he warned, the psychological moment for capturing the interest in part-time soldiering was rapidly passing: immediate action was needed.[16] The next day Churchill revealed his growing doubts about the wisdom of a foreign service obligation to the Army Council. An exasperated Wilson recorded in his diary:

> We have been months at this, with Winston's knowledge and approval. This morning he suddenly and unexpectedly ran out. He said he would get no more recruits, there would be a complete frost, etc., etc., and he wanted to revert to the Territorial Force of pre-war days. I said that I could not agree to 6 – 10 millions being spent on a sham.[17]

Churchill thereupon agreed that the two schemes should be put to the Cabinet, which would have to choose where the War Office had been unable to make up its mind. The difference between the two hinged on the nature of the foreign service obligation, for Wilson had managed to secure from Churchill an agreement that this should exist in some form. One scheme envisaged the Territorial liability for overseas service only coming into force after the passing of a general conscription act; the other made the Territorials liable for overseas service after the Regular Army Reserve had been called out by Royal Proclamation. In both cases the 'special class', supernumerary to the Territorial establishment, would also be created. The second alternative was clearly much more in line with the thinking of the military members of the War Office, for it meant the Territorial Force could be used in a moderate or even small war that would not warrant general conscription.[18]

The delay in reaching a final agreement had long since become an embarrassment to the War Office. Eight months had passed since Churchill had summoned the Territorial representatives to hear his general proposals, yet it seemed that little progress had been made. The Army Committee of the House of Commons was restive, and had already passed a resolution condemning the delay.[19] Field

[16] WO 32/2681.
[17] Entry for 2 December 1919, Wilson Papers.
[18] Army Council minutes, 259th meeting, 2 December 1919, WO 163/24.
[19] *The Times*, 29 October 1919.

Marshal Lord Haig had urged a speedy decision; so too had Lord Esher, in his capacity as Chairman of the County of London Territorial Association.[20] Questions were asked in Parliament, and letters written to the press. The plaintive cry in *The Times* (October 29), 'When, Sir, will this operation be completed?' was typical. These pressures and growing doubts made it necessary for the War Office to reassure the Territorial supporters that it fully intended to re-establish the Force.[21] Widespread fears that the War Office was less than enthusiastic about the Territorials were not calmed by the spate of reports in *The Times* to the effect that the Government was unable to make up its mind.[22]

The delay only served to deepen the suspicions of the Associations, and to feed the sense of grievance that many Territorials had. This had been building during the war, and the apparent inability of the Government to reach a decision on the future of the Territorials only reinforced the widespread feeling among them that their services had not been fully appreciated. Apart from the resentment that had been caused by Kitchener's contemptuous treatment of the Territorial Force as a whole, there were other grievances that made the Associations wary of the War Office's expression of goodwill towards them.

One decision that greatly affected the Territorials was the awarding of medals. In the first place the Government decided not to give any special medal to those Territorials who had been in the Force when war broke out and who had answered the call for volunteers for overseas service. Rather than make any distinction between Territorials and other volunteers, the Government simply lumped them all together and awarded them the 1914 and 1915 Stars as appropriate. Many Territorials felt that their special service, in preparing themselves for war during peacetime, deserved something better than that, especially when it was recognized that the ability of the Territorials to go into action had been of critical value in the early days of the battles in France and Belgium. As the Lincoln Association put it, 'many Territorials are possibly prouder of the fact that they were members of the Force prior to the outbreak

---

[20] Haig had said, on receiving the Freedom of the City of London: 'My message . . . is to urge you . . . to set up forthwith the organization of a strong Citizen Army on Territorial lines . . ..' *The Times*, 13 June 1919. Esher's comments were reported in *The Times* on 7 July 1919.

[21] *Ibid.*, 15 August 1919 (Deputy Chief of the General Staff), 6 December 1919 (Churchill).

[22] *The Times*, 15 and 21 November, 6, 17 and 18 December 1919.

of war, than that they were in a theatre of war in 1914 or 1915'.[23]

Secondly, some Territorials who had volunteered for overseas service at the beginning of the war had ended up with no medals at all. These were the men who were held back — against their wish — and put into training positions in Britain, where they performed invaluable service building up the vast national army that had finally brought victory. But their efforts were denied recognition, and the Government refused to strike a home defence medal. The result was that some who had volunteered for overseas duty but had been refused permission to go had less tangible sign of their willing service than the merest conscript who barely saw service across the Channel in the last months of the war. It was not enough to suggest, as one speaker did when the Sussex Association voted against a home defence medal, that it would 'cheapen and insult' the awards for those who did serve overseas, because 'every fit man who wanted to go could go'. As a commanding officer in Hampshire noted in 1922, almost 33 per cent of his officers and 62 per cent of his warrant officers and sergeants had been held back during the war: now they 'were almost ashamed to put on uniform and would leave the Corps on that account, as soon as their time was up'. A number of Associations, including Cambridgeshire, Oxfordshire, Hampshire and the Cities of Dundee and Glasgow, supported Essex in its attempts to have proper recognition given to those who served in a home defence role,[24] but just as many Associations (Buckinghamshire, Devon, Fife, Peebles, Stirling and Sussex) rejected the Essex resolution.[25]

Another of the grievances arose over the failure of the War Office to maintain the integrity of Territorial units. Even allowing

---

[23] Lincoln, 1 June 1920, TA 1/2. Support for a special Territorial medal came from the following Associations: Cambridgeshire, 6 October 1920, Minutes, vol. 2; City of Aberdeen, 6 October 1919, MD 4/4; City of Dundee, 18 February 1919, MD 7/5; City of Edinburgh, General Purposes Committee, 4 May 1920; Denbighshire, 8 July 1920, TA/D/6; Devon, 7 August 1919, 1715c/TA/2; Hertfordshire, 12 April 1920; Lanarkshire, 25 June 1920, MD 2/3; Perth, Finance Committee, 30 June 1920, MD 7/39.

[24] Hampshire, General Purposes Committee, 17 February 1922, 37M69/5; Cambridgeshire, 10 October 1919, Minutes, vol. 2; Oxfordshire, 1 November 1919, Acc. 727/5; City of Dundee, 21 October 1919, MD 7/5; City of Glasgow, 7 October 1919.

[25] Buckinghamshire, 6 November 1919; Devon, 24 September 1919, 1715c/TA/2; Fife, 12 December 1919, MD 7/25; Peebles, 17 October 1919; Stirling, 4 November 1919, MD 6/22; Sussex, 13 October 1919, D 912/7.

for the demands of war, many Territorials felt that the War Office had simply cast aside the undertakings it had given when the Force was first formed, despite the fact that one of the prime attractions of the Territorials had been the promise that men would be able to serve with their friends from their own areas. No one had expected that this could be an absolute guarantee, but there had seemed to be not even an effort to maintain units intact. The Secretary of the West Riding Association told Scarbrough that the following letter, from an officer of the 4th Battalion Duke of Wellington's Regiment, was 'typical of the feeling of a very great number of members of the Territorial Force'.

> As far as I myself am concerned, during the period I have served abroad, I have never once been attached to my own unit, or to any other Yorkshire unit . . .. It is impossible to believe that the posting of Officers and men to other than their own Units was accidental, necessitated by exigencies of the Service, or for any other reason than the desire of a certain school of Officers to break up all Regimental feeling, and to put the whole Army on one footing in the same way as in the Royal Navy. If this had been the declared policy of the Government it would be understood, but it looks very much as if it was an attempt to achieve a certain end by disloyalty and underhand means.[26]

It was true that the War Office by and large looked upon the Army as a whole, and did not concern itself with the distinctions that were so dear to many Territorials, but there was no deliberate plot to destroy the Territorial Force — once that is, that Kitchener had made the decision to bypass them and to create his own 'New Armies'. Nevertheless this treatment rankled, and after the war many Associations were determined to force the War Office to give iron-clad guarantees that the same would not happen in any future war.

Perhaps the most deeply-felt grievance related to India. At the very beginning of the war, a number of Territorial units, including some from Surrey and Devon, had been sent to India to relieve Regular troops on garrison duty there. Kitchener had assured them that this posting, which was suddenly announced after they had volunteered for service in France, would not affect any claim they might have for medals and honours. That promise was never kept.

---

[26] Excerpt quoted by Brigadier H. Mends to Scarbrough, 14 March 1919, Scarbrough Papers.

The 1/6th Devonshire Regiment, for example, served in India, Mesopotamia, Salonika, France and the Northwest Frontier from 1914 until well into 1919, but because its voyage to India was completed on 3 January 1915 — three days after the cut-off date — its claims for the 1914 – 15 Star were rejected, and its members were palmed off with the two medals given to every soldier. Notwithstanding Kitchener's undertaking, the War Office repeatedly refused to honour his commitment, on the grounds that to do so would 'open the gates' to other similar claims.[27] This sort of attitude, which showed so little understanding of the Territorial mentality, naturally aroused great resentment. A government spokesman admitted that 'a great many more Territorials have seen active service [in India] than is thought by public opinion',[28] but the ignorance and lack of sympathy for the Territorials' plight was not confined to the public at large. At a War Cabinet meeting in 1919 the Lord Privy Seal, Andrew Bonar Law, was quoted as saying that the Territorials in India 'had at least escaped all active duty and had saved their skin'.[29]

As if this was not bad enough, the Territorials who served in India felt that they had been positively discriminated against. As one Territorial put it:

> I cannot help feeling that the fact that I am a 'territorial' instead of a 'Kitchener' makes it much more difficult to get a decent job — it was the same in India. They select a few Territorial Peers and MPs for good appointments for eye wash for the world at large, but there is not a Territorial Officer living, who does not feel that the Territorials have been badly treated all through.[30]

Even worse was in store at the end of the war. Despite the War Office's promise that when demobilization began every consideration would be given to those who had volunteered for duty first, that undertaking was also scrapped on the grounds of economic and political expediency. Rather than apply the principle of 'first in, first out', the Government announced that it would release men on an industrial and commercial scale of priorities. The result was that some Territorials, for example the 1/6th Devons, were still in

[27] See the statement by the Secretary of State for War, Mr T. Shaw, on 24 March 1930: *Parl. Debs.* (Commons), 5th series, vol. 237, col. 81.

[28] *Ibid.*, vol. 114, col. 1052, 1 April 1919.

[29] War Cabinet 521(1), 28 January 1919, CAB 23/9.

[30] Quoted in a letter from the Private Secretary to the Secretary of State for the Colonies to Scarbrough, 24 April 1919, Scarbrough Papers.

India almost a year after the war had ended. It was hardly enough to be told that a shortage of shipping prevented their earlier return, especially since, when they did return, they were denied the public honours and welcomes that other troops, often conscripts, had received. The Territorials who had been 'banished to India', as one of their supporters put it to Scarbrough,[31] had every reason to feel let down and abused. One wrote plaintively: 'It's no good moaning. We Territorials are here in India. Nobody knows anything about us in England, and nobody seems to care about us. We were fools in the start and now must stand the racket.'[32] The Surrey Association unanimously passed a resolution condemning the 'shabby' treatment that the Territorials in India had received at the hands of the War Office,[33] but it made no difference. By 1919 the problems of demobilization and the wish to get back to a peacetime routine pushed aside the claims of the Territorials in India, and indeed of the Territorials as a whole, as making an invidious distinction between different sorts of volunteers, and between volunteers and conscripts.

As the delay in announcing the final proposals lengthened, there was a growing danger that such interest as there was in the Territorials in the country at large might disappear altogether. The Associations were becoming restive, and many passed resolutions deploring the effect that the delay was having on former members of the Territorial Force and on potential recruits.[34] Churchill was keenly aware of the damage that was being done by the inability of the War Office to reach a final decision, and he therefore suggested to his military advisers that a 'loop-hole of escape' could be found

[31] Lieutenant-General Sir Reginald Carew to Scarbrough, 19 January 1919, Scarbrough Papers. Carew was Unionist MP for Bodmin Division, Cornwall, 1910 – 16, and Inspector-General of the Territorial Force in 1914. Carew felt a special concern for the Territorials in India, for, as he explained to Scarbrough, 'I regret to say that I helped K[itchener] by telling the poor Terriers . . . who were inclined to trust me, that they *must* go, and that they could trust K . . .. I suppose you will be able to get the Terriers home some day . . . .'
[32] Quoted by Carew to Scarbrough, 19 January 1919.
[33] Surrey, 7 April 1919, Minutes, vol. 2.
[34] City of Dundee, 18 November 1919, MD 7/5; City of Edinburgh, 25 November 1919; City of Glasgow, 11 November 1919; County of Aberdeen, 21 November 1919, MD 4/45; County of London, 30 October 1919, A/TA/2; Derbyshire, 6 October 1919, D 530/3; Dumbarton, 16 December 1919, MD 9/1; East Lancashire, 6 June 1919, Minute Book 4; Monmouthshire, 23 October 1919, D 766.1; Sussex, 24 November 1919, D 912/7.

by opening recruiting at once on the basis of tentative conditions of service, including the main sticking point, an obligation for overseas service, thereby quelling the rumbles of discontent over the Government's inaction, and introducing in March the necessary legislation to amend the Territorial Act. If, in the intervening months, it was found that recruiting had been seriously affected by the inclusion of the foreign service obligation, the legislation could be dropped and recruiting could proceed on the basis of the pre-war conditions, that is, service for home defence only.[35] The response to this proposal was cool. The Parliamentary Army Committee was not prepared to accept the opening of recruiting before the final conditions of service had been published, and it further insisted that until general conscription had been imposed Territorial service abroad could only be in units that were maintained intact.[36]

Faced with this impasse Churchill appealed to the Cabinet for a decision. He admitted that though the advantages of an overseas obligation were 'overwhelming' from a military point of view, he thought it 'essentially unfair to ask men who are not soldiers to take on a liability to be sent away . . . for long periods while the mass of their fellow-countrymen pursue their ordinary avocations and bear no part whatever of the national burden'. Furthermore he had told the Territorial representatives in April that the Territorial Force would not be embodied and despatched abroad unless the emergency was sufficiently grave to warrant the introduction of general conscription. If the Government now went ahead and imposed a foreign service obligation as the War Office wanted, Churchill feared that charges of bad faith might arise and that public opinion might turn against the concept of the Territorial Force, with grave effects on recruiting. The proposal could be dropped and the Territorial Force could carry on along pre-war lines, but such an open admission of mismanagement and disagreement within the War Office would hardly commend the Force to the country or allay rumours of War Office hostility to its reconstitution. Churchill therefore specifically asked the Cabinet to solve his dilemma.[37]

When the Cabinet met on 7 January 1920, Churchill again reminded them that the Government was pledged to reconstitute

---

[35] Churchill to CIGS, AG, DGTF, 8 December 1919: WO 32/2681.

[36] *The Times*, 19 December 1919.

[37] 'Liability of Territorial Force for General Service', 5 January 1920. CP 388, CAB 24/95. Churchill had advised the Cabinet on 23 December of the urgency of reaching a decision, the more so since he was due to meet the Territorial Associations on 15 January to announce the Government's proposals. Cabinet 19(19), CAB 23/18.

the Territorial Force and that little time was available to arrive at a decision, since a public meeting had already been announced for 15 January. But the Cabinet was no more able than the War Office to reach agreement. The proposals were deceptively simple, their implications far-reaching. There were strong arguments on both sides. In support of a foreign service obligation there was the opinion of those who were closely in touch with the Territorial movement. They had made it clear that if the Force was reconstituted on pre-war lines, and not made liable for overseas service, it would not be taken seriously and recruiting would be poor. Those who hesitated for fear that Territorial units would be broken up and used as drafts for the Regular Army would be reassured by the creation of the 'special class' beyond the normal Territorial establishment. Against this argument was the assertion that a foreign service obligation would deter men from enlisting because of the dangers it would pose to their security of employment. Consequently the stable, responsible class that it was hoped would join the new citizen army would hold back, and the Territorials would be drawn from the elements who had previously filled the ranks of the Militia, mainly young or unemployed labourers. There was also a political consideration. If a foreign service obligation were to be imposed, amending legislation would have to be introduced in Parliament, giving the Government's opponents an opportunity to charge that the Force was being raised for intervention in Russia. Political dangers attended one course of action, the real possibility of the scheme's failure the other.

Various alternative proposals were made: that foreign service be confined within the bounds of the Empire; that Territorials be given a choice of liabilities; that the foreign service obligation run for only the first two years of a four year engagement; that the Territorials be liable for overseas service only after Parliament had passed a resolution approving the action; or that the Territorials be sent overseas only after general conscription had been introduced. Each of these suggestions had its shortcomings. The first unnecessarily restricted the area within which the Territorials could be used, and was an unsatisfactory solution for those who objected to any form of overseas service, within the Empire's boundaries or not. The second created administrative nightmares and destroyed the integrity of units, as would the third, for it established two classes within each unit. The fourth would not satisfy those who mistrusted the Government, for it seemed clear that no government would risk introducing such legislation unless it was certain of success; while the fifth did not meet the War Office's requirements for a moderate war, and in any case committed the Government to introducing conscription in an emergency situation, which, although it was agreed might be inevitable, was not a course the Government wished to state publicly. When it was clear that the Cabinet was making no progress, it appointed a sub-committee to wrestle with the problem and recommend a solution.[38]

When the Cabinet sub-committee first met, it made little headway. Two of its members, Churchill and F. G. Kellaway, the Deputy Minister of Munitions, were reluctant to recommend a foreign service obligation. The others, Auckland Geddes, President of the Board of Trade, and Lord Lee, Minister of Agriculture and Fisheries, were, in Henry Wilson's eyes, 'quite sound and good'.[39] *The Times* quickly became aware of a 'serious hitch', and reported on 9 January that from a position of virtual agreement within the Government, there had been a 'violent change' as the old fears about a foreign service obligation surfaced once more. In view of the widespread Territorial willingness to accept such an obligation, *The Times* reporter castigated the Government for its lack of political courage, and warned that unless it took the obvious course, the Territorials would be nothing but a 'sham factor in national defence'. The following day it announced that the War Office had postponed until 23 January the meeting between Churchill and the Territorial Associations that had been previously set for 15 January. This had been brought about, it said, by the 'marked divergence of opinion' that had emerged in Cabinet and which the sub-committee had so far been unable to resolve.

In fact the sub-committee was approaching agreement as the pressures on Churchill mounted. On 13 January he met a group of Territorial Associations' representatives, Territorial divisional commanders, and officers who had commanded Territorial brigades during the war. When the question of a foreign service obligation was put to them individually, there was overwhelming support for it: twenty-nine voted in favour and only two against.[40] Churchill later told the Cabinet of the vote but thought it of little significance, saying of those who had favoured a foreign service obligation that 'their views perhaps were somewhat vitiated by the fact that their wish was father to the thought'.[41] Shortly afterwards

[38] Cabinet 2(20), CAB 23/20.
[39] Wilson Papers, diary entry for 9 January 1920.
[40] Scarbrough to Wilson, 13 January 1920, WO 32/2681. Wilson's tally was slightly different: he recorded three dissenting votes. Wilson Papers, diary entry for 13 January 1920.
[41] Cabinet 8(20), Appendix III (4), 27 January 1920, CAB 23/20.

Auckland Geddes wrote to Churchill, saying that from discussions he had held with interested parties, he had reached the unshakeable conclusion that to reconstitute the Territorials on the basis of home defence without a foreign service commitment 'would be regarded as simply playing with the Force'.[42]

Churchill was not yet convinced, and in the absence of any decision, his meeting with the Territorial Associations, already postponed once, was further put off until 30 January. *The Times* claimed on 21 January that there had been a significant hardening of opinion in favour of foreign service, but Churchill still held out. He was supported by the Duke of Rutland, President of the Leicestershire Territorial Association, who wrote to him to say that the difficulties of imposing a foreign service obligation could be avoided if it was made voluntary, since 'the *vast* majority of men would volunteer for such General Service the moment the urgent necessity of their services was announced'. Churchill was delighted, and had a copy of Rutland's letter sent to Wilson:[43] he remained unimpressed. A further meeting of the subcommittee confirmed Geddes's and Lee's support for the foreign service obligation, but again no decision was reached. Wilson wrote gloomily in his diary: 'Winston is heading for Home Service obligation which will be his ruin'.[44] Two days later, just before the Cabinet was due to consider the matter in time for the Government's decision to be announced on the 30th, Churchill conceded defeat. He told a relieved Wilson that he now accepted the need for a foreign service obligation that would come into effect after an Act had been passed by Parliament authorising the dispatch of Territorial troops overseas.[45]

A meeting of Cabinet ministers was held on 27 January, and Churchill told them that a decision had to be reached that morning. He admitted that his conversion for a foreign service obligation had been a recent one, but said that now he was convinced that it was impossible to reconstitute the Territorials for home defence purposes only. The best policy was to make an unequivocal statement of the Government's policy, to ask recruits to accept an overseas service obligation, and to offer them, by way of protection, a guarantee that they would not be sent out of the country until Parliament had passed an Act declaring a state of emergency.

[42] Geddes to sub-committee secretary, 17 January 1920, WO 32/2681.
[43] Rutland to Churchill, 21 January 1920; minute by Churchill, 25 January 1920: WO/2681.
[44] Wilson Papers, diary entries for 23 and 26 January 1920.
[45] *Ibid.*, 26 January 1920.

Furthermore, to allay the most widespread of all Territorial fears, the Government should undertake to send them abroad only in their units. To prevaricate on the Government's position would risk giving rise to suspicions that the Force was being raised for internal strike-breaking purposes, and that, foreign liability or not, the Government would send the Territorials abroad if it wished. The problem of supplying drafts for the Regular Army would be solved not by adopting Scarbrough's cumbersome scheme of a 'special class' of Territorials, but by raising seventy-four battalions of the old Special Reserve, renaming them the Militia, and attaching them to the Regular Army. The Territorial Force could be reconstituted along these lines, assured of its role as the second line of the British Army, and confirmed as the sole basis for the expansion of the nation's military power — all within the budgetary limits laid down by the Cabinet the previous August. It would be necessary to recast the role of the Yeomanry, to reduce some of its units and to convert others, but the essential details that were so urgently needed had been worked out. All that was left was for those present to give their approval. The meeting was no doubt relieved to hear this, and after a short discussion decided to accept the proposals Churchill had presented.[46]

Three days later, on 30 January, Churchill unveiled the Government's plans. He emphasized the responsibilities that were to be placed on the Territorial Force ('the purpose of the Territorial Force shall be Imperial Defence, including our obligations to France and Flanders') and balanced against them the inducements and safeguards that the Territorials would enjoy. If a Territorial with military experience completed the maximum of fifty drills in a year, passed the musketry course, and attended the annual fifteen days' camp, he could earn a bounty of £5. A recruit would join under slightly different conditions, and could earn up to £4. These rewards were in addition to the pay at Regular rates that he would earn during camp. An overseas obligation would be imposed, but would come into operation only under stringent conditions. Not merely would a proclamation calling out the Army Reserve be required, but Parliament would have to pass an Act specifically authorizing the dispatch overseas of the Territorial Force. In addition Churchill promised that not only would Territorial units go abroad as units, but that as soon as their efficiency made it possible, they would fight in Territorial brigades and divisions. In

---

[46] Cabinet 8(20), Appendix III (4), CAB 23/20. The meeting was not one of the Cabinet but a 'Conference of Ministers'.

every sense the new Territorial Force was to be a self-contained, second line Army.[47]

These were welcome words to the Territorial representatives who had been waiting for a year to learn the Government's intentions. Yet relieved as the Associations were that a decision had been made, criticisms of the Government for the delay, the confusion, and the final scheme were not so easily silenced, especially when recruiting, which officially opened on 1 February, proved disappointingly slow. Notwithstanding Churchill's commendation of the bounty and rates of pay to be offered Territorials, the financial rewards were not quite as attractive as he suggested. In the postwar boom wages were high, so that for the steadily-employed man — the type the War Office wanted to recruit — service in the Territorial Army was not necessarily financially advantageous. Churchill admitted as much when asked to explain why in South Wales three battalions had managed to enlist only eighty-two men by the middle of May.[48] There were other criticisms too. Sir Francis Acland, who as Financial Secretary to the War Office from 1908 to 1910 had been intimately concerned with Haldane's original Territorial scheme, complained that the rates of pay were too high, with the result that 'instead of the Territorials being a real civilian force depending upon the goodwill and patriotism of the masses of the citizens they are going to become pinchbeck regulars dependent on money and organized on a purely military basis'.[49] On the other hand, several Associations cavilled at what they considered were the excessive number of drills needed to qualify for the bounty, especially in view of the fact that for the first few years at least, most of the men would probably have had wartime military experience.[50] Only one Association, Cambridgeshire, pointed out that if the Territorials were to be taken seriously as a force available for overseas service at short notice, then the prescribed number of drills was 'totally inadequate'.[51]

There were widespread fears that enlistment in the Territorial Force might jeopardize a man's employment. Many Territorials were worried that their employers might not be willing to grant them leave with pay to attend camp (or at least to make up the

[47] *The Times*, 31 January 1920.
[48] *Parl. Debs.* (Commons), 5th series, vol. 130, col. 2018 (22 June 1920).
[49] *Ibid.*, vol. 125, col. 1374 (23 February 1920).
[50] City of Glasgow, 2 February 1920; Dumbarton, 12 February 1920, MD 9/ 1; Inverness, 29 March 1920, MD 8/25; Perth, Executive and Finance Committee, 9 February 1920, MD 7/39.
[51] Cambridgeshire, 13 February 1920, Minutes, vol. 2.

difference between their civilian and military pay) or even grant them leave at all. Milne's sub-committee in March 1919 had recommended that there should be some sort of legal obligation on employers as a means of sharing the national burden of defence, but on closer examination it was thought to be impracticable. If employers were required to give special holiday and pay privileges to members of the Territorial Force they might refuse to employ them in the first place. If they did employ them and allowed them extra holidays and pay, there might be opposition from the foremen and other workers arising out of resentment over this preferential treatment. There was also the possibility that the granting of employment privileges to Territorial soldiers would be construed as a none too subtle form of pressure to get men into the Force. Small employers in particular would find it difficult to make the concessions that were relatively easy for large firms and govern-ment departments. In general the question of employers' legal obligations opened up so many other problems that it was not pursued further by the War Office. Several Associations however had called for such an obligation in 1919, and after Churchill had made the proposals public one Association, West Lancashire, demanded a War Office conference with the Associations, employers and labour to reach agreement on a common policy for those who wished to join the Territorials.[52] Nothing came of the suggestion then, but during the next twenty years there were periodic attempts to involve the employers more closely in Territorial affairs, both at the national and the local level.

Nor was the final form of the overseas liability greeted with unanimous approval. The Peebles Association rejected any form of overseas obligation, but most Associations recognized that without it the Territorial Force had no future. Their objections were on two main grounds. First, many agreed with Lanarkshire that the final terms did not give sufficient guarantees that the foreign service obligation would only be applied in extreme circumstances. They dismissed the argument that the specific sanction of Parliament was a sufficient safeguard, and they demanded that the War Office give a firm guarantee that no Territorials would be called upon to serve overseas 'unless and until' a General Service (i.e. conscription) Act had been passed. Almost as many Associations rejected the Lanarkshire motion, arguing that the injustices the Territorials had suffered in the war were admitted by the War Office, which would

---

[52] Denbighshire and Flintshire, 7 April 1919, TA/D/6; West Lancashire, 26 April 1920, Acc. 1469/3.

hardly dare treat the Territorials in the same way again.[53] Nevertheless, almost all the Associations set great store by the assurances that Churchill gave to respect the integrity of the Territorial units, as the battles — described in chapter 7 — in the early 1930s over the pledge were to show.

Many Associations argued that their troubles derived from the fact that their interests were not properly represented in the highest circles in the War Office. Their grievances arising out of wartime experiences, their frustrations over the delay in announcing the reconstruction proposals, and dissatisfaction with certain details of the scheme — these they felt would not have developed had the Director-General of the Territorial Force been a member of the Army Council. When the East Riding Association passed a resolution to that effect, it found support among many other Associations. Unfortunately, opinion was by no means unanimous on the subject, so that Churchill and his successors were able to resist these pressures. That they refused to make the Director-General a member of the Army Council was interpreted as further proof that the War Office did not take the Force seriously or listen to its requests and complaints sympathetically.[54]

[53] Peebles, 19 January 1920; Lanarkshire, 25 June 1920, MD 2/3; Bedfordshire, 16 July 1920, X 372/5/2; City of Glasgow, General Purposes Committee, 27 January 1920; City of Edinburgh, General Purposes Committee, 1 March 1921; Essex, Recruiting Committee, 12 January 1921; Inverness, 29 March 1921, MD 8/25; Kent, General Purposes Committee, 30 July 1920, MD/TA 3/4; Perth, Finance Committee, 30 June 1920, MD 7/39; Stirling, 6 July 1920, MD 6/22. Among the Associations that rejected the Lanarkshire resolution were: Cambridgeshire, 16 July 1920, Minutes, vol. 2; City of Aberdeen, 7 July 1920, MD 4/4; County of Aberdeen, 24 June 1921, MD 4/45; Lincoln, 8 March 1921, TA 1/2.

[54] Among the Associations supporting the East Riding resolution were: Buckinghamshire, 6 November 1919; City of Dundee, 5 February 1920, MD 7/5; City of Edinburgh, General Purposes Committee, 4 November 1919; County of Aberdeen, 21 November 1919, MD 4/45; Denbighshire, 13 February 1920, TA/D/6; Derbyshire, 5 January 1920, D 530/3; Devon, 10 December 1919, 1715c/TA/2; Dumbarton, 27 January 1920, MD 9/1; East Lancashire, 19 December 1919, Minute Book 4; Flintshire, 11 February 1920, TA/F/6; Lanarkshire, 19 December 1919, MD 2/3; Sussex, 12 January 1920, D 912/7; Warwickshire, General Purposes Committee, 1 February 1921, CR 1141/4. The East Riding resolution was rejected by the following: Cornwall, 5 February 1920, Acc. DDX 295/12; City of Dundee, 18 November 1919, MD 7/5; City of Glasgow, 2 December 1919; Fife, 12 December 1919, MD 7/25; Inverness, 15 December 1919, MD 8/25; Perth, Executive Committee, 5 November 1919, MD 7/39.

The unhappy state of relations between the War Office and the Associations was publicised by *The Times*. It reported that at a meeting of the West Riding Association in April, several speakers had charged that the War Office was deliberately sabotaging the recruiting campaign because it did not want the Territorial Force to succeed: having failed to kill it off at once, it was now withholding the information and support that was needed if the required numbers of recruits were to be obtained. To his utter embarrassment, Scarbrough was quoted at the meeting by Lord Harewood, President of the Association, as laying the blame at the feet of the Finance Department of the War Office and its penny-pinching attitude and dilatory methods. Scarbrough denied that that was his opinion, but there is no doubt that he had been very critical of the Finance Department.[55] In a leader on 29 April *The Times* doubted that the Government was ill-disposed towards the Territorials, but did think that 'as regards the War Office, there may be some ground for the persistent notion that the success of the Territorial Army is not desired'. Churchill was forced to deny the charge, and to defend the delay in announcing the terms of reconstitution,[56] but *The Times* was not convinced. An appeal by the King to the Lords Lieutenant and Lord Mayors, echoing Edward VII's original appeal that launched the Territorial Force in 1907, came 'opportunely at a time when official dilatoriness had brought the fortunes of the force to a low ebb . . .. [The] Government launched the new scheme in February in so half-hearted a fashion that the results . . . have been disastrous'.[57]

The Times had exaggerated, but not much. The post-war Territorial Force, which in 1921 officially became the Territorial Army, had got off to a shaky start. Not least of its handicaps was the mistrust between the War Office and the Associations that had arisen out of the Territorial experiences during the war and was exacerbated by the difficulty of assessing the nature of Britain's military requirements in the unsettled circumstances of the post-war world. In trying to allay that mistrust, and soothe the sense of grievance that many Territorials felt, the War Office saddled the new Territorial Army with handicaps that emerged only later, when the considerations that had made them a necessary part of the

---

[55] West Riding, 26 April 1920, Acc. 1469/3; *The Times*, 27 April 1920. Scarbrough to Harewood, 27 April 1920; to Churchill, 28 April 1920: Scarbrough Papers.

[56] *Parl. Debs.* (Commons), vol. 128, cols. 1876–7 (4 May 1920).

[57] 15 May 1920.

reconstruction scheme in 1919 and 1920 no longer had the same force. Liberal pay scales, generous financial grants to the Associations, pledges that restricted the use of the Territorials: all of these were fundamental to Churchill's scheme. All of them came under attack in the following decade.

4

Bayonets in the Streets?

Just as there were differences of opinion over the use of Territorials abroad so disagreements arose when the question of employing them within Britain was discussed. In some senses this was an even more thorny problem than that of foreign service, for a Territorial role in aid of the civil power, especially in the conditions prevailing immediately after the end of the war, would be highly visible and have an immediate impact on the general community. The industrial scene was volatile. Grievances resulting from demobilisa-tion procedures, and the prospect of widespread unemployment for returning troops, not to mention — at least in the eyes of the Government — the example of the Bolshevik Revolution, led to a situation in which the inevitable readjustments to the strains in society which the war had magnified but not initiated loomed as threatening challenges to the existing order. The huge growth in the membership of trade unions, which doubled from four to eight millions between 1912 and 1919, and the demonstrable power of those unions to extract enormous wage increases from the government during the war, raised the fear that labour would continue to press for unreasonable concessions to the point of disrupting, even halting, the normal business of the community. Even more disquieting, perhaps, were the returned servicemen's associations, many of which seemed dedicated to a radical restructuring of society rather than simply concerning themselves with such questions as employment and housing. In the Home Office, monthly reports on 'Revolutionary Organisations in Great Britain' pandered to the alarmist inclinations of the more right-wing members of the Cabinet.

For its part, the Army faced the prospect of civil strife with dismay. When a general strike was proclaimed in Glasgow at the end of January 1919, and the red flag was raised in the centre of the city, the Cabinet had to decide whether or not to use troops to quell it. While volunteers could be found to run the essential municipal services, they had to be protected against the possibility of attack from strike supporters. The police force had been seriously depleted during the war, and only the Army could provide the necessary protection. The military authorities, however, were far from sanguine. Apart from their natural reluctance to become involved in disputes of this nature, they could not be sure that the troops stationed in Scotland were reliable. The nineteen infantry battalions there were mainly second and third line units, many of them physically unfit and most of them not amenable to the discipline required should they encounter resistance from the strikers. They were, in the words of one War Office soldier, a dangerous and unique army, 'educated and ill-disciplined'.[1] A real test never came, for the strike collapsed when regular troops were quickly sent in before positions hardened.

Reassured by this show of strength, Churchill argued forcibly for the deployment of troops to crush a strike of electrical engineers that broke out early in February 1919. He was not prepared to make any distinction between an industrial emergency in time of war and in peace; these 'attempts of a well-organized minority to obtain extravagant concessions' had to be resisted, by armed force if necessary.[2] Again, however, the situation never developed that far, but Churchill had raised a question that became even more important as the expiration date of the Military Service Act approached. For once conscription no longer provided the requisite numbers of troops, not only for the defence of a swollen empire but for the manning of occupation zones in Germany and Turkey, then the burden imposed on the Army by the demands that it be available to act in aid of the civil power would become intolerable. The suggestion that the Military Service Act be extended to enable the Army to fulfil its foreign commitments was rejected on the grounds that it would intensify labour suspicions of the Government's motives, just as it was subsequently deemed 'inopportune' to discuss in Parliament the possibility of using troops to man essential services during prolonged strikes.[3]

Throughout the spring of 1919 there were mounting fears of a crippling strike by the Triple Alliance — the three largest unions, the miners, transport workers, and railwaymen. This was a formidable challenge and in response to it the Government established the Industrial Unrest Committee to coordinate emergency services

[1]   War Cabinet 522, 30 January 1919, CAB 23/9.
[2]   War Cabinet 525, 4 February 1919, CAB 23/9.
[3]   War Cabinet 537 and 551, 26 February and 25 March 1919, CAB 23/9.

and to provide protection for those who ran them. It also tried to break up the alliance by settling with the individual unions, so that when the railwaymen finally went on strike in September they were not joined by the miners or the transport workers.

Churchill was determined that military force should be used if necessary, and to the difficult question of conditions of overseas service he now added the requirement that the Territorials be available for use in serious civil disputes. Apart from his own inclinations that way, such a role for the Territorials would be a useful counter to those who argued that the Force was too limited and too highly paid. In any case, it was inconceivable to him that the Government could not meet the threat of a strike by the Triple Alliance by calling out the Territorial Force. He insisted that the draft regulations for enlistment in the reconstituted Force be rewritten to allow for the use of the Territorials to assist the civil power. But if it was 'inopportune' to discuss in Parliament the use of troops to maintain the lifelines of the state, what could be said of proposals to embody the Territorials when serious strikes were threatened? Scarbrough was sure that the old Territorial regulations prohibited the use of the Force in civil disputes, except under conditions of extreme national emergency, and Sir Charles Harris pointed out that the regulation in question had been included specifically to calm the fears of organized labour so that recruiting would not fall foul of union suspicions that the Territorials were being formed as a strike-breaking organization.[4]

Fortunately for the Territorial proposals, the railway strike lasted only seven days. The Strike Committee, the old Industrial Unrest Committee renamed for the railway strike, had not had time to test its embryonic organization, but the experience gained in September formed the basis of its subsequent plans. Field Marshal Earl Haig, Commander-in-Chief of Forces in Great Britain, urged the War Office to press the Government to establish a Civil Guard that could be embodied to reinforce the police, protect property and maintain order. Only as a last resort should the Army be called upon to assist the civil power. This plea was well received by the General Staff. The CIGS, the DCIGS and the Adjutant-General all stressed the undesirability of using troops during strikes, and

---

[4] Churchill to Peel, 8 July 1919; Scarbrough to DCIGS, 16 July 1919; Harris to FM, 6 August 1919; WO 32/11245. The suggestion that a Territorial obligation to undertake a role in aid of the civil power as a *quid pro quo* was made by Lt-General Sir J. S. Cowans, the Quartermaster-General: QMG to DGTF, 10 June 1919, WO 32/11245.

pointed to the likelihood that there simply would not be sufficient troops available in future civil emergencies. In that case it was all the more necessary that the Home Office begin organizing a Civil Guard immediately.[5]

At the end of October the Home Secretary, Sir Edward Shortt, submitted his general proposals to the Supply and Transport Committee, which had again changed its name from the Strike Committee so that its activities might appear more neutral and its deliberations not be confined to any particular strike. From consultations with local authorities throughout Britain, Shortt concluded that a Civil Guard would be very unpopular and at best sectional in its appeal. What was required was a force that could be recruited from all classes, including trade unionists, for the protection of life and property, rather than a para-military organization that was seen as a strike-breaking weapon. It was 'absolutely necessary' that the force be civil in organisation and control, that it be under the authority of the local police, and that it 'be made clear beyond the possibility of any misunderstanding' that its main purpose was to render assistance to the police so that it would not be necessary to call out military forces.[6] The Committee accepted the proposals, and passed them to the Cabinet. There the matter lay. Nothing was done.

It was left to Wilson to try to bring the gravity of the situation home to the Cabinet. Early in January 1920 he submitted a strongly-worded warning to Churchill, complaining that although the civil departments had concurred in his proposals several months previously, proposals that were designed to shift the burden of maintaining essential services from the Army to civil organisations, no progress had been made to meet the situation that had been predicted would arise in the new year. Despite all the warnings of the War Office, and especially of the Army Council, civil departments were all too clearly relying on the Army to provide assistance 'which it is quite beyond its power to afford'. Wilson spelled out 'in the plainest manner possible' the limitations under which the Army was operating. Although it was thought essential to maintain troop levels in Britain (excluding Ireland) at a minimum of 40,000, so that an effective force of 30,000 could be

[5] Haig to Secretary, War Office, 17 October 1919. Appendix to CP 111, 'The Employment of Troops in Industrial Disturbances', CAB 24/93; Note by CIGS, 6 November 1919, CP 111, CAB 24/93; AG and DCIGS to Secretary of State, 21 and 23 October 1919, WO 32/5467.

[6] CP 78, 'Citizen Guards', 31 October 1919, CAB 24/92.

mobilised in time of national emergency, there would be only 38,000 troops stationed in Britain in January and February, and this figure included nineteen conscript battalions. When the conscripts were demobilized in March, the troop level in Britain would fall to 25,000, many of them young soldiers with minimal training and weak discipline, lacking experienced senior NCOs. The figure of 40,000 was based on the assumption that adequate police forces would exist to form the first line of civil power. But no such police forces had been built up. Far from being able to assist the civil authorities in the area of transport and signal communications, the Army was entirely dependent upon the Ministry of Transport and the Post Office to provide these services if it was deployed in a civil emergency. Similarly the Army had no internal intelligence service (and Wilson thought it unwise that the Army should engage in gathering industrial intelligence), and had to rely entirely on the Home Office and Scotland Yard for appropriate information.[7]

Yet there seemed to be no sense of urgency, no effort to face up to the situation. Wilson felt he had made his point with both Lloyd George and Bonar Law when he impressed on them the 'necessity of increasing, doubling and doubling again if necessary, the police', and of putting any counter-strike measures in the hands of the civil rather than the military authorities. But Churchill seemed neither interested nor surprised when Wilson, on learning that Churchill had not read his memorandum, apprised him of the Army's complete inability to render assistance to the civil power. Churchill's answer to the problem, in the absence of the Territorial Army, on which he based his long-term solution, was to appeal for loyal volunteers to enlist in a force to be raised and administered by the Home Office.[8]

A similar proposal was made by the Permanent Under-Secretary at the Home Office, Sir Edward Troup, in collaboration with the Chairman of the Supply and Transport Committee, Sir Eric Geddes. They suggested the formation of a 'Special Guard' of 10,000, which would be enlisted for temporary duty, though they did not specify how they would be recruited or under what conditions of service.[9] Churchill's 'loyal volunteers' scheme differed in that he thought preparations for raising such a force should be

---

[7] CP 472, 'Capacity of the Army to assist the Civil Power in Industrial Disturbances', 3 January 1920, CAB 24/96.

[8] Wilson, diary entries 5 and 9 January 1920.

[9] Supply and Transport committee meeting, 15 January 1920, CAB 27/73.

made secretly to avoid provocation; though how volunteers could be raised quickly enough without prior publicity he did not say. It appeared, however, that the question of aid to the civil power fell into the 'too hard' category, and for the moment none of these proposals got very far.

Although Churchill had not paid close attention to Wilson's warnings, he had continued to pursue the possibility of imposing upon the Territorial Force the obligation to act in aid of the civil power in cases of extreme national emergency. Rumours circulated throughout the country that the Territorials would be liable for such duty, and when recruiting proved disappointingly slow, there were suspicions that men were holding back through fear that the Territorial Force would be used in a strike-breaking role.[10] Evidence of the disquiet building up came from the City of Dundee Territorial Association, whose Recruiting Committee had unanimously voted to approach the War Office for reassurances that would encourage lagging recruiting.[11]

For all the flat statements by the War Office that the Territorials could not be used in civil disputes, there was an ambiguity in the regulations. Scarbrough, who had earlier opposed using the Territorials in this way because of the effect it would have on organised labour, which he hoped would support the Force, pressed for a change in them. As they stood, the Territorial Force could be embodied once the Army Reserve had been called out by proclamation. Since the Army Reserve could be embodied in aid of the civil power, and since the Territorial Force, once embodied, came under normal Army discipline, it was possible to argue that the War Office had a loophole that enabled it to bypass its undertaking not to use the Territorials in civil disturbances. To allay suspicions and to reassure labour that they would not be enlisting in a strike-breaking organization, Scarbrough suggested that an additional safeguard be inserted in the Regulations, namely that after the Army Reserve had been called out, a further proclamation be required, and Parliament be given the opportunity to express its opinion, before the Territorials could be embodied and used to assist the civil power.[12] The Under-Secretary of State, Peel, had evidence of growing unease over this question, and with recruiting lagging

---

[10] *The Times*, 9 February 1920.

[11] Secretary, City of Dundee Territorial Force Association, to War Office, 16 April 1920, WO32/2676.

[12] Scarbrough to Peel, 30 March 1920, WO 32/2676. Scarbrough's earlier objections and his fears of the effect on labour's willingness to enlist were expressed in a memorandum, 30 September 1919, WO 32/2677.

badly, was anxious to issue the necessary reassurance to Territorial Associations and potential recruits.[13] Scarbrough's proposals for a second proclamation was a simple solution.

Churchill would have none of it. He agreed that the Territorials were not to be embodied for the 'suppression of civil disturbances or labour disputes', but insisted that these restrictions did not apply, and had never been intended to apply, in a 'grave national emergency such as an attempted revolution endangering the fundamental peace and safety of the entire country'. It was useless, wrote Churchill, to deny that this had been one intention in reconstituting the Territorial Force, for without such a capability, the Force would be of little use. To rewrite the regulations and rule out such a role would be a fundamental change of policy on which the Cabinet would have to be consulted.[14] Given the Cabinet's reluctance to establish a civil alternative to the employment of military power (which, in the circumstances outlined by Wilson meant using Territorial troops), it was unlikely that the War Office objections would meet with much sympathy.

Scarbrough was not convinced, but did admit that the rise of 'Bolshevik and revolutionary ideas' had injected a much more serious note into the situation. To this extent both he and Peel agreed with Churchill that in a national emergency the Government should have the power to embody the Territorial Army, but they pressed Churchill to recognize that the distinction between labour disputes and emergency situations was not matched by a corresponding procedural distinction. It was this that was giving rise to suspicions that the Territorials would be used in strike-breaking operations, and in an atmosphere of mistrust of the War Office's intentions and motives — a mistrust that went far beyond the question of the civil role of the Force — additional safeguards would provide the necessary reassurance, and remove at least one obstacle to recruiting.[15]

Churchill refused to budge, and eventually the War Office had to reassure the City of Dundee Association that there were adequate safeguards against the abuse of the power to embody the Territorials for assistance to the civil power.[16] In the face of Churchill's adamant rejection of his fears, Peel noted that: 'The real safeguard

[13] Peel to Churchill, 28 April 1920, WO 32/2676.
[14] Churchill to Peel, Scarbrough, 29 April 1920, WO 32/2676.
[15] Minute by Scarbrough, 30 April 1920; Peel to Churchill, 4 May 1920: WO 32/2676.
[16] WO to City of Dundee Territorial Force Association, 11 June 1920, WO 32/2676.

of the force lies in the fact that no sane Government would embody it, unless it was sure that the feeling of the country justified so grave a step.'[17] This was not likely to reassure those who already mistrusted the Government's motives, especially as the distinctions that Churchill insisted prevented the Territorials being used in a strike-breaking role were not as clear as he imagined. In the unsettled industrial atmosphere that marked post-war Britain, with the Home Office circulating intelligence reports on subversive and revolutionary movements and the Supply and Transport Committee drawing up plans to combat attempts to overthrow the existing order, it was difficult to distinguish between prolonged industrial disputes and genuine national emergencies in which the security of the state was threatened. What of a general strike? Did the use of this weapon, the most powerful in labour's industrial arsenal, constitute that 'grave national emergency' that Churchill argued would justify calling out the Territorials to assist the civil power? Churchill, with his known record of anti-labour sentiments and policies, was hardly the man to decide.

The test came in April 1921. A strike by the miners precipitated the situation that the War Office had predicted for months. Throughout 1920 Wilson despairingly pressed the Cabinet to establish a civil force to provide the services that were even more beyond the capability of the Army than had been the case in 1919 when Wilson had privately fulminated against the 'criminal folly' of the Government's inaction.[18] Again nothing was done, so that when the strike was called in April, hasty measures had to be enacted to meet heavy demands for protective services.

Despite military and political objections to reducing Britain's troop commitments overseas, the Cabinet decided that the 'risk at home from Sinn Feiners, Communists and other dangerous elements' justified the risks involved in withdrawing two battalions from Malta and four from Upper Silesia. Even this would not make sufficient troops available, and steps were to be taken to enable the Government to call out the Army Reserve as quickly as possible, by passing the necessary legislation in a single day. If the situation deteriorated further, the Cabinet thought that it might be necessary either to embody the Territorial Army or create a special force to augment Regular troops. The Army Council then consulted the

[17] Peel, minute, 31 May 1920, WO 32/2676.
[18] CP 1853, 'The Internal Situation and Military Precautions', 13 September 1920, CAB 24/111; Wilson, diary entry, 3 January 1920.

General Officers Commanding Territorial Divisions, and on the basis of their opinions advised against embodying the Territorials. The reason for this was very much in line with the arguments put forward earlier by Scarbrough and Peel, that although legally the Territorials could be called out after the Army Reserve had been mobilised, 'it had been practically stated by those appealing for recruits that the Territorial Forces would not be used for the maintenance of internal order'.[19] Charges of bad faith and strike-breaking would inevitably arise if the Cabinet chose to embody the Territorials.

With that avenue blocked, the Supply and Transport Sub-Committee looked at the other alternative, that of creating a separate force. The problem it faced here was that for over a year it had done virtually nothing to implement the recommendations made by the Army and the Home Office. Now, when the crisis was upon it, the Cabinet had to improvise quickly. The results were unfortunate. There was no Civil Guard in existence, even in skeletal form, no organization of a civil nature around which Churchill's 'loyal volunteers' could rally. There was only the Territorial Army, composed of civic-minded volunteers. It was natural that the form, if not the name, should provide the instant nucleus which the Cabinet needed. It was therefore decided that should the Miners' Federation refuse to continue negotiations and the situation deteriorate further, Army, Naval and Air Force Reserves would be called up, and the War Office would prepare to raise a Defence Force.[20]

In response to an increasingly critical situation, Lloyd George announced in Parliament on 8 April that a Defence Force would be raised to meet the challenge posed by the strike. The Government made a 'special appeal to patriotic citizens' to enlist, 'not for the purpose of interfering in any wage dispute, but solely to support the Police in the fulfilment of their duties to the community'. The Force would be raised for a period of service of ninety days, at normal Army rates of pay and allowances.[21]

Almost every opinion previously given on the subject of auxiliary forces used in civil disputes had stressed the necessity of keeping them away from military control. Nevertheless it was decided that the Defence Force would come under Army command. The

[19] Cabinet 17(21)3, 4 April 1921; Conclusions of a Conference of Ministers, 6 April 1921, Cabinet 22(21), Appendix III(3), CAB 23/25.
[20] Cabinet 22(21), Appendix III(3), CAB 23/25.
[21] *Parl. Debs.* (Commons), 5th series, vol. 140, col. 697.

Army Council advised the Cabinet that the Government had 'practically stated' that the Territorials would not be used in these circumstances. Yet members of the Territorial Army were to be 'specially invited' to enlist. The Home Secretary had urged that it be made 'clear beyond the possibility of any misunderstanding' that the main purpose of a Civil Guard was to do away with the need to call out the military forces. In the same breath as he announced the formation of the Defence Force, Lloyd George told Parliament that he had advised the King to call out the Military Reserves. The following day the Cabinet was told that several hundred Marines and four battalions from Ireland had been sent to Scotland.[22] Recruiting for the Defence Force was to take place at Territorial drill halls and head-quarters, using Territorial permanent staff specifically assigned to that task. Although Territorials who wished to volunteer their services in the Defence Force would have to resign from the Territorial Army, their service in the Defence Force would count towards fulfilling their Territorial obligations and they would automatically be readmitted to the Territorial Army at the end of the ninety day period if they so wished. Technically the Government had remained true to its pledge not to use the Territorial Army in internal disputes, but only at the cost of employing the most transparent of devices.

Enlistment in the Defence Force began on 9 April and ended nine days later. There are no precise figures for the numbers ultimately recruited, but the response was such that after four days 40,000 had signed up.[23] It is impossible to say how many of these came from the Territorial Army: at best a few details from scattered Territorial Associations can be pieced together. In East Lancashire almost 20 per cent (1,767 out of 8,931) of Territorial men enlisted in the Defence Force; in Derbyshire the figure was also 20 per cent (273 out of 1,443), and there Territorials made up almost 41 per cent of the Defence Force. In Leicestershire and Rutland over 30 per cent of the Territorials (1,124 out of 3,110) joined the Force, where they made up an average of half the strength of each unit raised; while in Lanarkshire enlistments were just over 12 per cent (96 out of 766).[24] This response hardly fulfilled Churchill's hope that large

22 Conclusions of a Conference of Ministers, 9 April 1921, Cabinet 22(21), Appendix VIII (3), CAB 23/25.
23 Conclusions of a Conference of Ministers, 13 April 1921, Cabinet 23(21), Appendix II, CAB 23/25.
24 East Lancashire, Recruiting and Discharge Committee, 22 April 1921, M 73/3/30; Derbyshire, General Purposes Committee, 2 May 1921, D 503/4; Leicestershire and Rutland, 5 May 1921, Acc. 819/3; Lanarkshire, Recruiting Committee, 20 May 1921, MD 2/3.

numbers of 'loyal volunteers' from among the ranks of the Territorials would answer the Government's call.

Recruitment was carried out at drill halls and headquarters, which the War Office had 'asked' Associations to place at the disposal of the Defence Force authorities. Technically the buildings belonged to the Associations, and at least one — West Lancashire — had previously indicated that its premises were not available to the War Office for non-Territorial use. But when the request was made, it seems that all the Associations responded, even though there were complaints (for example from the Durham Association) that buildings had been virtually requisitioned. Just as the Government maintained the fiction that the Defence Force was entirely independent of the Territorial Army, so Associations could claim — unconvincingly — that the loan of buildings did not involve the Territorial Army in the activities of the Defence Force.[25]

In fact the two organizations were inextricably interwoven. Apart from the use of Territorial buildings, permanent instructors were seconded to the Defence Force, which was raised by having each Territorial unit (where required) 'throw off' a Defence Force unit, which adopted the same name as its Territorial parent. Officers from the Territorial Army transferred wholesale to the Defence Force, which thus cut so deeply into Territorial activities that a number of Associations all but stopped recruiting until after the Defence Force was disbanded.

Towards the end of April the Government decided that transportation difficulties arising out of the strike made it impossible to hold scheduled Territorial camps, except for those planned for weekends, until after the middle of June. On 10 May *The Times* reported that financial stringency was causing the War Office to consider the cancellation of all camps, but the report was denied two days later, and the following month, after representations from Territorial Associations, numbers of permanent Territorial staff serving with the Defence Force were returned to their Territorial units so that training would not be unduly curtailed. The possible cancellation of camps for the whole of the summer was a serious blow to the Territorials, for in many counties these were to be the first camps held since the Force had been reconstituted in 1920. In the first year of recruiting camps were made optional and attendance at them was not a requirement for obtaining the bounty. Slow recruiting, difficulties in organization, and the feeling that most Territorials

[25] West Lancashire, 19 January 1920, Acc. 2074, Minute Book 1908 – 1922; Durham, 3 May 1921, Minutes, vol. 2.

would not welcome a return to life under canvas quite so soon after so many of them had been demobilized led many Associations and commanding officers to decide against camps in 1920. A second year without the benefit of eight or fifteen days' continuous training would have been fatal, however, both to the attractiveness of the Territorial Army to its members and potential recruits and to those who supported it in the face of sniping and often ill-informed criticism.

While those who joined the Defence Force had some exposure to training and sustained discipline (however slight) before it was disbanded on July 2nd, most Territorials had neither the inclination nor the opportunity to break from the routine of their normal lives for three months. The 7th and 8th Middlesex Battalions of the Defence Force, for instance, camped on Hounslow Heath from early April until the end of June, but less than 10 per cent of London's Territorials, according to *The Times* report of 10 May, had answered the call. Since recruiting in London was among the slowest in the country (and remained so throughout the 1920s and 1930s) it was particularly important that camps be held there. Even if the War Office did relent, and most camps were held, the mere fact that cancellation of camps on the pretext of transport difficulties had been considered raised old doubts about the Government's commitment to the concept of the Territorial Army. If there were problems in moving large numbers of Territorials to distant camps, why (as it was asked in 1927 when exactly the same reason was given for the cancellation of camps) could not units hold local camps: they might have lacked the attraction of a seaside location, but at least they would enable enthusiastic troops to train together for some days rather than several hours once a week.

Despite a few grumbles from those who felt that the War Office had taken their assent too much for granted, most Associations willingly cooperated with the War Office. The Director-General of the Territorial Army, Sir Noel Birch, admitted to the Surrey Association that in the rush to establish the Defence Force, the Territorials had unavoidably, though regrettably, been involved. Several Surrey members objected that the use of Territorial unit titles for Defence Force units had given the impression — which would ultimately harm the Territorials — that the Territorial Army had been embodied 'in connection with trade disputes'.[26] Surprisingly, however, this charge was not levelled against the Territorials, and for the moment there was general agreement that the

[26] Surrey, 25 April 1921, Minutes, vol. 2.

raising of the Defence Force would benefit the work of the Associations.

Of more immediate concern to the Associations was the effect that service would have on those who had left the Territorial Army to join the Defence Force and who would subsequently wish to rejoin their Territorial units. Although the Prime Minister had said that time spent with the Defence Force would count towards fulfilling Territorial obligations, the War Office had not offered any detailed guidelines on how this was to be done. The Council of County Territorial Associations recommended that service with the Defence Force should be counted as the equivalent of the total drills required to earn the annual bounty (apart from completing the course in musketry), and that attendance at Territorial camps be made optional for such soldiers. Conversely, Territorials belonging to units which had not held camps owing to the activities of the Defence Force were not to be denied the full bounty. Not until two days after the disbandment of the Defence Force did the War Office release its policy. Provided men re-enlisted in the Territorial Army within a month, their service would be counted as continuous, and they would be granted full credit for time spent with the Defence Force.[27]

Even before this policy had been decided upon, Associations looked to the Defence Force to bring in extra recruits. Not only did they hope that those who had left the Territorial Army would return, but that they would encourage others to follow them from the Defence Force. Apart from the taste of quasi-military life that the Defence Force offered, a taste that the Territorials could satisfy, there was the added attraction that men who had not been Territorials but who joined up upon discharge from the Defence Force, could earn the Territorial bounty simply by firing an elementary musketry course. Some Associations virtually suspended recruiting during the spring and summer of 1921. Surrey eased up on recruiting, fearing that since the 'right class' of man had gone into the Defence Force, the Territorials would be left with a poor selection from which to choose; but Gloucestershire reported a marked increase in enlistments, even before the Defence Force was demobilised. In the short term the raising of the Defence Force seemed to have had little adverse effect on the Territorial Army, and was thought by a number of Associations to have been of some benefit.[28]

[27] CCTA, Business and Finance Committee, 27 April 1921; *The Times*, 5 July 1921.
[28] Surrey, 25 July 1921, Minutes, vol. 2; Gloucestershire, General Purposes Committee, 20 June 1921, D 2388 1/2.

Time showed otherwise. Within a few years, almost every Association was bemoaning the poor quality of recruits that it had enlisted in the previous two years. Rates of discharge on the grounds of undesirability jumped significantly. Durham explained its high wastage rate as the delayed result of choosing quantity rather than quality in the first year of recruiting, and also because it had taken on many men from the Defence Force who proved to be unsuitable. Sixteen per cent of its soldiers were discharged in 1922 – 3 as being undesirable, while between 1922 and 1924 one of its units discharged over a quarter of its strength. In Leicestershire and Rutland, the joint Associations reported that by July 1922 they had dropped 22 per cent of their recruits taken in since recruiting began in 1920. In 1924, when those who had joined at the commencement of recruiting in 1920 were completing their four year term, Derbyshire recorded a net gain of only 31 recruits for the first six months: 271 had enlisted since January but 240 had been discharged, many of them for being 'undesirable'. In West Lancashire the Association recorded severe financial losses on its clothing account occasioned by 'an unsuitable class of man' abusing the clothing issue, and voted to raise its recruiting standards in the future. This was a common sentiment throughout the Territorial Army, but it proved more difficult than expected to attract a higher standard while keeping numbers up; so that in 1924 the Essex Association deplored the necessity — experienced by 'practically all Associations' — of striking off large numbers of men (about 15 per cent), some of whom were 'undesirable'.[29]

There were repercussions too in the labour movement. After the wrangles over the question of assisting the civil power it was the height of folly to use the Territorials so blatantly in a role that could be construed as strike breaking. By 1925 the War Office was aware of the price that it was having to pay for this precipitate government action. A study of the Regular Army's requirements reached the conclusion that on mobilization a large body of skilled tradesmen would be needed to act in a support role behind the frontline troops. For this purpose, the War Office proposed to create a Supplementary Reserve of a technical nature so that a minimum of delay would be experienced in a future emergency.

[29] Durham, 30 October 1923, Appendix 2; 14 November 1924, Appendix 6, Minutes, vol. 2; Leicestershire and Rutland, 4 July 1922, Acc. 819/3; Derbyshire, 7 July 1924, Acc. 530/4; West Lancashire, Recruiting and Discharge Committee, 7 July 1922, Acc. 2074, R&D Minutes, Bk. 2; Essex, 16 January 1924.

Union resistance to recruitment was led by the National Union of Railwaymen and the Transport Workers' Union. They feared that the Supplementary Reserve might be called out in circumstances similar to those of the strike in 1921, and that unionists, now embodied in the Supplementary Reserve, might be called upon to run services that would in effect help break the strike. The Secretary of State for War, Sir Laming Worthington-Evans, emphasized that the War Office had 'no ulterior motives' and appealed for union support, but to no avail. Although he repeated Churchill's pledge — for what that was now worth — that Supplementary Reservists would not be used in aid of the civil power, he also stuck to Churchill's line that no Government could deny itself the right to employ Reservists to assist the state in an extreme national emergency. But after the experience of 1921 the unions had every reason to claim that the distinction was less than clear. The only way in which their suspicions could be allayed, they insisted, was for a guarantee to be given that the Supplementary Reserve would be embodied for overseas service only. This the War Office was reluctant to do, since all other classes of reservists and the Territorials were recruited on a non-restrictive basis.[30] The result was that both unions resisted attempts to recruit their members for the Supplementary Reserve, and numbers remained very low for some years.

The War Office was not unsympathetic to the suspicions that bedevilled the formation of the Supplementary Reserve. In July 1925, when it seemed that a coal strike was impending, some thought was given to the measures that might be necessary to maintain essential services and preserve order. One report in the War Office deprecated any suggestion that the Territorials should be used as the nucleus for another Defence Force. It was argued that the use of Territorial staff and facilities in 1921 in this way was 'hardly in accordance with the *spirit* of the provision that it shall not be used to deal with civil disturbances'. In any case, the Defence Force had been a 'waste of money and energy', an over-reaction on the part of the authorities. Worse, from the Territorial point of view, was the influx into the Territorial Army of large numbers of 'undesirables' from the Defence Force, whose presence in Territorial units made recruiting very difficult in the face of parental disapproval. The conclusion of the report, endorsed by

[30] Worthington-Evans, 'Supplementary Reserve: Memorandum by the Secretary of State for War', 6 February 1925, CP 66(25), CAB 24/171; 6 April 1925, CP 197(25), CAB 24/172.

the Adjutant-General, was that 'It is difficult to over-estimate the harm done to the T.A. by the Defence Force.'[31]

These questions became of immediate concern in the spring of the following year, when the miners went on strike and a general strike was threatened. Despite the lessons that had been learnt from the 1921 experience about the harmful effects of unprepared-ness, and the warning signals that had been apparent for some months, little had been done to meet the new dangers. In April, the Under-Secretary of State of War, Viscount Onslow, advised against following the example set in 1921 in creating a Defence Force, and allowing its members to join the Territorial Army on demobilisa-tion. 'I was Civil Commissioner in the S.W. District (Bristol) in 1921', he wrote, 'and I had some opportunity of observing the peculiarities of certain members of the Defence Force. We do not want these people in the T.A.!' These sentiments were supported by the CIGS and the Adjutant-General, and also by the Permanent Under-Secretary, Sir Herbert Creedy, who added: 'The Defence Force as then raised was very expensive and none too efficient.'[32]

When the General Strike began on 3 May, it was decided that the Territorial Army should not be embodied to assist the civil power. That much at least had been learned from 1921. As the DGTA, Sir Hugh Jeudwine, told Scarbrough, the legality of so using the Territorials was outweighed by the difficulties inherent in the embodiment procedure. By the time the situation had deteriorated to an extent that justified calling out the Territorials, it might well be too late for them to have any useful effect.[33] Instead the War Office decided to use regular troops. But that did nothing to solve the problem of maintaining order in the community if, as expected, the strike was a prolonged one. Lack of preparation, despite the mounting warning signs throughout 1925 and the early months of 1926, forced the Cabinet to improvise. The Territorials might not be embodied, but their partially trained man-power, their buildings, and ready-made organization were too valuable an asset to be bypassed in the circumstances. True, the name 'Defence Force' had too military a ring and was perhaps suggestive of a degree of military involvement that the War Office wished to play down. But what could be more appropriate, at a time when the constitutional foundations of the state were under attack, than that

---

[31] Memorandum by Captain J. C. Latter, 13 July 1925, WO 32/2674.

[32] Memorandum by Viscount Onslow, 3 April 1926; minutes by CIGS, AG, Creedy: WO 32/2674.

[33] Jeudwine to Scarbrough, 6 May 1926, Scarbrough Papers.

a body of citizens should rally to uphold the law and maintain the normal services of the community. A 'Civil Constabulary Reserve', deployed by the Home Office rather than the War Office, and operating in civilian clothes rather than military uniforms, was the answer.

The War Office could take comfort from this decision in that it seemed to have convinced the Cabinet that control of additional forces for use in civil disputes should fall to the civil (i.e. police) rather than to the military authorities, but its enthusiasm was not unbounded. The example of the Defence Force in 1921 created little enough confidence in the ability of the Territorials to render effective aid to the civil power, and there were the long-term effects to consider. Jeudwine wrote to Onslow: 'I think that we should ensure that should it be at any time necessary to raise again a force of this nature it should on no account be emptied into the TA as in the past. We are only now emerging from the cloud it cast over the TA.'[34] Churchill dismissed these fears as groundless, and in any case minimal when weighed against the threat the general strike posed. Writing to Worthington-Evans, he said:

> Do not, I beg you, speaking with the knowledge of so many years of military affairs, be misled by silly War Office objections against this measure [using the Territorial Army]. The Territorial Army will recover after the conflict is over, but even if it suffers for some years it will not have suffered in vain. Such an embodiment will immediately give you the necessary mass of men to afford the widespread protection which is essential, and will enable you to keep the regular units concentrated . . . It is far better to take too many precautions than too few.[35]

The Territorial Army was already involved, as on 1 May the War Office had requested all County Associations to place their drill halls and other buildings at the disposal of the Regular Army.[36] What remained to be decided was the extent of that involvement.

After meeting several times on 7 May the Cabinet agreed that regular troops should be used only as a last resort. Before that became necessary, the full strength of the police forces should be deployed, augmented where necessary by special constables. London

---

[34] Jeudwine to Onslow, 3 May 1926, WO 32/2674.
[35] Churchill to Worthington-Evans, 7 May 1926: quoted in Martin Gilbert, *Winston S. Churchill*, vol. v, *1923 – 1939* (London, 1976), p. 161.
[36] War Office to Territorial Associations, 1 May 1926, WO 32/2674.

was authorised to enrol as many as 50,000 specials, and behind these front lines there was to be established a Civil Constabulary Reserve (CCR). Although the Territorial Army (and the Army Reserve) was not to be embodied as such, the CCR was to be based upon the existing Territorial organisation. Territorial units were to be asked to volunteer *en masse* for duty with the CCR, which would form the nucleus of a special section of the police forces. Until the situation became clearer, recruiting for the CCR was to be restricted to Territorial soldiers or to ex-military men, 'known and trusted at territorial headquarters'. If it did become necessary to embody the Territorial Army, those serving in the CCR would immediately revert to their Territorial units, while non-Territorial members of the CCR would join the Special Constabulary, thus preventing the emptying into the Territorial Army of men who, however carefully they had been screened, might subsequently prove to be unsuitable, creating those problems of recruitment and retention that had plagued the Territorials since the Defence Force experience of 1921.[37]

Those who volunteered for service with the CCR were paid five shillings a day, a generous rate designed to compensate them for the disruption to normal routine, and equipped with steel helmets, brassards, and truncheons. Recruiting opened on different days at Territorial drill halls throughout the country. The Government's intention was to raise up to 300,000 men in units consisting of five officers and 500 other ranks, and to concentrate them at what were provocatively called 'storm centres'. The response was heartening. In Hertfordshire 313 applicants were registered between 3 pm on 10 May and 10 am the following day, before recruiting was halted. In Middlesex plans were made to raise three full companies, around the area of the 7th Middlesex Battalion, and within hours of the beginning of recruiting on 12 May, 'hundreds of men' had enlisted. This successful appeal was repeated through the country where it was thought that additional forces would be needed.[38]

Barely had recruiting begun, however, than the general strike collapsed. The CCR was disbanded on 15 May. A few of its members had been involved in clashes with strikers and strike sympathizers, but most had done little more than don their helmets and fall in at their 'storm centres'. Even this limited exposure was enough to raise doubts about the wisdom of the Government in

[37] Cabinet 25(26), 11 am, 7 May 1926; 26(26), 9 pm, 7 May 1926, CAB 23/52.
[38] Hertfordshire, 30 July 1926; Col. E. J. King, 'A History of the Territorial Army and Air Force Association of the County of Middlesex', typescript

raising the CCR. The London District report concluded that:

> they were undoubtedly looked on as a species of strike breaker and 'black and tan'. They did not in consequence give the same confidence to workers, and in attacking them strikers did not feel they were up against the law in the same way as with police.[39]

So much for the claim of the chairman of the Essex Territorial Association, Brigadier-General Colvin, that the establishment of the CCR was 'eloquent testimony to the value of the Territorial Army'; and there was an ironic truth in the boast of the County of London Association that the raising of the CCR had been 'nothing other than a masterpiece of organisation, a circumstance which had not passed unnoticed in Whitehall in again evidencing the possibilities and various uses to which Territorial organisation . . . could be put to use in a moment of emergency'. Other Associations saw their useful role in a very different direction. The Warwickshire Association staged a tattoo in Birmingham, which both stimulated recruiting and was instrumental, it suggested, 'in helping to maintain the peaceful conditions which prevailed in the Midlands throughout a period of acute industrial crisis'.[40]

Again, as in 1921, the attempt to separate the Territorial Army from the temporary force was not successful. Although the CCR was under the authority of the Home Office, its recruitment and administration were the responsibility of the War Office. Even though its members did not wear military uniforms, the fact that they were recruited exclusively from Territorial units and concentrated at Territorial drill halls destroyed the official pretence. The Territorial Army had been embodied in all but name. In spirit the Government had called upon Territorials to volunteer as units; in place of the order it felt politically unable to give it relied upon a coercive *esprit de corps*. Those who volunteered their services with their Territorial units were praised for coming to the aid of the state, yet as one military member of the Essex Association emphasized, it had to be made 'very clear that those joining the Territorial

---

(1943), pp. 31 – 2. Copy in the Middlesex Territorial Association records. King was Vice-Chairman of the Middlesex Association, and commanded the three Middlesex CCR companies that were raised.

[39] 'London District Report on the General Strike, May 1926'. 18 November 1926, WO 32/3455.

[40] Essex, 14 July 1926; County of London, 27 October 1926, A/TA/3; Warwickshire, General Purposes Committee, 16 July 1926, CR 1141/4.

Army were under no obligation to assist in a civil capacity, and . . . there was no slur on those who did not join the [Civil Constabulary] Reserve'.[41]

Despite the unfortunate identification of the Territorial Army with the Government's efforts to combat the general strike, Churchill was probably right in arguing that any adverse effects that arose out of using the Territorials — whether as Territorials or disguised as the CCR — would soon pass. While the Territorial Army did not enjoy the recruiting boom that followed the disbandment of the Defence Force in the middle of 1921, neither did it suffer from the previous influx of undesirables. Recruiting generally remained steady throughout 1926, and the fluctuations that did occur were probably due as much to the cancellation of some camps in the summer of 1926 (the result, the War Office claimed, of a lack of transport) and the abolition of the bounty in 1927. How much residual hostility to the Territorial Army remained in labour circles, and was heightened by the experience of 1926, is almost impossible to say. Certainly the War Office continued to have problems in recruiting skilled tradesmen to join the Supplementary Reserve, and the earlier objections of some unionists to joining it must surely have been confirmed by the Government's insistence on the maintenance of essential services during the general strike; but the reason for the declining fortunes of the Territorial Army during the late 1920s and early 1930s must be sought elsewhere.

The collapse of the general strike and the crushing of the unions through the vindictive Trade Disputes Act of 1927 brought a measure of calm if not a sense of justice to the industrial scene. The Home Office, while aware that the bitterness engendered by the general strike was another and major impediment to a lasting industrial harmony, could at least be reassured that the police forces had been able to handle the great majority of disturbances. There had been only a minimal requirement to use troops and the future need for them had been 'rendered so much the more remote'. References to the possible use of the Territorial Army, and even of the Regular Army, in aid of the civil power grew less frequent, until by 1931, in their Annual Review of Imperial Defence, the Chiefs of Staff noted, probably with some satisfaction, that there was little likelihood that calls would have to be made on military forces, Territorial or Regular, to assist the civil power.[42]

41 General J. T. Wigan, Essex Territorial Association meeting, 14 July 1926.
42 'Observations by the Home Office on Internal Security', 10 June 1927, COS 97, CAB 53/13; 'Papers Prepared for the Use of the Chiefs of Staff in

A question that warranted serious consideration was the maintenance of internal order just prior to or immediately after a declaration of war. That was a difficult problem, for if the Regular Army were outside the country, the Territorials would be the only troops available to maintain internal security, should panic set in or should there be resistance of any kind to the Government's policy. But if the Territorials were to fulfil their primary role as the second line behind the Regular Army, ready to go overseas to reinforce an expeditionary force, then who would be left to aid the civil authorities? The CCR could not be reconstituted, at least on previous lines, since the vast bulk of its members had been drawn from the Territorial Army. When these questions were first raised by Onslow in 1927, they were not of immediate relevance and could be pondered at leisure.[43] That was not the case in the late 1930s, when the possibility of having to dispatch an expeditionary force to the continent clashed with the need to provide adequate home defence, especially against attacks from the air. The Territorial Army was fundamental to both.

---

their Sixth Annual Review of Imperial Defence, 1931', Section 4, Home Office memorandum, 17 April 1931, COS 267, CAB 53/22.

[43] Memorandum by Onslow, 13 May 1927, WO 32/3456.

5

The Power of the Purse

The greatest obstacle to the fulfilment of the aspirations of the Territorials was the constant threat, all too often carried out, of cuts in government expenditure. Barely had the Territorial Army been re-established after the war than the power of the purse was used to undermine and restrict the dreams of its latter-day founders. The most pervasive complaint in Territorial circles throughout the interwar period was that the Treasury, either directly or in the guise of the Financial Member of the War Office, was always trying to find ways of reducing expenditure, and that the Territorial Army was the most vulnerable target. Whether it was a question of the bounty, or of marriage allowances, or re-equipment, or improved accommodation — all of which Territorial supporters argued were central to the well-being of the Force — these matters always resolved themselves on the issue of money.

Those who pressed for the reconstitution of the Territorials after the war claimed that for the relatively small amount of money involved, the Territorial Army offered the greatest degree of second-line security behind the Regular Army that a voluntary system could provide. If, as had been accepted by 1921, the Territorial Army was to be the sole basis for the expansion of the nation's military forces in time of war, then expenditure upon it could not be regarded as a frill, or approved as a grudging afterthought. On the contrary, the Territorials constituted the vital buffer that could reinforce the Regular Army within several months of the outbreak of a major war while the bulk of the nation's man-power was being mobilised and trained. If improvised measures such as Kitchener's 'New Armies' were to be discarded, as they had been in the early 1920s, then the Territorial Army was an indispensable element in the military posture of the nation.

And if this line of reasoning was accepted, the economy argument could be used as an added justification for expenditure upon the Territorial Army. Its supporters constantly argued that far from costing the state inordinate amounts of money, each Territorial soldier was in fact subsidizing the country, since his military service was voluntary and largely unpaid, as was that of the bulk of each County Association which raised and administered individual units. It was often claimed that not only was the Territorial Army the best 'insurance policy' that Britain could have, but that it was also the cheapest. Demands for a reduction in Territorial expenditure were always met, therefore, by cries of 'false economy'.

Critics of the Territorial Army could answer variously, and they did. They could accuse those who formulated the conditions of the reconstitution scheme of undue generosity, even extravagance, in drawing up the scale of pay for drills and attendance at camp. While there were some who attacked the very notion of paying citizen soldiers anything beyond the barest compensation for expenses, preferring instead to rely upon the appeal of patriotism and comradeship to bring in the necessary numbers, most recognized the unreality of that position in the changed conditions of post-war Britain, and accepted that some sort of pay — 'bounty', 'proficiency grant', whatever it was called — was right and proper. What that scale should be was quite another question.

Secondly the Associations were frequently criticised for their financial demands upon the Treasury, a charge that rankled among men who volunteered their services in a cause they felt — often bitterly — had little public or even official support, or that was at best taken for granted. If the Associations were sometimes unduly jealous of their independence, particularly in financial matters, it was precisely that which made them a ready target for the Treasury. The Associations enjoyed a very special financial position. Their grants, which were made on an annual basis, could be expended within very broad limits, according to each Association's understanding of its own needs. While training grants were clearly tied closely to the military requirements laid down by GOC-in-Cs of each division, the Regular officers responsible for the training of the Territorials, the expenditure of such block grants as 'Clothing' and 'Buildings' fell largely within the discretionary powers of each Association. Furthermore, the grants were continuous, so that individual Associations could, by careful management or minimal expenditure, accumulate large surpluses that were carried over beyond the end of each financial year. Some Associations, of course, especially those who had to recruit in scattered rural areas, or those who undertook heavy building programmes in districts where land prices were high, consistently ran at a loss. But others, whose numbers remained steady and strong, were able to build up

87

considerable capital reserves. The financial position of each County Association was published annually from 1922 on, and the accounts show that Associations such as Cheshire and Durham each had reserves of over £20,000.[1]

It was these reserves that became the focus of attack. In times when economy was the order of the day, it was difficult to argue that Associations could not bear a cut in their annual grants if they were able to accumulate substantial funds each year. Either the annual grant was too large in relation to the needs of the Associations, or else the Associations were holding back necessary funds, thereby interfering with the efficiency of the Territorial units. In any case, from a centralised Whitehall perspective, there was no reason why Associations should need these reserves. The role of the Territorial Army was determined by the War Office, and grants were made to enable the Associations to raise and administer the units required to fulfil that role. The accumulation of surpluses, which gave some Associations virtual financial independence, was a blow to the War Office's assertion of predominance as well as an offence against the canons of Treasury control and financial orthodoxy. As the demands for economy became irresistible, therefore, the Associations found that not only were their annual grants reduced, but that when they occasionally volunteered in a spirit of patriotic example (duly balanced by a hesitancy lest an undesirable precedent be set) to donate some of their surpluses to the War Office, they only added further weight to the arguments of their critics that the scale of annual grants to the Associations was too generous in the first place.

Thirdly, there was the charge that in view of the strategic calculations (or guesses) of the Cabinet — the 'ten year rule' and all that flowed from it — virtually any money spent on the Territorials was a waste, given the restrictions on the employment of the Territorial Army that had been built into the 1920 reconstitution scheme. Henry Wilson's criticism that the Territorials were a 'sham' was frequently echoed throughout the 1920s. In the battles of economy the War Office fought to protect the interests of the Regular Army first. Lacking a clear and well-defined role of immediate import, the Territorials were inevitably sacrificed.

The terms of the Territorial reconstruction had barely been agreed

---

[1] In March 1921 the Cheshire Association had a surplus of £35,622; Durham's was £20,622. Cmd. 1740, 'Statement Showing the Financial Position of Territorial Army County Associations on 31st March 1921', *Parl. Papers*, 1922, XII.

upon when the collapse of the post-war boom forced the Government to look for ways to reduce expenditure. In August 1921 Sir Eric Geddes, a former Minister, was appointed to head a committee to recommend substantial savings to the Cabinet. In the wake of a great war, with the general mood of the country weary of military matters, it was not surprising that the services suffered most severely. Even before the Geddes axe fell it was clear that the Army would be a prime target for recommended cuts, and so the War Office began a searching enquiry into its expenditure in the hope that it might be able to forestall the worst of the Geddes proposals, rumours of which soon began to circulate.

For the Territorial Army and its supporters it was an anxious time. The adoption of the 'ten year rule' in 1919 vitiated the need, at least in official thinking, for a capability to reinforce an expeditionary force overseas. The primary role of the Territorial Army was to act as the vehicle for the expansion of the Regular Army in a major war, but that possibility had now been ruled out. The wrangles between Churchill and his War Office colleagues over the question of using the Territorials in civil emergencies had left the General Staff dissatisfied. The Territorial Army was therefore in a weak position to resist inroads on its budget.

There was a number of ways in which economies in Territorial expenditure could be effected, but each naturally had its drawbacks. Those who in 1919 and 1920 had been lukewarm to the terms of the Territorial reconstitution could now renew their attacks, this time shielding themselves behind outside insistence for overall national economies. Given the pronouncements of the Cabinet on the lack of urgency for a major overseas capability, defenders of the Territorial Army found it difficult to defend what increasingly appeared as a privileged position.

The proposed cuts on which there was least disagreement related to the support units such as signallers, hospitals, field ambulances and veterinary companies. Since there was little likelihood that the Territorial Army would be operating overseas in the foreseeable future, these could be disbanded or reduced, with considerable saving but at little risk. Of course there were bound to be some protests, for it was not pleasant to tell men who had answered the call in 1920 that their services were no longer required, but this was the least painful area in which cuts could be made. Others were not so easily found.

There were only two areas in which substantial savings could be made without devastating the efficiency, such as it was, of the Territorials. Either overall numbers could be cut, or the cost per man could be reduced. In the latter case a reduction of the bounty was the obvious answer. The scale of payments fixed in 1920 had appalled the Financial Section in the War Office and caused some unease in the Treasury; they went far beyond a reasonable compensation for expenses incurred and were more in the nature of 'come hither' rewards. The circumstances of 1921 therefore provided justification for attacking this unwarranted, indeed undesirable, extravagance, even, as Sir Charles Harris argued, 'at the cost of taking some risk'.[2] If the bounty was withdrawn from new recruits and reduced by one-third for men already enlisted, there would eventually be an annual saving of £300,000 while the immediate saving would be £105,000.[3]

Against this attractive proposition, however, had to be balanced the impact that such cuts would have on what remained of the Territorial Army. The DGTA, Sir Noel Birch, agreed with the critics who protested that to reduce the bounty for those already enlisted would be a 'breach of faith', an opinion shared by the Judge Advocate General.[4] (The term continually crops up in Territorial records. The County Associations jealously guarded the interests of their soldiers, and were quick to interpret any attempt by the War Office to change the conditions of service as a 'breach of faith'.) Apart from this, there was the objection that recruiting would seriously decline, since men would be unwilling to incur possible losses in spending their free time in military training. The argument could be made, however, that a reduction in the bounty would keep in the Territorial Army and attract to it only those who were motivated by reasons other than purely financial rewards, so that while numbers might decline, overall quality would improve.

The other means of achieving large savings was by reducing the establishment of the Territorial Army as a whole. It was clear by 1921 that the original projections of the reconstitution scheme were unrealistic. The slow recruiting of 1920 had proved to be not the exception that Territorial supporters claimed but the norm, so that almost two years after recruiting began numbers had come nowhere near what had been expected. While some areas, especially in the north of England and south Wales, had built up strong units, others had been much less successful. Even this relative failure had not produced parallel savings, since Regular staffs and

[2] Minute by Harris, 21 June 1921, WO 32/5283.
[3] Minute by A. E. Widdows, 8 November 1921, WO 32/11257.
[4] Note by Birch, 30 September 1921; JAG to DGTA, 9 November 1921: WO 32/11257.

support services had been maintained at the levels laid down in 1920.[5]

The wholesale abolition of units therefore promised the greatest savings. It also seemed most consistent with maintaining the efficiency of the units that were retained. Rather than a reduction of ancillary units across the board that would have left the fourteen Territorial divisions 'so completely emasculated as to render each and all valueless from the point of view of war', the Quartermaster-General proposed that the number of formations in each division be reduced. The Adjutant-General, Sir George Milne, went much further and suggested that seven (i.e. half) of the Territorial divisions be abolished outright so that the rest could be properly equipped and trained.[6] This avenue, however, was rejected on political grounds,[7] or, as the Secretary of State put it when subsequently announcing the Territorial cuts, 'to select one division for disbandment would mean to select one part of the country and to give it no opportunity of expressing the military spirit which is common to every county'.[8] Behind this statement was the realisation that however the cuts were decided upon, there would be an outcry from the particular unit and the county in which it was raised.

Eventually on both questions a compromise was reached, but with the inevitable result that no-one was satisfied. Proposals to reduce the numbers of infantry and yeomanry units brought an angry response from Churchill, now at the Colonial Office. Not only would it 'violate the undertaking' he had given in 1920 (another 'breach of faith'), he said, but it would entail the 'mutilation of the Territorial Force and the injury to local patriotism'.[9] The difficulty was that if a proper geographical distribution was to be combined with a substantial reduction then some units which had done well in recruiting since 1920 would have to be disbanded, while others, much less successful, would be saved simply to retain a Territorial presence in their area.

[5]   The Interim Report of the Geddes Committee, submitted to the Cabinet on 14 December 1921, pointedly referred to this anomaly. CP 3570, CAB 24/131.

[6]   QMG and AG to Under-Secretary of State, 12 August 1921, WO 32/11257.

[7]   'Report of the Committee on the Reduction of Expenditure upon the Territorial Army', 21 September 1921, WO 32/11257.

[8]   *Parl. Debs.* (Commons), 5th series, vol. 151, col. 2241 (15 March 1922).

[9]   'Reduction of the Infantry of the Territorial Force: Memorandum by the Secretary of State for the Colonies', 28 August 1921, CP 3259, CAB 24/127.

There had already been one round of reductions in 1920 – 1. Before the war there were fifty-five Territorial Yeomanry regiments, few of which had seen service in the role for which they were trained. Although after the experiences of the Great War there were those who claimed that the cavalry had a useful role to play (and from the perspective of the requirements of imperial policing there was some justification for their view), the experience of continental war led most observers to the conclusion that in a future war the cavalry would be much less useful than in the past. The War Office had therefore decided to reduce the number of yeomanry regiments in the Territorial Army to a mere ten. Of the remaining forty-five, one voluntarily disbanded, while thirty agreed to convert to artillery batteries, signals or armoured car companies. When it was announced that the remainder, redundant in the eyes of the War Office, would be disbanded, there was an uproar. The yeomanry was by far the most popular of the Territorial arms, and although some regiments had been slower than expected in rebuilding after the war, their overall recruiting record was much better than that of the infantry. Nevertheless, there could be little justification for maintaining these units apart from considerations of traditions and local pride. They had to go, and they did, although pressure on Churchill caused him to retain an additional four regiments, to a total of fourteen.

At the same time there were reductions in the number of infantry battalions. Nineteen were converted into other arms, and one was turned into an officers' training corps. A further twenty were either disbanded or merged with other units, while all battalions suffered a reduction in establishment. In general these changes had been agreed upon, albeit reluctantly, by the various County Associations, who could hardly argue against the poor recruiting figures in the units concerned. There were some protests, especially in cases where strong battalions had been sacrificed in order to spread the losses geographically. Thus the merger of the 6th and 7th Manchesters was met with dismay and anger, as these battalions belonged to the 42nd Division, the strongest in the country. That Division had the proud record of being the first Territorial Division to go on overseas service in 1914, when, confounding the predictions of those who denigrated the preparedness of the Territorials, it embarked only five weeks after the outbreak of war. Concessions to sentiment and tradition, such as allowing merged units to retain their distinctive uniforms and badges and to maintain separate headquarters, had helped to soothe wounded feelings of pride, but it was risky to think that the County Associations would be prepared to accept another round of abolitions and mergers with so little sustained ill-feeling.[10]

The Geddes Committee submitted its preliminary report to the Cabinet in December. Of its recommended defence cuts of £75 millions, £20 millions were to fall on the Army. Although no section of the Army escaped unscathed, the bulk of the cuts were directed against the Regular Army. Infantry battalions, cavalry regiments, artillery batteries, and engineer and auxiliary units were all to be reduced by a total of 50,000 officers and men. In contrast the Territorial Army escaped comparatively lightly. The Committee noted that although the Territorials were smaller in number than in 1914, the cost per man had more than doubled. But this alarming trend did not lead them to recommend a reduction in the Territorial establishment. Instead they argued that since there was no immediate prospect of war, and even less likelihood of an invasion of Britain, the Territorial Army could be maintained at a lower level of preparedness — by spending far less on permanent staff, those Regular officers and NCOs attached to Territorial divisions and units for training purposes. The cost of this staff in 1921 was £1,135,000; it would be reduced to £1,000,000 as the abolition and merger of units was effected, but the Geddes Committee recommended that no more than £500,000 should be spent in this area.[11]

As speculation on the contents of the report began to mount, Scarbrough, now Chairman of the West Riding Territorial Association, wrote in alarm to Churchill:

> I have no doubt that the cut must fall heavily on the Territorial Army, but I am alarmed at the rumours floating about, which include a drastic reduction in the length of the annual training, and even go as far as the actual abolition of the Force.
>
> From my experience of the Military Members of the Army Council I have little doubt that they would welcome abolition and if thereby they can save something substantial for the Regular Army they will probably press for it, and if successful, destroy the one thing that keeps the voluntary spirit alive in the Country.[12]

---

[10] See the statement by the Secretary of State for War, *Parl. Debs.* (Commons), 5th series, vol. 193, col. 1286 (15 March 1921), and the critical article by Gerald B. Hurst, 'A Great Victory for the Economists', *The Nineteenth Century and After*, XC (July – December 1921), 598 – 606.

[11] CP 3570, CAB 24/131.

[12] Scarbrough to Churchill, 17 January 1922, Scarbrough Papers.

Some of Scarbrough's fears would have been confirmed had he known of a meeting of the Territorial Divisional GOC-in-Cs which Birch convened at the War Office in the utmost secrecy to discuss the implications of the Geddes recommendations and to suggest other ways of saving money. Although there was no talk of abolishing the Territorial Army, there was a suggestion made that the County Associations should be abolished. It was rejected overwhelmingly, but it was agreed that any reductions in establishment or changes in conditions of service should be imposed on the Associations and not discussed with them beforehand. The divisional commanders felt that some of the Associations were wasteful and extravagant in their administration, that smaller ones should be amalgamated for the sake of efficiency and economy, and that if the bounty had to be reduced, the savings should be made on payment for attending drills rather than for annual camp. Reductions in permanent staff could be made if the training standard of officers and NCOs was maintained; the training of the men for war during peacetime was 'not essential' since all plans included a period of six months after embodiment before Territorial troops would proceed overseas.[13] (So short were the memories of 1914.)

Scarbrough was quite right in his assessment of the Army Council. The Geddes Committee's call for swingeing cuts in the strength of the Regular Army evoked a furious response from the General Staff, who found a vent for their anger in the comparatively light treatment afforded the Territorials. The proposed reductions in the permanent staff attached to the Territorial Army, the General Staff noted caustically, would ensure that 'the military value of the force shall be even less than it is at present'. The Geddes Committee, it charged, had ignored the growing responsibilities of the Regular Army and, in a manner that was almost cavalier, had pressed for reductions that would restrict dangerously its operational ability, while 'they pass almost in silence the policy of spending £5,000,000 a year on a force which under present conditions is of no practical value in upholding the authority of the British Government at home or abroad'. It was not a question, the General Staff disingenuously emphasized, of hostility to the Territorial Army, but a matter of priorities unhappily forced on the War Office by the calls for economy:

> The General Staff have already pointed out that the whole *raison d'être* of the Territorial Army has been definitely ruled

[13] 'War Office Conference of G.O.C.-i-Cs', 3 January 1922, WO 32/11257.

out by the Cabinet's decision that a great war was out of the question for 10 years or more. This wipes out any chance of invasion. The Territorial Army cannot find out overseas garrisons, it cannot provide drafts, it cannot furnish reinforcements for an Eastern campaign, and it cannot be used for the preservation of internal order. It therefore fulfils none of the essential tasks which the maintenance of the British Empire demands. On the contrary, it is absorbing money to find which regular units are to be abolished. It is therefore, impossible to justify the retention of the Territorial Army in its present form on military grounds.

Either there had to be a change in the terms of service so that Territorials could provide reinforcements for the Regular Army in a 'small war' overseas, or some new role had to be found that would give the Territorial Army a clear and valued position within Britain's defence posture. Since the first alternative had been, in the words of the General Staff, 'exhaustively discussed' before the Territorial terms of service had been drawn up and had been found impossible to accommodate within the political and military restrictions imposed upon the Force, the second alternative became increasingly attractive to the War Office.

A Force that was effectively limited to home service could be utilised for defence against the enemy not, as previously, from the sea, but now from the air. Anti-aircraft defence was primarily the responsibility of the Royal Air Force, but it required a complex support system of ground troops to man anti-aircraft guns, operate searchlights, and provide the necessary communications. Here was the logical role for the Territorial Army. Restricted as they were in their ability to be deployed overseas, the Territorials could be employed at home — and probably near their homes — in a role that might well be of vital importance in the opening stages of a war. The experiences of bombing raids during the Great War, and especially the havoc caused by the lack of preparations to meet the threat, had influenced the General Staff to begin thinking along these lines even before the Geddes Report was issued. The Army Council had already approved the establishment of two Territorial Anti-Aircraft Divisions, but apart from taking the decision nothing had been done. The funds were not available. Lip service was paid to the need to create strong anti-aircraft defences based on the Territorial Army, but in reality very little was done until the latter half of the 1930s. Before then it was the familiar story that, desirable as this development might be, there simply was not the money to carry it out.

In the meantime the General Staff pointed to the infantry, artillery and cavalry units in the Territorial Army and suggested that rather than reduce the numbers of permanent staff attached to the Territorials, an entirely wrong-headed approach in their minds, the Territorial establishment itself should be reduced by abolishing some of those units that had conspicuously failed to win local support and had very weak recruiting figures. A leaner Territorial Army, backed by local enthusiasm, trained by a keen and efficient permanent staff, and with an increasing role to play in a vital aspect of home defence, would, so the General Staff argued, be more economical on a continuing basis and more attuned to the defence needs of the country.[14]

Reasonable as this was in light of the decisions made by the Cabinet and the needs for economy (whether or not the specific recommendations of the Geddes Committee were accepted), it was quite another matter to put it into practice. Even before a Cabinet committee was appointed to consider the Geddes Report and the General Staff objections to it, Churchill proposed an unwieldy compromise. Rejecting a purely financial approach to the question, he suggested that not only should there be no further reductions in the Territorial yeomanry, apart from some amalgamations on a squadron basis, but that regiments that had already converted to other arms should be given the option to change back to their yeomanry role if they were willing to accept certain conditions of service, namely that they should be liable to assist the civil power in times of emergency (which Churchill defined much less loosely than most of his former War Office advisers) and that in the event of a small war they should be liable for overseas service without the passing of an act of Parliament.[15] This was in answer to the objection of the General Staff that since the yeomanry, together with the rest of the Territorials, could only be used in very restricted circumstances, 'further expenditure on it is unjustified'.[16] Birch admitted that given the option of reconverting most yeomanry regiments would take it, thus entirely upsetting all the rationalisation that had been worked out in 1921. The General Staff was adamant: there could be no question of retaining unwanted yeomanry regiments

[14] 'Interim Report of the Committee of National Expenditure. Paper by the General Staff', 20 January 1922, CP 3619, CAB 24/132.
[15] DCIGS to CIGS, 27 January 1922, WO 32/11257.
[16] 'Note on the Reduction of the Infantry and Yeomanry of the Territorial Force', n.d. [November 1921]. Wilson's sarcastic evaluation of Churchill's proposal was that it was 'quite charming'. Minute, 4 November 1921, WO 32/11257.

while Regular units were being disbanded and reduced. It would be a case, wrote Lord Cavan (shortly to succeed Wilson as CIGS), of 'putting sentiment before efficiency.'[17] Nor could there be any amalgamation of regiments on a combined squadron basis. Apart from the fact that this would still retain unnecessary numbers of yeomanry, it would be all but impossible to get agreement on the siting of headquarters, titles, and such matters as were of particular importance to county regiments. Having suffered the opprobrium resulting from the contractions of 1921, the War Office was not about to reopen that question. As the Deputy CIGS noted: 'County feeling runs very high in these days.'[18]

Although he was chairman of the Cabinet committee set up to examine the Geddes proposals, Churchill made no headway in his fight to protect the yeomanry or the Territorial Army as a whole. The Committee's final report attacked much of the thinking behind the recommendations, but in the final analysis it was forced to accept most of what the Geddes Committee suggested, only scaling down the cuts from twenty millions to sixteen millions. Scarbrough had expressed the hope to Churchill that 'in the broader interests of the country you will [not] be a party to any forms of reduction which would really emasculate and possibly kill the second line which you created',[19] but there was little comfort to be had for the Territorial Army. Churchill's report concluded:

> Very serious reductions have been effected in the size and standard of maintenance of the Territorial Army. . . . The reductions will deeply affect the efficiency of the force and will be extremely unpopular. We do not see how they can be avoided in the existing circumstances.[20]

The Cabinet's decision on reductions and savings was communicated to the Territorial Associations at the beginning of March, and announced in the House of Commons two weeks later. Worthington-Evans, the Secretary of State for War, stressed that in finding ways of saving some £1,175,000 out of a current Territorial budget of £6,825,000, the Cabinet had been guided by certain

---

17 Cavan to CIGS, n.d. [? January 1922], WO 32/11257.
18 DCIGS to CIGS, 27 January 1922, WO 32/11257.
19 Scarbrough to Churchill, 17 January 1922, Scarbrough Papers.
20 'Report of a Committee appointed to examine Part I (Defence Departments) of the Report of the Geddes Committee on National Expenditure', 4 February 1922, CP 3692, CAB 24/132.

principles. There could be no question of disbanding any of the fourteen Territorial divisions, since the essence of the scheme was that it should cover the whole country and offer every area the chance to volunteer its services. Similarly all fighting units were to be retained, and reductions were to be made in the expenses of ancillary services — the signals, service, medical, and veterinary corps. As far as possible there would be no shortening of the period of annual training, which would remain at fourteen days. Critics of the restricted role of the Territorials were to be assuaged — hopefully — by the announcement that a greater part would be played in anti-aircraft defence by the creation of half a group of Air Defence troops, consisting of 220 officers and 2,708 men.

These changes, however, would account for only 60 per cent of the required savings. The remainder were, as Churchill predicted, bound to be much more unpopular. The infantry establishment was to be cut from 280,680 to 210,637 men; although no units would be abolished, the strength of the individual units would be reduced to 600 other ranks, and officers were to be recruited only to 75 per cent of the war establishment. Artillery batteries would be cut from six to four guns, while there would be some reductions (though not as extensive as the Geddes Committee had recommended) in the numbers of permanent staff attached to Territorial units.

The bounty for men was to be drastically reduced. The £5 that it had been possible for a trained Territorial to earn in the course of a year (plus his pay during annual camp) was cut to £3 for a trained man and £2.10s for a recruit. Perhaps the hardest hit were the officers. Their daily messing allowance while in camp was abolished outright; they were put on the same footing as Regular officers, and also given a flat grant of £1. Even worse, their allowances for incidental expenses incurred in the course of the year's training, previously rarely sufficient to cover their costs, were halved.[21]

This was a bitter pill for the Territorials to swallow, but on balance they had emerged from the economy campaign better than might have been expected, given the hostility of the General Staff and the widely-acknowledged fact that they were unlikely to be needed to repel an invasion or to serve overseas in the near future. The calls for economy throughout the nation were so strong that

[21] War Office to County Associations, 1 March 1922, WO 32/11257; Speech by Worthington-Evans, *Parl. Debs.* (Commons), 5th series, vol. 151, cols. 2240 – 1 (15 March 1922).

support for cuts in government spending became almost a test of patriotism, supplanting even the protection of the special interests of the Territorial Army. Many members of the County Associations were themselves businessmen, anxious to see a reduction in government expenditure and a lowering of taxation rates. Of course, they defended the Territorial budget and argued against capricious cuts, but in the end resigned themselves to the inevitable with the consolation that by accepting the government's course of action they were undertaking yet another sacrifice for the good of the nation.

But although there was cause for relief that the cuts had not been more savage, there could be little reassurance that more serious inroads would not be made if further calls for economy began to be heard. An 'economical force', a 'national insurance policy' — these were fine-sounding sentiments, but what did they mean in the context of Britain's defence requirements in the 1920s? Who could possibly justify the expenditure of five million pounds on a Territorial Army that had so little apparent relation to Britain's needs? The emphasis throughout the 1920s was much more on extra-European, colonial commitments, ventures for which the Territorials were peculiarly unfitted. Against the claims of the Regular Army on increasingly limited funds the Territorials were poorly placed to compete. Even with its powerful constituency, the Territorial Army could not take its continued existence for granted. As the CIGS, Lord Cavan, said in a speech shortly after the cuts had been announced: 'This voluntary army must be treated with sympathy and understanding, for there is a real danger of its melting away.'[22]

---

[22] Speech at the annual banquet of the Royal Academy of Arts, *The Times*, 1 May 1922.

6

Reduction and Recrimination

The Territorials had little sympathy or understanding from the Government over the next few years. Continued calls for economy forced the War Office to focus its attention on the needs of the Regular Army; the Territorials were left to make do as best they could with what was left. It was never enough, especially when the Secretary of State several times emphasized the important role the Territorials would play in the expansion of the country's forces in time of national emergency. Such assurances rang hollow as each reduction in expenditure was imposed, as each government decision affecting the Territorials in some way or other was announced without adequate consultation with the Associations. As a result the Government had its way: expenditure was substantially reduced, but at the cost of the goodwill and strong morale in the units and County Associations that was so necessary if the Territorial Army was to be a success.

The effect of the bad feeling that developed towards the end of the 1920s was a delayed one. Not until the 1930s, when the long discarded possibility of an expeditionary force was revived, did the viability of the Territorial Army become a pressing matter for the War Office. By then, however, the accumulated distrust and feeling of neglect that permeated many Territorial units and Associations was too deep to be assuaged by glib promises of renewed interest, particularly when increased expenditure was all but ruled out by the demands of economic recovery from the depression. A combination of 'pinpricks' and 'hammer-blows', compounded by an apparent War Office belief that the support, however grudging, of the County Associations could be virtually taken for granted, led to a confrontation. When the War Office pressed for a fundamental revision in the terms of enlistment for the Territorials in 1932 it received a rude shock: its proposals were rejected. That rebuff marked the beginning of a long but steady rehabilitation of the Territorial Army from the low point of the late 1920s.

The savage cuts in Army expenditure following the report of the Geddes Committee had so reduced the Regular Army that the General Staff felt there could be no further cuts without endangering efficiency and the Cabinet accepted this view.[1] In future it would fall to the Territorial Army to bear the brunt of any additional reductions. None were called for on financial grounds for several years, and the Secretary of State for War was authorised to deny specifically that reductions were contemplated, in the hope that this would put an end to the rumours and stabilise recruiting numbers, which had fallen off badly as the uncertainty spread.[2] However, a reordering rather than a reduction of expenditures became necessary in 1923. On the recommendation of the Geddes Committee, and at the insistence of the General Staff, the Territorial Army was required to undertake an anti-aircraft defence role in the Air Defence of Great Britain [ADGB] scheme that was being set up. The Director-General of the Territorial Army was assured that these troops would not be raised by abolishing a number of Territorial infantry divisions, for the War Office now based its home defence plans on the possibility of an air attack combined with an invasion force of 10,000 in the Colchester-Shorncliffe area. To meet the threat Territorial infantry levels had to be maintained at their existing strength.[3] The suspicion remained, however, that the War Office might be forced to resort to abolition of some units. The initial ADGB troops were to be established in the Southeast of England — in London and its approaches, precisely the areas where recruiting for Territorial infantry units was weakest. It was tempting to abolish those units which had been struggling since the war to reach a respectable strength and to channel the funds thus saved into producing the £450,000 required to maintain the 15,000 AA troops.

Towards the end of 1923 the question of abolishing Territorial infantry divisions was again broached. A poor response to the appeal for AA troops raised doubts over the ability of the Territorial Army to supply the necessary numbers, in which case responsibility for manning ADGB installations would have to fall to the Regular Army. In that case there could be no justification for

---

[1] 'Our Military Strength in Relation to Our Military Commitments: Memorandum by the General Staff', April 1923, Annex to CP 200(23), CAB 24/159.
[2] Cabinet 31(23), 13 June 1923, CAB 23/46.
[3] DGTA to CIGS, 5 July 1923; CIGS to DGTA, 2 August 1923: WO 32/11271.

maintaining expenditure on the Territorial Army at what the General Staff already considered to be an unwarranted level. It was suggested that the rate of conversion of Territorial drill halls and the provision of anti-aircraft equipment be slowed down until such time as recruitment revived sufficiently to show that AA troops could be raised through the Territorial Army.[4] It was a vicious circle. The less money was spent on providing modern equipment and attractive practice halls (together with social facilities), the more reluctant men were to enlist, and the less likely it seemed that the Territorial Army was the most suitable medium through which to raise the necessary troops. If the numbers were not forthcoming, there was no reason to maintain a number of weak infantry divisions whose usefulness in an overseas role was circumscribed by the terms of enlistment and whose unwillingness to convert to home defence anti-aircraft duties had been so forcefully demonstrated.

The Director-General of the Territorial Army admitted that abolition might become necessary, even at the cost of stirring up 'deep resentment and strenuous opposition', but he went on to say that 'if destruction of Divisions and reconstruction of Territorial formations on a new plan should be closely followed by further destruction and further reconstruction, without any definite end in sight, the effect on the Territorial Army will certainly be to induce a most dangerous spirit of discontent and discouragement'.[5] The military implications of abolishing infantry divisions, particularly in the home counties area, and the political uproar that would result was enough to convince the Army Council that other means of raising AA troops would have to be found. In December it was decided that the costs involved would have to be an additional item on the Army estimates and that Territorial units would not be reduced to provide AA troops.[6] For the moment those 'other means' did not have to be found. The ADGB scheme got off to a very slow start, and the raising of AA troops was given a low priority until the funds to purchase modern equipment became available.

For the next two years the Territorials enjoyed a degree of stability. The unrealistic hopes of the 1920 scheme had been tempered

[4] R. Paterson (Finance, WO) to DGTA, 28 October 1923, WO 32/11271.
[5] DGTA to Under-Secretary of State, WO, 10 November 1923, WO 32/11271.
[6] Army Council, 326th meeting, 19 December 1923, WO 32/11271. This decision was endorsed by the Committee of Imperial Defence, 179th meeting, 14 January 1924.

by the sobering recruiting figures of the first two years, and the outright hostility of the War Office had given way to a resigned acceptance of the 'second line'. For the moment the Territorials were left alone. There were no demands for additional expenditure cuts, and apart from the question of AA troops, there seemed to be no controversial policy issues to be decided which might have an effect on the Territorial Army. There was a minor flurry in 1924 when the short-lived Labour Government cancelled the capitation grant given annually to Cadet units. This provoked a storm of protest, much of which was repeated in 1930, when official recognition was withdrawn from the Cadets, again by a Labour government. However this action had little real effect on the Territorials, other than to confirm the evident fact that the Labour movement had little sympathy with military organisations, even those such as the Cadets whose connections with the country's military forces were tenuous at best. Though many of them privately admitted that the Cadets were of dubious value to the Territorials, the general reaction of the Territorial Associations was to decry yet another attack — albeit an indirect one — on the Territorial Army and the sources from which it could draw its support.

By 1926 the picture had changed. Further cuts in defence expenditure were demanded, and there was little that the War Office could do to resist them. Early in the year it withdrew the per capita grant of five shillings paid to each Association for the upkeep of its clothing supplies. That saving, amounting to £36,000, was quickly followed by calls for much more massive cuts. The Earl of Derby, a leading spokesman for the Territorial Associations, accepted the need for national economy, but insisted that the Territorials should not be made to bear a greater proportionate cut than the Regular Army and that the weight of reductions should fall as much on the training as on the administrative grant.[7] The Secretary of State agreed that the Associations as a whole should determine exactly where cuts should be made. He probably hoped to avoid inflaming feelings against the Government and the War Office more than was inevitable. All he required was that the cuts be made in such a way as to cause the least possible disturbance to the Territorial Army, and — more important — that they be effective immediately and produce 'an actual cash saving for the coming year'.

When the Associations met under the aegis of the Council of County Territorial Associations to consider how the savings were to

---

7   Derby to Worthington-Evans, 22 January 1926, Derby Papers, Correspondence with Individuals: War Office 1926.

be made, there was surprisingly little evidence of animosity, for the total of cuts demanded by the War Office — £160,000 — was proportionate to that imposed on the Regular Army. There could therefore be no justification for previous complaints that the Territorials were being singled out by an unsympathetic War Office. Nor was there any disagreement when the Vice-Chairman of the CCTA, Brigadier-General Sir William Bromley-Davenport, who had met the Secretary of State to discuss the level of cuts, rejected out of hand any idea that the reductions could be made by abolishing units, either by wiping out one battalion in each brigade or one company in each battalion. Yet in the long run some measure of abolition or at least reduction might have been the best solution. Had the weakest units been abolished or reduced to cadre levels, the smaller grants available for both training and administration would have been more effective in providing adequate training and social facilities. As it was, when reductions were ruled out as a means of saving money, the increasingly restricted funds were spread more thinly, with serious effects on recruiting. However, this was not a realistic option in 1926, when the demand from the War Office was for 'immediate cash savings in the coming year'.

Bromley-Davenport recommended that Training Grants be cut by almost thirty-eight per cent to £100,000, that grants for land purchase and the erection and renovation of buildings be halved to £50,000, and that grants for hiring horses for preliminary (i.e. pre-annual camp) drills be reduced by ten per cent, saving £11,000. A further £39,000 could be found by reducing the per capita clothing grant by four shillings. The remaining £9,000, he suggested somewhat hesitantly, could be made up if Associations volunteered to donate five per cent of their surplus funds (which in 1926 totalled £360,000) to the Government. This was a bold proposal, for these surplus funds had been jealously guarded by those Associations that had managed to accumulate them and keep them out of reach of the War Office and Treasury. The suggestion was not lacking in self-interest, however, for Bromley-Davenport argued that not only would this prevent units from being disbanded to save money but that it would make the surplus funds 'more than ever safe. For seeing them put to so splendid a purpose, no Government would ever have the face to lay a finger on them.'[8]

There was little disagreement, for in fact there could be none. It was unthinkable, only four years after the cuts of 1922, that units might be reduced or abolished outright, and once that avenue was

[8] CCTA, 10 February 1926, Minutes, 1923 – 1933.

rejected, Bromley-Davenport's suggestion provided the only solution. The sole dissenting voice was that of Colonel John Brown of Northamptonshire, a long-standing critic of the power of the Associations in Territorial matters. He questioned the wisdom of cutting the training grant, arguing that these were the only funds available to unit commanders to conduct weekend camps and other forms of training outside the annual camp. Already the grant was too small, and if it were to be reduced further, the efficiency of the Territorial Army would suffer. As he later wrote to Basil Liddell Hart, the *Daily Telegraph* Military Correspondent, 'the weekend exercises and winter training are [the] basis of the present efficiency of TA units and as the bulk of this money gets down to the keen men it may be considered a reward for enthusiasm and efficiency . . .. The fact is that at the Council the bulk of members are Secretaries of the Associations and very few of them are in touch with the units.'[9] In one sense Brown was right: many members of individual Associations tended to think in terms of bricks, mortar and clothing stores, but this was one of the prime responsibilities of the Associations, and the authority in local affairs that went with it undoubtedly encouraged public spirited men to serve on the Associations. If the authority of the Associations were to be reduced and unit and divisional commanders given much more control of training funds, as Brown wished, then, Derby warned the Permanent Under-Secretary at the War Office, 'you won't get business men to serve any longer on the Associations'.[10]

Apart from training the other major responsibility of the Associations was the raising and maintaining of individual units. Every enquiry, official or unofficial, into recruiting that was carried out between the wars indicated that the inadequacy and unattractiveness of so many Territorial drill halls and social clubs was a major factor in poor recruiting levels. If the grants for lands and buildings were cut more than the fifty per cent Bromley-Davenport recommended, a course that Brown seemed to prefer, numbers might well have dropped even more, whether or not extra training was held. At this stage, only four years after the Territorials had been reconstituted in the face of considerable opposition from the General Staff, there was a measure of safety in numbers. Not until recruiting campaigns had decisively failed and there had been further reductions in expenditure did the Associations and the War Office make a virtue of

[9] Brown to Liddell Hart, 11 February 1926, Liddell Hart Papers 1/115/3.
[10] Derby to Sir Herbert Creedy, 22 April 1926, Derby Papers, Correspondence with Individuals: War Office 1926.

necessity and begin to stress quality over quantity.

Derby warned the CCTA to avoid 'kicking against the pricks', and, undoubtedly anxious to avoid a confrontation with the War Office, which they could only lose and out of which they might suffer greater losses, the meeting quickly accepted Bromley-Davenport's recommendations on cuts in expenditure and agreed to donate five per cent of their surplus funds to the Government.[11] It was an astonishingly easy victory for the War Office. In effect it had extracted major concessions from the Associations without giving anything in return. But it was also too easy, for it led the War Office to believe that the Associations would be equally pliable in the future. That assumption was quickly proved wrong, and in the process the distrust and ill-feeling between Whitehall and the Associations reached a peak.

No sooner had the Associations accepted the cuts than the Territorials suffered another blow. When the General Strike was called in May, the Territorial Army was not embodied to assist the civil power in the maintenance of order, but selected units were asked to volunteer en masse as members of the Civil Constabulary Reserve. (See above, chapter 4.) The effect of this transparent device was a delayed one: it added weight to the long-standing suspicion of the Territorials on the part of organised labour, which saw them as a home defence body designed to protect the *status quo*. Any ideas Labour might have had that a successful Territorial movement would be the best protection against the introduction of conscription were overshadowed by the fear that the Territorials might again be embodied to carry out a Conservative policy of internal repression. Not for many years could the Territorial movement hope to find any strong support in Labour circles: in the meantime the Territorials were held to be a manifestation of the militarism that was such anathema to Labour (even though much of the rank and file in the inter-war Territorial Army came from the working class).

A much more immediate effect came in the summer of 1926. Two weeks after the collapse of the General Strike, the War Office announced that all annual camps that were scheduled to be held before July 15 had been cancelled.[12] The ostensible reason for this decision was that the strike had interfered with coal production and deliveries to such an extent that supplies were insufficient to permit Territorial units to undertake long train journeys to their

---

[11] CCTA, 10 February 1926, Minutes, 1923-1933.

[12] Speech by Worthington-Evans, *Parl. Debs.* (Commons), 5th series, vol. 197, col. 232 (22 June 1926).

training site. Nor was it possible, the War Office claimed, to rearrange those camps, either for a period after July 15 or to a locality that did not involve excessive train travel. Exactly why this could not be done was not explained, and the suspicion spread that the Government had taken advantage of the chaos resulting from the General Strike to save some money at the expense of an acquiescent Territorial Army. This interpretation was strengthened by a remarkably insensitive letter from the War Office to the Associations, in which the Army Council denied that its decision had been dictated by the wish to save money on training, and insisted that the sole consideration had been that 'affecting national transport' — which did not explain why it had refused to sanction local camps which involved no transport other than marching. The letter concluded:

> The Army Council are concerned at the loss of training and of consequent efficiency which must accrue to the Territorial Army and at the disappointment and inconvenience caused to many members of all ranks; but they are aware that they can rely upon the Territorial Army to accept uncomplainingly and in the right spirit decisions arrived at in the national interest.[13]

This was too much to expect. The summer camp was the high point of the Territorial year, and by far the biggest single recruiting factor. Weekly drills were all very well, but it was only large scale concentrations of troops at summer camp that made battalion, brigade, and sometimes divisional exercises possible, and only then could the Territorials truly become more than 'Saturday night soldiers'. The Army Council's offer to provide additional funds for weekend camps was a poor substitute for fifteen days' annual camp, especially when the sum barely made up what had been cut from the training grant in February. There were other considerations which the Army Council had overlooked. It was more than a matter of mere 'inconvenience' for many Territorials: they planned their holidays around the annual camp and, if the location was an agreeable one (near the sea, for example) arranged for their families to stay nearby. With the cancellation of camps, they risked the loss of the bounty and the allowances they could earn while in camp. For many of them it was this money that enabled them to take their families for a holiday each year. Now that was threatened. Even though the Government made it possible for men to earn their

---

[13] *The Times*, 14 July 1926.

bounty by doing extra drills this could not compensate for these losses.[14]

The Army Council's hopes that the Territorials would accept the decision 'uncomplainingly and in the right spirit' were quickly shattered. They did complain, not least because the reasons put forward by the Army Council were so unconvincing. The Chairman of the Staffordshire Association, most of whose units had their camps cancelled, rejected the coal shortage argument and publicly and bluntly accused the Army Council of being unwilling to provide the necessary funds.[15] The Staffordshire Association passed a resolution 'to express the feeling of deep dismay' at the action of the Army Council,[16] and persuaded the Council of County Territorial Associations to do likewise.[17] Looking back it is a little surprising that the protests were so muted. The explanation perhaps lies in the composition of the Associations. Their most active members were politically conservative and sympathised with the Government's interpretation of the General Strike as an extra-constitutional threat to the country. Thus, although dismayed by the War Office's decision, they did not judge it as harshly as might otherwise have been expected. Certainly when the camps were again cancelled in 1931, the Associations were much less accepting.

The cancellation of summer camps in 1926 was an indication — though largely unrecognized at the time — of things to come. Even before the War Office announced its decision on camps, the Chiefs of Staff had met and heard the Chief of the Imperial General Staff, Sir George Milne, recommend a reduction in the size of the Territorial Army and a recasting of its training priorities. In May he explained to the Chiefs of Staff that unless substantial cuts were made there would be a deficit of one million pounds in the coming year, and that took no account of expenditure connected with the defence of the naval base at Singapore and other ports on imperial routes to the east. Not did it allow for the costs of anti-aircraft defences in England, even though there was some possibility that the rate of establishing these might be slowed down. The Territorial Army consisted of fourteen infantry divisions together with

[14] See *The Times* leader ('Territorial Camps'), 19 June 1926; also the letter by Major C. R. Bland, formerly of the London Rifle Brigade (14 June 1926), who wrote that the cancellation of camps would be a 'catastrophe'.

[15] Lieut.-Colonel Hon G. A. Anson, letter to *The Times*, 19 August 1926.

[16] Staffordshire, 24 July 1926, D 969/1/3.

[17] CCTA, 17 November 1926, Minutes, 1923-1933.

cavalry, artillery, and the usual support services, but that organisation had been established in the immediate post-war atmosphere: it had assumed that in a major war the Territorials would be required to act as the second line behind the Regular Army. The likelihood of the Territorials carrying out such a role had so diminished that there was no longer any justification for maintaining so many divisions for overseas service. The only way in which funds could be found for raising and equipping anti-aircraft troops was by cutting down on the Territorial establishment.[18]

When the Chiefs of Staff presented their 'Annual Review of Imperial Defence' to the Cabinet in June, they followed Milne's recommendation, but with a significantly different emphasis. The Locarno Treaty of 1925 imposed at least a semblance of stability on France's border with Germany, and though the Treaty saddled Britain with a commitment to resist forcible changes in the border, the obligation was shared with the other signatories, making it — in the words of the 1928 Review — a 'somewhat indefinite liability'.[19] The ability of the Territorials to reinforce the Regular Army in a European commitment was thereby rendered much less important. Additionally — and this was the significant change — a friendly France meant that Britain no longer had to guard against air attacks from that quarter, fear of which had prompted the Chiefs of Staff in 1923 to press for increased expenditure on anti-aircraft defences. The funds released by reduction of the Territorial units earmarked for an expeditionary role need not therefore be used for anti-aircraft defences. Now the Chiefs of Staff recommended that the expansion scheme for the Royal Air Force be postponed until 1935-6, and no further work be carried out on the inner and outer anti-aircraft artillery zones that were to have been established around London, until the situation was reviewed at some unspecified time in the future. Instead the savings would be used for 'research and experiment' (especially on mobile armoured forces) and 'to supply the Regular Army with the supplementary units, equipment and training grounds, which it now lacks'.[20]

This would be a major change of policy, and no hasty decisions

---

[18] COS, 30th meeting, 27 May 1926, CAB 53/1.
[19] COS, 'Imperial Defence Policy: A Review of Imperial Defence, 1928', 25 June 1928, CP 348(28), CAB 24/198.
[20] COS, 'Imperial Defence Policy, 1926', 22 June 1926, COS 41, CAB 53/12.

could be taken. It was clear to the War Office, however, that somehow its spending priorities had to be reordered even if the Treasury demanded no further cuts. Worthington-Evans was determined that if cuts had to be made, they would be the result of careful planning rather than the hasty decisions that had been the War Office response to previous calls for economy. As soon as the Chiefs of Staff had completed their review and made their recommendations, he appointed a sub-committee of the Army Council to look at the finances of the Territorial Army and to anticipate calls for reductions. The operations of this committee were subsequently the subject of a bitter dispute between the Associations and the War Office.

The CIGS, Milne, underlined the parlous state to which the Territorials had been reduced. Except for the extreme and unlikely emergency of a European war, the Territorial Army would be unable to mobilise and take the field abroad in less than six months. Even if it could be ready before that, there was insufficient shipping to transport the troops within six months, so that expenditure on the Territorials could not be cut down without seriously weakening the overall military power of the country. The committee agreed that some units could be abolished outright. These included two yeomanry regiments and a number of supporting units — ordnance corps, hospitals and veterinary stations. These savings, however, amounting to £44,000, came nowhere near the figure of about £250,000 which the War Office thought necessary to fulfil the needs of the Regular Army. There were four ways in which large reductions could be made, which, taken together, would produce the required savings.

The first possibility was the abolition of the bounty. This had the advantage of producing immediate and substantial savings which would become even greater as the bounty was phased out completely. Even the War Office flinched from the breach of faith involved in withdrawing the bounty from serving men, but by not paying it to those who re-enlisted after a certain date or to new recruits, up to £80,000 could be saved in a single year, and eventually this would rise to £332,000 when the phasing out was complete. The Committee recognized that recruiting would suffer a severe if temporary setback, but thought that eventually it would reach its former levels.

The second possibility was summer training, one of the largest items in the Territorial budget. Each unit went to camp for fifteen days a year, although there was provision for men who could not get that much leave to attend for only eight days. If the normal length was cut to eight days, there would be considerable savings on pay and allowances and the hire of horses and grounds. On purely political grounds this was perhaps preferable to the abolition of units, for at least there would be an equality of sacrifice rather than the singling out of individual units to bear the brunt of the cuts. Milne was adamantly opposed to shortening the period to eight days. As it was the Territorials could hardly claim a high degree of military expertise, and if their one extended period of training was cut to eight days, the effective time available would be only four days, since two days at either end were usually taken up with establishing and then dismantling the camp site. Milne's argument was another variation of the General Staff position of 1921 (which as Adjutant-General he had helped draft), when commenting on the Geddes Committee's recommendation that the permanent staff attached to the Territorial Army be reduced by half. This, the General Staff replied, would ensure that 'the military value of the force shall be even less than it is at present' — and that, in Milne's estimation in 1926, was clearly not very great. The committee agreed, and that option was dropped from further consideration.

The third means by which substantial sums could be saved was through the reduction of establishments across the board. As with training, it was decided that the efficiency of the Territorial Army and its ability to expand rapidly in times of emergency could only be maintained if the establishment of officers and NCOs was kept at existing levels. For the rank and file, however, it was another matter, and the committee recommended that the establishments of infantry battalions be reduced from 680 to 500 other ranks, and that proportionate cuts be made in all other units.

Finally there was some discussion of the possibility of telescoping the fourteen infantry divisions into seven, but this was opposed by Milne who wanted at least the skeleton of a large Territorial Army kept in existence, even though there were no funds to give it an efficient life. The committee pursued the idea no further, except to add that the two London divisions, among the weakest in the whole Territorial Army, could perhaps be amalgamated, with a saving of £114,000. London was unique in Territorial circles in that the original anti-aircraft units were established there, so that if one of the infantry divisions was abolished there would still be every opportunity for men to serve in the Territorial Army, and to serve in fact in an arm which was becoming increasingly important.

In October the committee submitted its recommendations to the

Army Council. It urged that the bounty be withdrawn; that establishments be reduced; that the two London divisions be telescoped into one and certain other small units be abolished; that economies made in 1926 be carried over into the following year; and that grants for travel to annual camps be reduced.[21] These were far-reaching proposals, and Worthington-Evans understandably hesitated to accept them without trying to gauge the response of the Territorials, who were still angered by the sudden cancellation of camps.

Rather than place such an explosive package before the Associations as a whole Worthington-Evans decided to sound them out indirectly, by consulting with senior men in the Territorial movement. He later claimed, when defending himself against charges that the War Office had sprung the cuts on the Associations without giving them any real chance to examine them, that Bromley-Davenport had been involved in the committee discussions from the time of its inception.[22] That involvement, however, was fleeting and very occasional, and it was not until early in 1927 that Derby, Bromley-Davenport, and Colonel R. E. Golightly, the Chairman, Vice-Chairman, and Secretary respectively of the Council of County Territorial Associations, were informed of the extent of the cuts that the War Office was contemplating.

No doubt to the relief of Worthington-Evans, Derby told him that he personally agreed with the abolition of the bounty, and from talking to Territorials in West Lancashire, he found that many Commanding Officers shared his dislike of it, and would look upon its withdrawal as the least objectionable means of saving money. Derby offered his strong support to the War Office in facing up to the 'howl that there always is' but gave the impression that any adverse reaction would be limited and easily withstood. Although he was reluctant to approve of reductions in establishment, he admitted that they could be justified, and suggested that a combination of the abolition of the bounty and cuts in establishments would satisfy the War Office demands, especially as those already drawing the bounty gradually left the Territorial Army. His only reservation was over Golightly's endorsement of the proposal to reduce camps to eight days, but

[21] 'Army Council Sub-Committee on Financial Aspects of the Territorial Army', October 1926, WO 32/2670.
[22] *Parl. Debs.* (Commons), 5th series, vol. 203, cols. 883 – 5 (7 March 1927).

that, Worthington-Evans assured him, was no longer under serious consideration.[23]

The War Office, then, had reason to believe that while the cuts it wished to make would be greeted with understandable dismay the Associations would accept them as resignedly as they had cuts in the past. It was rudely disabused of this notion when the CCTA was told of the proposed reductions. Bromley-Davenport laid the War Office proposals before the Associations' representatives at the quarterly meeting on 9 February. No notice of the announcement had been given, and Bromley-Davenport added to the sense of shock by implying that he had been briefed by the Secretary of State only that very morning. It was grim news that he had to tell the Associations. Expenditure cuts of £160,000, which the Territorials had accepted the previous year on the understanding — they thought — that they were for one year only, were to be increased to £231,000. An increase of that magnitude required 'something of a much more drastic and radical character'. Fortunately the War Office had decided against abolishing units or reducing selected ones to cadre levels, but the only other way in which the cuts could be made was by a combination of the withdrawal of the bounty and the reduction of establishments, plus some smaller economies.[24]

The meeting was stunned by these sudden revelations. Bromley-Davenport wrote to Derby, who was unable to attend:

> It is a bad business! . . . [The] Council have taken it *very* badly. The attack was led by Scarbrough in a violent speech which aggravated feelings at a moment when calmness and consideration were required.[25]

Scarbrough described the proposals as a 'bolt from the blue', a case of the War Office holding a 'pistol at their heads', and called on the Associations to fight them 'tooth and nail'. It was impossible to agree to them at such short notice, he claimed, especially when they were 'calculated to destroy the efficiency and the spirit of the Territorial Army, and to reduce Commanding Officers to a state of

---

[23] Derby to Bromley-Davenport, 30 January 1927; to Worthington-Evans, 30 January, 5 February 1927; Worthington-Evans to Derby, 2 February 1927, Derby Papers, Correspondence with Individuals: War Office 1926.

[24] CCTA, 9 February 1927, Minutes, 1923-1933.

[25] Bromley-Davenport to Derby, 10 February 1927, Derby Papers, 4/51, 52.

despair'. Bromley-Davenport pleaded in mitigation of the War Office's action that there was no other realistic course open, but the meeting would have none of it. Speaker after speaker rose to denounce the proposals, and Scarbrough's motion to appoint a sub-committee to examine the cuts and, if possible, to recommend alternative economies, received unanimous support.[26]

It was one thing to rail against the War Office plan, but quite another to suggest how the money was to be saved. Scarbrough's committee (he had been made chairman) rejected the reduction of establishments and the abolition of the bounty. In the case of the latter, it emphasized that the granting of the bounty was of much more than purely monetary significance: 'it was also intended as a recognition of the increased obligations undertaken by the new Territorial Army.' Particularly galling to the committee was the fact that while the War Office proposed to withdraw the bounty from Territorials, it continued to pay much higher bounties to members of the Supplementary Reserve, who usually carried out their annual training with the Territorial Army. In place of these cuts, which formed the backbone of the War Office's economies, the committee recommended that the Associations surrender twenty-five per cent of the accumulated clothing reserve funds to the War Office and that the annual grant to the Associations be reduced by six per cent. These would yield cuts of £200,000, which together with those smaller economies that the committee accepted, would produce the overall savings required by the War Office. However, as the committee noted, it was not simply a matter of financial reductions. The Associations had the right to be consulted by the Army Council before the implementation of any decisions that would drastically affect the Territorial Army: 'in neglecting to do so the Army Council have shown a want of confidence which is much to be regretted'.[27]

These proposals were rejected by Worthington-Evans on 21 February, on the grounds that they were not a continuing solution to the problem facing the War Office, for they could not be repeated on a yearly basis, whereas the abolition of the bounty would provide an immediate saving of £64,000 and eventually at least £350,000. The only other way in which comparable savings could be made was through the large scale disbandment of units,

[26] CCTA, 9 February 1927.
[27] 'Report of the Special Committee of the Council of Territorial Associations', annex to minutes of special meeting, 1 March, 1927, Minutes, 1923 – 1933.

but this was rejected out of hand by Scarbrough's committee. Instead Worthington-Evans offered a compromise: if the Associations would accept the abolition of the bounty, the War Office would drop its plans — for the coming year at any rate — to save £140,000 by the reduction of establishments. Bromley-Davenport had anticipated this impasse, and told Derby that he was certain that if the Associations would agree to the bounty being withdrawn, the War Office would drop its threat to cut establishments.[28] There was not much else the Associations could do, and Scarbrough's committee recommended that they bow to the inevitable and accept the Secretary of State's offer. In making it, Worthington-Evans stressed that to be an effective economy measure the withdrawal would have to be made quickly to prevent an influx of recruits hoping to qualify for the bounty before it was abolished. Nothing more was said on the matter, and the committee left under the clear impression that there would be no final decision until the Associations had discussed the proposal at a meeting set for 1 March.[29]

In fact the decision had already been taken, and consultation with the Associations had been little more than a formality. On the very day the committee met Worthington-Evans, he signed an Army Order abolishing the bounty for all men enlisting or re-engaging in the Territorial Army on or after 1 March. The Associations were told of the new policy on 24 February, and reacted to this *fait accompli* with howls of outrage. When the need for cuts had been announced earlier in February there had been strong objections voiced by many Associations. Special meetings were called to discuss the perfidy of the War Office, which, it was widely held, had deliberately misled the Associations and again undercut the Territorial Army. From Aberdeen to Kent, from London to Northumberland, Associations protested that the abolition of the bounty would have a 'disastrous' effect on the Territorials, that it would 'kill' recruiting. Not only would numbers suffer, there would also be a decline in efficiency, since now there would be no incentive for a soldier to attend drills and musketry courses. Even more of the very limited time at annual camp would have to be spent in learning basic movements instead of more difficult manoeuvres at the battalion and brigade levels. While most Associations were

---

[28] Bromley-Davenport to Derby, 20 February 1927, Derby Papers, 4/51, 52.
[29] 'Supplementary Report of the Special Committee', 22 February 1927, addendum to CCTA minutes, 1 March 1927.

gloomy about the effects on recruiting, not all shared their dire predictions. The City of Glasgow preferred to see the bounty withdrawn rather than have establishments reduced, but it was one of the few Associations that had filled its establishment and had waiting lists in several units. Kent agreed, but in this case it feared that its poor recruiting record would become even worse: the agricultural workers on whom it relied heavily would simply not be able to afford to join the Territorial Army if the bounty, which represented more than two weeks' average wages, were withdrawn. But whether they inclined to one course or another, all the Associations deplored the War Office's action, and were determined, in the words of the Cornwall Association's resolution, to fight the proposals 'tooth and nail'.[30]

The prevailing mood at the CCTA meeting on 1 March was therefore one of bitterness and anger over the high-handed War Office attitude, particularly after the special committee had warned Worthington-Evans of the resentment caused by an apparently deliberate and slighting neglect to consult the Associations properly in the first place. Bromley-Davenport, deputising for Derby, tried to appeal for calm at a time when 'their natural feelings of indignation' ran high, but his plea was ignored. The objections to the War Office action were two-fold. Many Associations argued that the Territorial soldier would be financially out-of-pocket, and that recruiting would therefore suffer badly. This was particularly so in those counties where the population was small and scattered, and where travelling costs were consequently high. Since grants to defray the costs of going to drills had been reduced in 1925 and 1926, the abolition of the bounty was the last straw. The

---

30 See City of Aberdeen, special joint meeting with County of Aberdeen, Kincardinshire and Banffshire, 14 February 1927, MD 4/6; Kent, General Purposes Committee, 24 February 1927, MD/TA 4/5; City of London, General Purposes Committee, 16 February 1927, 12,606/2; Northumberland, 15 February 1927, NRO 408/6; City of Glasgow, General Purposes Committee, 15 February 1927; Cornwall, 16 February 1927, DDX 295/12. For similar motions protesting the expenditure cuts and the abolition of the bounty in particular, see Cambridgeshire, 26 February 1927, Minutes, vol. 3; Derbyshire, 15 February 1927, D 530/5; Devon, 16 March 1927, 1715c/TA3; East Lancashire, 4 February 1927, M 73/2/6; Gloucestershire, 14 February 1927, Acc. D 2388 1/3; Middlesex, 28 February 1927, 994/5; Oxfordshire, 26 February 1927, Acc. 727, Minutes, vol. 6; Suffolk, 24 February 1927, LA2: 1205/13; Warwickshire, General Purposes Committee, 15 February 1927, CR 1141/4; West Lancashire, 25 February 1927, Acc. 2074, Minutes, vol. 2.

representative of the Northumberland Association accused the CCTA officials and the Associations of the home counties — the weakest in the country — of conspiring to economise in ways that would least affect their under-strength units. No one followed up the charge, but there was clearly a feeling that the Council had not been vigorous enough in pressing its objections to the War Office plan and in suggesting alternatives.

Secondly the Associations were angered by what they regarded as yet another attempt by the War Office to bypass them, even though they were by statute the official administrators of the Territorial Army. Not only was the abolition of the bounty 'monstrous and unjust', as the Lanarkshire Association put it, but a 'distinct breach of faith' and a 'dangerous menace' to the Territorial Army's ability to fulfil its role as the second line behind the Regular Army. This time the Associations were not so ready to accept the War Office action without a vigorous protest. They passed a unanimous resolution condemning the abolition of the bounty and disclaiming any responsibility for its effects on the future of the Territorial Army, and deploring the fact that such a 'momentous' decision should have been taken without due consultation with the Associations. Further the Council appointed a deputation to the War Office to press for a reconsideration of the bounty abolition, and it established another special committee to enquire into the whole question of Territorial finances, in the hope that similar precipitate actions in the future could be avoided and the finances of the Territorial Army be placed on a more secure and regular basis.[31]

The sense of outrage was not diminished by the Secretary of State's assurance that the Army Council had intended no slight in rejecting the Associations' advice.[32] Increasingly the abolition itself took second place in the scale of grievances to the method by which it had been accomplished. Bromley-Davenport reported to Derby a growing realisation that the effects on recruiting would be severe but temporary,[33] although this view was a typical example of the London-based perspective that had been criticised at the CCTA meeting. The Scottish Associations were unanimous in opposing the withdrawal of the bounty, but were split over the question of its impact. Large urban Associations such as Glasgow preferred to accept it rather than see a reduction in establishments, but almost

---

[31] CCTA, 1 March 1927, Minutes, 1923–1933.

[32] *Parl. Debs.* (Commons), 5th series, vol. 203, cols. 883–4 (7 March 1927).

[33] Bromley-Davenport to Derby, 2 March 1927, Derby Papers, 4/51, 52.

all the other Associations argued that their units, raised in many very small detachments in rural areas, would find it very hard to maintain their numbers.[34] No one could be sure, but what was clear beyond doubt was that relationships between the War Office and the Associations were at an all time low. *The Times*, outspoken in its defence of the Associations, attacked the unsympathetic treatment it had consistently suffered at the hands of the War Office. In a leader entitled 'Starving the Territorials', it wrote:

> The Territorial Army is far too important an element in the defences of the country nowadays to be treated in this niggardly and high-handed fashion . . .. At the present moment the Army Council is not merely looking a gift horse in the mouth; it is extracting its teeth one by one . . .. It is high time the public should demand their proper recognition, and that there should be an end to the policy of slights and pinpricks.[35]

The deputation that went to the War Office on 16 March insisted that even if Worthington-Evans believed there was a division of opinion among the Associations as to the effects of the abolition of the bounty, the Army Council ought to give greatest weight to the views of the CCTA. Its views were unanimous. Withdrawing the bounty discriminated unfairly against those who could not re-engage in time, and it created two classes of men within the ranks, a situation that would be inimical both to recruiting and to discipline. Henceforth Territorial soldiers would be out-of-pocket, a serious matter for working-class units in particular, and completely at odds with the undertakings and spirit of the reconstitution proposals made by Churchill in 1920. At that time it was recognised that the additional obligations placed on the new Territorial Army, especially that of overseas service prior to the introduction of a General Service Act, should be compensated for by the provision of some sort of bounty. The case for such a payment was strengthened by the increased standards of efficiency and the number of drills needed to reach that standard required of a force now officially designated as the second line behind the Regular Army. If the withdrawal of the bounty went ahead, commanding officers would find it impossible to maintain proper efficiency levels, for the loss of the bounty at a time when foreign service

---

[34] 'Report of a special meeting of the Scottish Committee of the CCTA', 16 February 1927. Copy in the Lanarkshire Territorial Association Papers, MD 2/4.

[35] *The Times*, 3 March 1927.

commitments were still enforced would be regarded as a 'breach of faith'.

Worthington-Evans bristled at that accusation, protesting that 'they all ought to realise that there was no intention of committing any breach of faith or of altering any existing contract'. Perhaps, but this answer hardly met the main objection: men who could not re-engage before the sudden announcement of the bounty withdrawal were to be placed in the invidious position of having to subsidize their service to the state out of their own pockets. And that they could not afford. That was an alteration of the contract which Churchill had explicitly offered the new Territorial Army in 1920, and which had been tied to the foreign service obligation that was still in force. In the narrow legal sense Worthington-Evans was quite right, but his reply illustrated the wide gap that existed between Whitehall and the Associations, and even more the individual units. He admitted that he had some misgivings as to the effects on recruiting, but pointed to the fact that after the bounty had been drastically reduced in 1923 the huge drop in enlistments that had been predicted had not materialised.

A more serious consideration was the effect on efficiency: he seemed quite willing to consider the deputation's proposal that an efficiency grant be made to each soldier who fulfilled his obligations by attending a certain number of drills, going to camp, and firing the annual musketry course. This at least offered some hope that while numbers might be reduced, those remaining would continue to try to become efficient. In fact they might improve their efforts since the grant could be more closely tied to performance than the bounty had been. Here was one means by which Worthington-Evans could carry out his promise to 'do his best to see in what way anything could be done to soften the blow'.[36]

It did not take him long to realise that the War Office had to make some conciliatory gesture to the Associations. Bromley-Davenport gleefully wrote to Derby that public clamour had forced the Secretary of State to back down, and to restore half the bounty under the new name of 'proficiency grant'.[37] Thus he could claim that he was open to representations from the Associations, despite the charges of lack of consultation that had been levelled against the War Office. No one would lose face. The War Office stuck to its demands that the Territorials should bear their share of defence

[36] 'Report of the Deputation to the War Office: Abolition of the Territorial Army Bounty', 16 March 1927. Copy in the Derby Papers, 4/51, 52.
[37] Bromley-Davenport to Derby, 29 March 1927, Derby Papers, 4/51, 52.

cuts; the Associations' insistence that they be involved in 'momentous' policy changes was vindicated; and both sides could and did proclaim their common interests in maintaining and strengthening the efficiency of the Territorial Army. Yet the perceptive onlooker might well have realised that the War Office would not give in so easily. Its prime object had been to make heavy cuts in the Territorial estimates, and the abolition of the bounty was only one means to this end. Others such as the reduction of establishments or the outright abolition of units had been dropped when it seemed that the Associations would accept the loss of the bounty. Whether they would be revived once the War Office had been thwarted over the bounty remained to be seen.

The Associations had shown that they were not prepared to be taken for granted by the War Office and that they expected to be consulted fully on major changes of policy. A year before the confrontation over the bounty, when the Associations had been asked to recommend substantial cuts, Derby had warned the War Office of the growing feeling of frustration in the Associations. They felt they were being bypassed and left with less and less autonomy in the administration of county Territorial affairs. If the War Office persisted in undermining the Associations, Derby cautioned, businessmen would refuse to serve on them and the whole structure of the Territorial movement would collapse. A year later he advised Worthington-Evans that there had been widespread hostility to the War Office over the bounty issue and the continual calls for cuts. Some felt that the Army Council was 'anti-Territorial', despite Derby's assurances to the contrary and his efforts to convince the Associations that 'the War Office realised the full value of the Territorial Force'.[38]

The War Office was already taking steps to patch up relations with the Associations. Even before the compromise over proficiency pay was announced the Under-Secretary of State, Viscount Onslow, suggested that some sort of monthly council could be established to act as a 'safety valve' for the Associations' grievances, most of which Onslow thought were imaginary. Creedy too saw the need for more regular consultation with the Associations but cautioned against setting any precedent that might later be interpreted as 'taking them into administrative partnership

[38] Derby to Creedy, 22 April 1926; to Worthington-Evans, 25 May 1927, Derby Papers, Correspondence with Individuals: War Office 1926, 1927; comments by Derby at the CCTA annual meeting, 25 May 1927, Minutes, 1923 – 1933.

with ourselves in the determination of Territorial Army policy'. That there was a sense of distrust over the bounty question was acknowledged by Worthington-Evans. He admitted as much when he told Derby that he hoped the proficiency grant would be 'received with pleasure and relief', and that the War Office could 'expect peace and renewed effort to secure harmony all round . . .'. Onslow was wary of admitting the right of the Associations to be consulted on every issue, and suggested instead that no action be taken until the CCTA Finance Committee had presented its report. Then a decision could be made.[39] Unfortunately, the Associations failed to pass the War Office test.

The Finance Committee presented its report to the CCTA in September. Since it had been appointed in the wake of the outcry over the cuts proposed by the War Office on the implicit understanding that if given a reasonable time the Associations could find more acceptable ways of effecting economies, the War Office was understandably surprised if not annoyed by its recommendations. The Committee concluded that the only cuts that could be made, and then reluctantly, were in the training grant. But that had already been ruled out by the War Office, which looked to administration, pay and allowances to bear the brunt of the cuts. The Associations on the other hand claimed that these had consistently suffered disproportionate reductions. Unable to recommend any specific economies, the Committee lamely suggested an overall cut of 2½ per cent in administrative grants, and then asserted, as if to justify this unhelpful conclusion: 'The Territorial Army is already a very cheap form of National Insurance, and if the country wishes to maintain an efficient and contented Force it must be prepared to pay a reasonable sum for its maintenance.'[40]

Derby had warned Worthington-Evans that reductions in the administration grant could not be made, and that any savings would have to come from the training grant. If the funds for administration were cut, Derby said, 'I think it will mean the gradual disappearance of the Territorials altogether.' When he received the report, Worthington-Evans made no attempt to hide his profound disappointment from Derby: the Associations had taken so long

[39] Onslow to Worthington-Evans, 21 and 29 March 1927; Creedy to Worthington-Evans, 25 March 1927: WO 32/9699; Worthington-Evans to Derby, 24 March 1927, Derby Papers, Correspondence with Individuals: War Office 1927.

[40] 'Report of the Committee to enquire into the whole circumstance of Territorial Army Finance', annex to CCTA special meeting, 30 September 1927, Minutes, 1923-1933.

and could then only recommend cuts amounting to a trifling £30,000. If the War Office followed the report's recommendations the result would be that while the Regular Army suffered savage reductions, the Territorial Army would go virtually untouched. That was an intolerable situation. The War Office was entitled to expect that the Associations would cooperate and accept their fair share of the cuts in a 'similar spirit of abnegation'. Derby, however, was not prepared to be browbeaten. He told Creedy that the War Office should be thankful for what it had got, that a 'great many of them [in the CCTA] were prepared to say we could make no reduction and to tell the Secretary of State to do his damnedest'. Privately, as he told Golightly, he tended to agree with the die-hards, for he was convinced that unless they dug their heels in, Worthington-Evans would demand reductions in establishment. Creedy tried to reassure Derby that the War Office was motivated by the need to maintain a 'proper balance between the two Armies' and not any 'spirit of animus' as the Associations clearly thought. But Derby was no longer the champion of War Office support he had been only a short time before. He warned Creedy that if Worthington-Evans pushed too hard and demanded much greater cuts than the Committee had recommended, 'He will have the resignation not only of the Council but probably of most of the Associations.' To Worthington-Evans himself he put it another way: 'Any further reductions must to my mind spell the death knell of the force, or else some of it will have to be scrapped.'[41]

The worst fears of the Associations were not realised, for whe.. the Army Estimates for 1928 were presented in the House c.. Commons, Worthington-Evans announced that of the addition.1 economies imposed on the Army as a whole, the Territorials woui 1 bear only £30,000, which represented a decrease of 2½ per cent i 1 the annual administrative grant. Apart from some minor reductions of casualty clearing stations the Territorial Army escaped otherwi.e untouched.[42] This was no mean victory for the Associations.

Why had the War Office given way? Certainly it was not because they suddenly realised that the Territorial Army had greater claims to funds than had the Regular Army, nor that the Territorials had an

[41] Derby to Worthington-Evans, 23 August, 3 November 1927; Worthington-Evans to Derby, 1 November 1927; Creedy to Derby, 7 October 1927; Derby to Creedy, 3 and 10 October 1927; Derby to Golightly, 1 October 1927: Derby Papers, Correspondence with Individuals: War Office 1927; 4/51, 52.
[42] Parl. Debs, (Commons), 5th series, vol. 214, col. 1271 (8 March 1928).

especially valuable role to play. If anything, the opposite was the case. In July 1927 the Cabinet ruled that Army Estimates should be based on the assumption that Britain would not be engaged in a European war within ten years and that preparations should be directed towards involvement in extra-European theatres. A year later, at the insistence of the Chancellor of the Exchequer, Winston Churchill, the rule was extended so that the ten year period advanced on a daily basis.[43] In these circumstances the ability of the Territorials to reinforce the Regular Army in a continental expeditionary force was far less important than it had been when the Territorial Army was reconstituted after the First World War. Its usefulness in an extra-European war of medium or small size was strictly limited, if indeed it existed at all.

The answer probably lies in the political pressure that the Associations were able to exert. The furore over the bounty question had demonstrated its strength. Derby's warning was not a casual one. Feelings were running very high, and the War Office had shown itself vulnerable to political opinion, especially opinion rooted in every county in the country. Rather than force the issue it dropped its demands for further cuts and tried to restore good relations with the Associations. Much as it resisted the Associations' claims to participate in the formulation of policy, it recognized that they were indispensable to the Territorial movement. Furthermore, the War Office did not want to seem to push the Territorials too hard. Logically there was no reason why the Territorial Army should not carry a proportionate share of expenditure cuts, but in one sense the Territorials were a special case. They gave their time freely for military training, and especially after the abolition of the bounty, often at some financial cost to themselves. The Associations were quite right in arguing that each cut imposed on the Territorial Army was at the direct expense of the soldiers. Coming immediately after the Associations had accepted the abolition of the bounty (even though half of it had been replaced by the proficiency grant), and at a time when it was widely believed — and not only by the Associations — that the Army Council was 'anti-Territorial', additional cuts would have been seen as the final blow. The War Office could afford — and probably had to afford — to be generous. It had learned not to take the Associations for granted, but, as subsequent events were to show, it had not learned the lesson well.

[43] Cabinet 45(27), 28 July 1927, CAB 23/55; Cabinet 39(28), 18 July 1928, CAB 23/58.

7

The Fight over the Pledge

The next five years, 1928 – 32, were the most difficult period for the Territorial Army since its reformation in 1920. The successive cuts in expenditure during the 1920s had already trimmed the fat from its organization, yet the calls for further economies continued. The attack on one article of faith of the Territorials — the bounty — and the sniping at another — annual camps — was soon to be overshadowed by frontal assaults upon both the annual camp and the basic conditions of service. The Associations could hardly be blamed for thinking that the War Office was hostile to the Territorial Army, and was trying to strangle it slowly after failing to abolish it outright in the previous decade. From its perspective the War Office was no less justified in reducing the Territorials to a bare minimum and channelling the funds saved to a Regular Army that was starved of adequate financial support, modern equipment and decent accommodation. As the possibility of a major continental involvement receded even further into the distance there was little reason to maintain the Territorial Army at the strength and efficiency that Churchill had envisaged in 1920. As the military imperative unquestionably lessened, anti-military sentiments began to strengthen, so that the Territorial Army, once a focal point of local pride, became increasingly an irrelevance at best and, in some quarters, a symbol of a discredited militaristic patriotism.

The combination of the abolition of the bounty in 1927 and the cancellation of many camps the previous year led to a heavy fall in recruiting in 1927. The automatic savings thus achieved enabled the War Office to reduce its demand for expenditure cuts for 1928 to a mere £30,000, or 2½ per cent of the Associations' annual administrative grants.[1] There was no guarantee, however, that this respite was other than a temporary one, or that continued falls in recruiting would produce their own justification for further

[1] *Parl. Debs.* (Commons), 5th series, vol. 214, col. 1271 (8 March 1928).

reductions. The Associations were therefore gratified to have the reassurance of the War Office that the Territorial Army had a clearly-defined and valuable role to play. That assurance came in several ways.

Duff Cooper, Financial Secretary at the War Office, repeated the Government's pledge not to use the Territorials as drafts for the Regular Army in time of emergency. Territorial units would remain intact, and reinforcements for the Regular Army would be provided by the reserves and by new recruits who would enlist for general service.[2] This was welcomed by the Associations who feared, perhaps more than anything else, that their units would be split up and used to feed Regular formations. That it was in fact no answer at all to the dilemma that had long bothered the General Staff — how to reinforce the Regular Army in an intermediate war that required more troops than the reserves could supply yet did not justify a General Service Act — was for the moment passed over. At this stage the Associations were anxious for any sign of support in the War Office, whether or not it was hedged with implicit restrictions.

The second and more direct assurance came from the Chief of the Imperial General Staff, Sir George Milne, in a speech to the CCTA in May 1928. Milne reiterated the Government's policy that the Territorial Army would be the 'sole means of expansion' in a national war. Every Territorial unit would 'throw off' a second unit, which would provide reinforcements where needed. There would be no repetition of the experience of 1914, when Territorial divisions were sent overseas as soon as war broke out. Instead the Territorial Army would have at least six months to recruit to full war establishment, to acquire the necessary equipment, and to carry out proper training, so that there would be no more 'naked divisions' sent to the field as had happened in the First World War. The War Office had a programme to modernize the equipment of the Territorial Army, but the process would be a slow one. Experiments were continuing with new types of equipment which had to be tested thoroughly before any firm commitment to issue it could be made. It would be an expensive business, and the Army could not afford to make mistakes by acting precipitately. On the question of the pledge not to use the Territorials as drafts for Regular units, Milne accepted 'in toto' the reassurances already given.[3]

[2] *Ibid.*, col. 1332.
[3] 'Address by the C.I.G.S. to the Central Council, Territorial Army Association, May 23rd, 1928', WO 32/2672.

This, as Derby told Worthington-Evans, was 'just what we wanted to know and . . . [it] will put the whole force on its mettle'. Others were not so sure. Although they welcomed Milne's statement, they were anxious that his reassurances be made public and not treated, as Milne had requested, as 'absolutely private and confidential'. The War Office was not anxious for a public debate on the issue, and Derby agreed with them, but changed his mind after being reminded by Scarbrough that what was important about Milne's remarks was not that he had repeated the two pledges given earlier to the Territorial Army, but that for the first time the pledges had been endorsed by the Chief of the Imperial General Staff rather than by the Secretary of State.[4] Their strength would be all the greater if they were made public; then the War Office would shrink from revoking them in the future. Firm as the assurances seemed to be, Milne had left an opening, but it was one whose dimensions had yet to be explored. In committing the War Office to honouring the undertaking given to the Territorials he had said: 'But how this pledge can be carried out needs consideration.' No one had directly questioned that at the time, but the call for a public reiteration of the pledges was an indication that not even Milne's statement had assuaged the long-standing fears of the Associations that had been exacerbated by the distrust and bitterness arising out of the recent cuts and cancellations.

Nor was the assurance that the Territorial Army would be the sole vehicle for the expansion of the nation's military forces in time of war necessarily as gratifying as it might first have appeared. The Associations had emphasized that role in the aftermath of a great war, when memories of Kitchener's treatment of the Territorial Force still rankled, and when it seemed distinctly possible, at least to Territorial supporters, if not to the War Office, that some sort of expeditionary force might be needed to intervene in the convulsive situation of the post-war world. The Associations demanded, and got, firm assurances that Territorial units would not be shunted aside, as had happened in 1914. In the struggles with the War Office over the terms of reconstitution in 1919 and 1920 that had seemed of vital importance.

It seemed to be less so by the end of the 1920s. The possibility of military intervention no longer centred on full scale expeditions; instead the focus of attention shifted much more to areas such as

[4]   Derby to Worthington-Evans, 23 and 29 May 1928; Scarbrough to Derby, 24 May 1928: Derby Papers, Correspondence with Individuals: War Office 1928.

Afghanistan, where by 1928 according to the Chiefs of Staff, there was a major threat to British interests that might require a military response.[5] If from the perspective of 1920 this appeared to be a swing away from a repetition of the experience of continental war that was uppermost in the Associations' minds, it was in fact a reversion to the imperial strategy that had dominated British military thinking in the nineteenth century. That strategy had centred on small and intermediate wars, which required a moderate degree of reinforcement (if any) for the Regular Army rather than the mobilisation of the whole nation's manpower. How the Territorials could fulfil that role, given the War Office pledge to retain their units intact and not to permit transfers, had yet to be determined. Once a continental strategy involving a huge expeditionary force had been ruled out, both by circumstance and increasingly by inclination, then the question of how to employ the Territorials in a limited war became ever more important.

Nor could the Territorials have found comfort — even had they wished, which recruiting figures in AA units generally indicated they did not — in a home defence role that had been allotted to them in AA and coastal defence. The necessary funds for equipping the AA units in particular had never been made available and were not likely to be in the near future, and by 1928 Trenchard, the Chief of Air Staff, was suggesting that anti-aircraft defences for Britain be given a low priority.[6] As the economic squeeze continued, and indeed became worse by 1930 when Territorial grants were reduced by a further £236,000, the Territorial Army became even more vulnerable to financial pressure and open to charges that expenditure on it was not justified.

The financial cuts of 1930, and rumours of further cuts in 1931, provoked an angry outburst from the Associations. By now that was the inevitable response to what had become annual reductions, and the War Office was not unduly alarmed. Rather more disturbing, however, was Derby's reaction, for he had consistently championed the War Office and tried to answer the widespread accusation that the Army Council was hostile to the Territorials. In January he wrote to Creedy protesting at the latest cuts, which had fallen heavily on the clothing grants to the Associations:

5   'A Review of Imperial Defence, 1928, by the Chiefs of Staff Sub Committee', 25 June 1928, COS, 1965, CAB 53/16.
6   COS, 73rd meeting, 6 July 1928, CAB 53/2.

Personally I think this reduction is the last straw and I do not see how we are going to carry on . . . . There is an impression abroad that the present Government, and I am afraid even the last one did [sic] not really care much about the Territorial Force and would not be sorry to see it more or less disappear.[7]

Creedy denied that the War Office was unsympathetic to the Territorials, and added that the previous cuts had been 'minor administrative economies' which could not be repeated. The 'great savings' that now had to be made could be realised only by a substantial reduction in numbers or by severe cuts in the budget.[8] Since the Associations had always vigorously opposed reducing establishments or abolishing units, the War Office had no choice but to impose economies across the board. Training grants could not be reduced further without weakening the efficiency of the Territorials, so that the Associations had to bear the brunt of the cuts.

Derby was not convinced, and when at the end of 1920 it was announced that additional cuts were being planned, he wrote again to Creedy:

I have had to write a pretty strong letter to the Secretary of State with regard to Territorial Finance . . . .. really we have come to the parting of the ways. We have had many difficulties in the past but for the first time I saw a distinct disposition on the part of all present at our meeting to chuck up the sponge and to have nothing more to do with it. We really cannot go on any longer if all these reductions are to be made. There has been a reduction in the per capita grant of over 30% in the last four years.[9]

As it turned out, the Territorials did rather better in the Army Estimates of 1931 than they had expected. Falling prices and the lower cost of living enabled the War Office to save substantial sums without calling on the Associations for extraordinary economies.

Nevertheless it was a difficult time for the Territorial Army. More than the cuts themselves, the Associations resented the lack

---

[7] Derby to Creedy, 1 January 1930, Derby Papers, Correspondence with Individuals: War Office 1930.

[8] Creedy to Derby, 3 January 1930, Derby Papers, Correspondence with Individuals: War Office 1930.

[9] Derby to Creedy, 21 November 1930, Derby Papers, Correspondence with Individuals: War Office 1930.

of sympathy and the apparent indifference of the Government and the country at large to what they were trying to do. This was particularly so with the Labour government. Labour had never been enthusiastic about the Territorial Army, or indeed about any military organization. By the end of the 1920s enthusiasm for disarmament, which in some quarters shaded into outright pacifism, led to a highly charged though erratic campaign against manifestations of 'militarism'. In March 1930 the Secretary of State of War in the Labour government announced that the annual capitation grants made to cadets in the various youth organizations run on military lines would be withdrawn, and that henceforth the War Office would not officially recognise these bodies. They would be allowed to use Territorial drill halls only for those activities that did not involve military training of any kind, and as far as possible all connections with Territorial units would be severed.[10] There was no question of this being an economy measure — it saved only £15,000; it was a direct attack, in the eyes of the cadets' supporters, on the inculcation of civic virtues through military training, an attack that might well be extended to the Territorials themselves. Claims that the cadets were a valuable source of recruits for the Territorials were not convincing, and there was an undeniable logic to the Secretary of State's argument that if the value of the cadet movement was primarily educational and social, then the necessary funds should come from the Board of Education and the Home Office. What rankled, though, was his statement that he had 'an unconquerable aversion to children of tender years being drafted into semi-military formations'.[11] There was an uproar in the conservative press, and even those Associations who saw little direct military value in the cadet movement joined the condemnation of the Labour government's action. Here was proof, if any was needed, that Labour was no friend of the Territorial Army.

Further evidence came in the Army Estimates of 1931. The Secretary of State announced that in future Territorial officers, irrespective of rank, would receive only 10s. a day allowance while in camp, as opposed to the normal pay and allowances they had previously drawn.[12] This was seen as a purely class-directed policy, for NCOs and men would continue to draw their full pay and allowances. The complaint of one commanding officer of a London Territorial battalion was typical: a four day Easter camp would

---

[10] *Parl. Debs.* (Commons), 5th series, vol. 237, col. 87 (24 March 1930).
[11] *Ibid.*, col. 3177 (17 April 1930).
[12] See 'Army Estimates', *Parl. Papers*, 1931, XIX.

cause him to lose at least £9 or £10 on the new rate, when even the previous rate did not cover his full expenses.[13]

But any hopes for more favourable treatment at the hands of the Conservative-dominated National Government were dashed soon after it took office in August 1931. In September Duff Cooper, Financial Secretary at the War Office, told the House of Commons tha̅t the grave financial situation in the country made it necessary to realise savings of at least one million pounds in Territorial grants. The Regular Army could not absorb cuts of that magnitude, and the only means by which the reductions could be made was to suspend annual training in camp for the Territorials in 1932. The consequent saving on clothing and equipment would permit the War Office to reduce grants to the Associations in the hope that camps could be held the following year when the economic situation had improved. In addition, to ensure that the automatic grants to Associations in 1932 did not increase as recruiting picked up in expectation of camps that year, limitations would be imposed so that unit strengths could not exceed in 1932 the numbers that had been provided for in the 1931 Estimates.[14]

This came as a great shock to the Territorial Army, which had had no advance warning that the War Office was planning such drastic economies. Coming so soon after the loss of the bounty and the series of cuts that had bitten deeply into the individual soldier's training and accommodation, it was bound to lessen the appeal of service with the Territorials. Recruiting, which was beginning to pick up again after the setback caused by the abolition of the bounty, fell off sharply, so that in 1932 only a very small number of units reached their 1931 strength and had to turn away prospective recruits. For units such as those in the West Riding whose turn it was to camp near the sea — always a good recruiting attraction — it was especially disappointing; Scarbrough called it a 'bad blow'.[15] Some units did arrange to go to camp, using the increased funds that the War Office had made available for training outside the annual camp period. Thus the London Rifle Brigade trained for a week with the 2nd Battalion The Somerset Light Infantry, but its strength nevertheless declined from 328 at the end of 1931 to 280 at the end of 1932. Part of the reason for this decline lay in the fact that the grants were not sufficient to cover all expenses; officers in

[13] *Daily Mail*, 14 April 1931.
[14] *Parl. Debs.* (Commons), 5th series, vol. 256, cols. 1034 – 5 (17 September 1931).
[15] West Riding, 16 November 1931, Acc. 1469/4.

the LRB received only a very small daily allowance while other ranks were paid for only four out of the seven days.[16]

Despite the dismay of the Associations, they bore the news calmly and with few of the outbursts that had accompanied the cancellation of some camps in 1926 or the abolition of the pledge in 1927. In this hour of national economic crisis the Associations accepted the loss of camps as their contribution towards restoring the country to a healthy state. This was the least they could do. But implicit in their stoic resignation to yet another imposition on their sense of duty was the understanding that this economy measure — the most drastic of all — was not to become a regular feature of spending cuts. At the same time as the Associations were preparing to weather a severe drop in recruiting the War Office was studying proposals to effect radical changes in the terms of service under which Territorials enlisted. During the 1920s there had been a growing concern in the War Office that the Territorial Army as reconstituted in 1920 was unsuited to the most likely situation that military planners could envisage, an intermediate sized war. A committee was established under the chairmanship of the DGTA, Sir Reginald Stephens, to examine these restrictions on the employment of the Territorials and to recommend ways of bringing the terms of service into line with War Office requirements. For the purpose of its enquiry the Stephens committee considered the use of Territorial forces in a war outside Europe that would involve a '1st Territorial Army Contingent' of eight infantry divisions and one cavalry brigade, together with supporting units. This contingent would be formed by embodying the whole of the Territorial Army and then choosing those units which would proceed overseas after mobilization, while the rest of the Territorial Army would remain embodied and would raise its units to full peace establishment. Thus the Territorials would constitute that second line behind the Regular Army which they had always aspired to be, and which the War Office had committed itself to uphold.

But in making that commitment the War Office had also made promises which it increasingly realised could not be kept. The Territorial and Reserve Forces Act of 1907 laid down that in time of war no Territorial soldier could be transferred without his consent. For example a soldier serving in the 4th or 5th TA Battalions of the Royal West Kent Regiment could not be transferred to either the 1st or 2nd (Regular) Battalions of that Regiment, nor could he be

[16] A. T. M. Durand and R. H. W. S. Hastings, *The London Rifle Brigade, 1919 – 1950* (Aldershot, 1952), pp. 30 – 1.

transferred to a totally different regiment such as The Buffs. The exigencies of war notwithstanding, many Territorials felt that the complete neglect of that regulation had been the crowning insult in Kitchener's (and his successors') abuse of the Territorial Force during the war. Determined that never again should their units be split up or used to supply drafts for other units (Regular or — even worse — New Army units), the Associations had insisted on firm guarantees after the war. In return for accepting a foreign service obligation, they had exacted from Churchill in 1920 a promise that Territorials would only proceed overseas with their own units, that they could not be compulsorily transferred to any other unit, and that 'attachments' to other units would be purely temporary and made only in cases of great need. Together these undertakings constituted the 'pledge'. To the Associations they were the guarantee that the integrity of Territorial units would be preserved, and that the Territorial Army would fight as an integrated second line. To the War Office they were the major obstacle to the employment of the Territorial Army in a war of intermediate size. As long as they remained in force, the Territorials could never act as reinforcements for the Regular Expeditionary Force.

The Stephens committee recommended that the first priority of the War Office should be the immediate cancellation of the pledge. Henceforth the form that recruits had to sign ('Notice to Recruits') should contain a statement that if war broke out legislation would be introduced making all men then serving who had not enlisted while the pledge was still in force and all men who enlisted after the appropriate Act had been passed liable for general service, i.e. liable to be transferred where and when the War Office saw fit. Unless this was done the War Office would be completely hamstrung in its ability to use the available manpower as the developing situation dictated.[17]

The CIGS, Milne, welcomed the recommendation, saying that the enforcement of the pledge during mobilization or even embodiment would 'complicate administration to such an extent as would be almost disastrous'. However, he added:

> [The pledge] was given at a time when post-war feeling ran high during the reconstitution of the T.A. At that time the very greatest importance was attached to it, and the resuscitation of

[17] 'Employment of the Territorial Army in War: Report of General Sir Reginald Stephens' Committee', annex to Army Council Précis No. 1360, 26 May 1931, WO 32/2673.

the T.A. was practically conditional on its being granted . . ..
Cancellation is a matter which must unquestionably be dealt
with with considerable discretion.

There were two ways in which the pledge could be withdrawn.
Either the War Office could announce that after a certain date it
would not apply to new recruits, or it could postpone cancellation
until the moment of crisis was at hand, when recruits would flock to
the Territorial Army before war was declared. The first alternative
might arouse wide-spread resentment among the Territorials and
severely impede recruiting, effects that the second course would
largely minimise. The disadvantage of the latter course was that the
withdrawal of the pledge in a period immediately prior to a formal
declaration of war could not be made retrospective, so that upon
embodiment and mobilization there would be two classes in each
Territorial unit: those who were serving under the pledge and who
could not be transferred without their consent and who could
proceed overseas only in their own units, and those liable for
general service. Despite the risk of immediate, though probably
temporary, discontent in the Territorial ranks, the first alternative
was infinitely preferable, for the existence of two classes in a
wartime Territorial Army would be 'administratively impossible'.[18]

Milne's wish to have the pledge withdrawn as soon as possible
was endorsed by the Adjutant-General and the Master-General of
the Ordnance.[19] It was also supported, of course, by the DGTA,
Stephens, but he raised several possible objections. One was that
even if the pledge were withdrawn immediately it would not
prevent two classes from developing within the Territorial Army.
Those already serving would have to be allowed to re-engage for a
further four years under the protection of the pledge, so that
although within four years after the pledge had been withdrawn
most men who had enlisted under it would have completed their
term of service and left, there would still be some ('naturally the
keenest') who would re-engage for another term. The only way of
drawing them into the general service category would be to ask
them to transfer voluntarily, which most would probably do (just as
in 1914 large numbers of Territorials — also the 'keenest' — had
voluntarily undertaken overseas service).[20]

[18] CIGS to PUS, 4 August 1931, WO 32/2673.
[19] AG to PUS, 22 September 1931; MGO to PUS, 9 September 1931: WO
32/2673.
[20] DGTA to PUS, 7 October 1931, WO 32/2673.

The more serious objection arose from the firm and unconditional promises that Milne had made to the CCTA in 1928.
Although he now claimed that 'there is no question of ''going back
on our word'' ', the withdrawal of the pledge would amount to
precisely that, notwithstanding his insistence that: 'It is merely a
matter of adopting new conditions of service for new entry.' The
only way around it, Stephens suggested, was to issue a public
statement that circumstances had changed to nullify the assurances
given by the CIGS in 1928, and that it was necessary to withdraw
the pledge.[21]

Clearly, as Milne had said, the War Office had to move
cautiously. When the Under-Secretary of State, Lord Stanhope,
approached Derby and Bromley-Davenport to sound them out, he
admitted that 'the Territorial Army has had so much to put up with
of late that any further burden would inevitably be viewed with
grave suspicion'. Once summer camps had been resumed, however, the War Office wanted to proceed to withdraw the pledge so
that the Territorial Army could be drawn fully into the mobilization
plans being prepared by the General Staff. But the proposal
Stanhope put to them differed from those previously discussed in
the War Office in one crucial respect. Milne, for example, had been
at pains to emphasize that there was no intention of the War Office
'going back on its word', or of withdrawing the pledge from those
already serving under it. Stephens had widened this to the extent
of allowing all pledged men to re-engage under the pledge even
though it had been withdrawn for new recruits. Although this was
in keeping with the spirit of the commitment made by Churchill in
1920, which had presumably been offered for an indefinite period,
it would have left the War Office with the very problem it was
trying to solve, that of having 'non-fluid' men in the Territorial
Army unavailable for postings at large.[22]

Derby's initial reaction was to warn against any precipitate move
by the War Office that might stir up disaffection among the
Territorials. 'There are a lot of people', he wrote, 'who are just
hanging in the balance as to whether they will go on with the
Territorial force or not and they might use this as an opportunity
for going.' The situation was so delicate that neither Derby nor
Bromley-Davenport were willing to commit themselves on paper:
on so important a matter they could not speak for the Associations

---

[21] DGTA to PUS, (?) November 1931, WO 32/2673.
[22] Stanhope to Derby and Bromley-Davenport, 15 January 1932, WO 32/
2678.

without carefully consulting them, but the War Office had insisted on the utmost secrecy.[23]

Several days later the three men met at the War Office. Bromley-Davenport tried to dissuade Stanhope from doing anything about the pledge that year, but Derby, less pessimistic than at first, now thought that the War Office could proceed without much trouble, and even withdraw the pledge from those serving under it. Derby was all too well aware of the distrust of the War Office that existed in Territorial circles, and realised that if the War Office should propose such a drastic change it might well be rebuffed. He therefore offered to put the proposal himself at the May meeting of the CCTA: he would 'bring up as his own idea the impossible state of affairs created by the pledge and explain the whole position', or, as he had put it when he initially heard of the War Office discussions, 'I promise to be the lightning conductor if there is a storm'.[24]

He soon discovered, however, that he had been too sanguine in his advice to Stanhope. Various discreet enquiries had shown that while there would not be the 'slightest difficulty' in withdrawing the pledge from new recruits or from those who re-engaged after its abolition, there were considerable dangers in altering the terms of those already serving. Each man would have to be asked individually, and since feelings (and resignations) were running high over the loss of camps, it was an inopportune moment to ask the Territorials to accept yet another restriction. Stanhope was relieved to hear that there would be little opposition, and added that of course the War Office had never intended to interfere with the rights of men serving under the pledge.[25] It seemed only a matter of time before the War Office had its way.

At the CCTA meeting in May, Derby went to great lengths to allay suspicions that he was merely acting as the mouthpiece for the War Office. The result was that he protested too much:

> I want you to clearly understand that this has not been done at the instigation of the War Office. It is entirely off my own bat and on my own initiative and I do not want anybody in this room to think that the War Office is deliberately trying to

23 Derby to Stanhope, 18 and 20 January 1932, WO 32/2678.
24 'Notes of a meeting at the War Office', 27 January 1932; Stanhope to Secretary of State, 27 January 1932: WO 32/2678; Derby to Thwaites, 13 December 1931: Derby Papers, Correspondence with Individuals: War Office 1931.
25 Derby to Stanhope, 3 May 1932; Stanhope to Derby, 6 May 1932: Derby Papers, Correspondence with Individuals: War Office 1932.

circumvent all its own pledges . . . . If there is a lingering doubt in your minds that it is a put-up job please put that aside . . . . I want you clearly to understand and, again, I repeat, there is no intention whatever on the part of the War Office of forcing any change on the Territorial Army . . . . I hope you will not think that I have taken upon myself something that I ought not to have done.

Scarbrough did think so. Referring to the proposals as a 'bombshell' that had a 'disturbing effect', he implied that Derby was by no means their sole originator as he had claimed. The suggestions that Derby had put forward, he said, would constitute a 'serious breach of faith' and the complete repudiation of solemn undertakings re-affirmed by successive Secretaries of State. They were not to be cast aside lightly, especially when camps had just been cancelled and there were rumours that there would also be no camps in 1933. The proposals would do 'grave injury' to the future of the Territorials by harming recruiting, and therefore had to be resisted on grounds both of expediency and principle. He was wholeheartedly supported by Colonel Evelyn Wood, representing the City of London Association, who warned that if the pledge was simply scrapped, there would be widespread bitterness and 'to the man in the street, who probably does not have a very full knowledge of the facts, it will look like another case of the historical scrap of paper of 1914'.

Derby had hoped to contain the discussion and to circulate his proposals to all Associations for study in time for the next meeting in November. Scarbrough's attack sank that possibility, and eventually it was decided to send out copies of the proposals together with a transcript of the discussion at the May meeting. Although the majority of speakers, including Lord Cobham (Worcester), Major-General J. E. B. Seely (Hampshire), and Colonel John Brown (Northamptonshire), supported Derby's endorsement of a swift end to the pledge as the only means of bringing the Territorial Army into line with War Office requirements, there had not been the unanimous acceptance that Derby had wanted.[26] He tried to reassure Stanhope that the meeting had gone well, and dismissed Scarbrough's intervention:

On the whole I think people were with us . . . but the only man

[26] CCTA meeting, 25 May 1932, Minutes, 1923–1933. A copy of these minutes is also in WO 32/2678.

dead against us and making mischief as he always does, was Scarbrough. However luckily everybody knows what bad judgement he has and I do not think he will do much harm . . .. Scarbrough is thoroughly mischievous and there is no doubt whatever he will deliberately make misleading statement [sic] with a view of prejudging the case. I really do not know any man whom I would trust less than him and it makes one mad when one knows that, with the experience he had at the War Office during the war, he must realize that the pledge cannot possibly be allowed to go on.

Derby promised to 'back you up through thick and thin' to override the resentment that would undoubtedly arise, for 'to have an Army saddled with such restrictions as the Territorials have is worse than having no Army at all'. Barely more than a week later, however, fearing that the opposition might be greater than he had originally anticipated, he suggested that the War Office set down the limits of the changes it was trying to make, what it wanted and what it was prepared to accept.[27]

Resistance to drastic changes to the pledge soon emerged. Scarbrough told Derby that he had wrestled unsuccessfully with the problem back in 1920, when his proposal to create a 'special class' that would be available for draft-finding purposes was dropped; unless it was established provision could not be made for reinforcing Regular units nor for maintaining Territorial units in the field. But while Scarbrough recognized the War Office's difficulty, he was not prepared to see the pledge swept away and the Territorial Army exposed to a policy that would emasculate its divisions. The concept of a 'special class' was also endorsed by Colonel Evelyn Wood, who submitted a strongly-worded plea for the retention of the pledge under all circumstances. He argued for a National Reserve which accepted an 'honourable obligation' to serve where required by the War Office, so that while the Territorial Army remained pledged (or at least that part of it that had enlisted during peacetime), there would be a large pool of manpower available for the War Office to use as it saw fit. But the pledge had to remain inviolate, for its abolition would result in a Territorial Army 'reduced perhaps to the tithe of the present skeleton, if not its total destruction'.[28]

[27] Derby to Stanhope, 25 May and 2 June 1932, Derby Papers, Correspondence with Individuals: War Office 1932.
[28] Scarbrough to Derby, 27 June 1932: Wood, 'Memorandum re "The Pledge" ', n.d. [June 1932]: WO 32/2678.

Derby thought there was a 'good deal' in Wood's suggestion, though he rejected, as did Stanhope, Wood's prediction that the abolition of the pledge would destroy the Territorial Army. To R. B. Paterson, the Director of Finance at the War Office, however, Wood's memorandum was simply a typical example of the attitude of the 'Obscurantists', who persisted in refusing to face up to the unrealistic situation created by the pledge. The War Office had to decide for itself if and when the pledge should go, and whether it should risk the resignations, non-re-engagements and decline in recruiting that Wood and his supporters had warned would follow. Paterson was not convinced that an unpledged Territorial Army would necessarily be any smaller. He agreed with Derby that the majority of the Territorials would loyally accept a change if the reasons for it were properly explained to them, and in any case, notwithstanding Scarbrough's insistence that Territorials attached enormous importance to the pledge, enquiries that Paterson had generated tended to show that most were 'practically unaware of its existence'. The unfortunate result of public statements by Scarbrough and Wood was to arouse opposition where none had previously existed. In those circumstances the War Office would find it impracticable to require the withdrawal of the pledge from the entire Territorial Army — serving, re-engaging or enlisting — after a certain date. This was the most desirable course, but if it could not be pushed through, Peterson and the DGTA were prepared to accept that after a given date all enlistments and re-engagements should be on a non-pledged basis. The very minimum that was acceptable to the War Office was to pass legislation so that all men enlisting after a state of emergency had been declared would be for general service only, but this of course left the peace establishment still pledged, and would require a 'second bite of the cherry' later on, just what Derby and the War Office wanted to avoid.[29]

In the hope that the opponents of the abolition of the pledge were in a small minority, Stanhope summoned representatives of a cross-section of the County Associations to the War Office to sound them out. It quickly became evident that there was a wide divergence of opinion, and that in Scotland especially opposition to the proposed changes was likely to be strongest. Edinburgh and Glasgow warned that recruiting would fall off badly if the pledge

---

[29] Derby to Stanhope, Stanhope to Derby, 24 and 28 June 1932; minutes by Paterson, 12 April and 29 June 1932; DGTA to DRO, 29 June 1932: WO 32/2678.

was withdrawn from new recruits, whereas Worcester thought that recruits paid little attention to the pledge. Short of testing these predictions, there was no way that the War Office or the Associations could be sure. But the Associations that were represented at the War Office meeting were sure of several things. One was that there would be widespread resentment if the pledge was not retained for men re-engaging. The second was that the War Office would have a much easier job of selling its new policy if it was able to announce at the same time that camps would definitely be held in 1933. Several Associations, including those from Scotland, could not understand why such drastic changes were necessary at this time, but even they agreed that the Territorials would probably accept the changes if they were properly explained, however reluctant they might be to surrender their rights vested in the pledge.[30]

Derby was disappointed that the response had not been more positive, and advised Stanhope that he dared not press harder for fear of arousing much stronger opposition. His suggestion — to minimise the objections to the imposition of an arbitrary cut-off date and the War Office's need to have as small a number of pledged Territorials as possible — was that no man should be able to claim the protection of the pledge who had not served in the Territorials for at least three months before their embodiment in time of emergency. This would keep clear of the pledge's restrictions that large body of recruits who would normally be expected to flock to the colours in a period of tension but before the actual outbreak of war. And if the War Office could not get the pledge as such withdrawn, perhaps it could widen its terms, so that Territorials would become available for transfer to other battalions of the same regiment (or the same corps in the case of the artillery and engineers). This would go some way toward giving the War Office the fluidity it needed while keeping men in units from their own areas. A compromise such as this would be all the more acceptable to the Territorial Army if it could be linked with a favourable announcement on camps.[31]

Both Derby and Stanhope were anxious to keep the discussion with the Associations open and not to allow them to prejudge the issue on the basis of false or incomplete information. Derby appealed to the Associations not to reach any conclusions before

[30] 'Note of a Conference with Secretaries of certain Territorial Army Associations at the War Office', 7 July 1932, WO 32/2678.

[31] Derby to Stanhope, 7 July 1932; Stanhope to Derby, 12 July 1932: WO 32/ 2678.

the Adjutant-General, Sir Archibald Montgomery-Massingberd, had put the War Office case. To minimise speculation developing from stories in the press, he enlisted the help of the editor-in-chief of the *Daily Telegraph*, Lord Camrose, to head off any premature disclosure by Liddell Hart, the paper's military correspondent. Eventually the War Office released a statement confirming that discussions about the pledge were taking place with the Associations, and firmly denying that there was any intention, no matter what the final outcome, of using Territorials as drafts for Regular units.[32]

Once the proposals became a matter of public discussion, there were increasing signs that Derby had been much too sanguine in his advice to the War Office. Reports came in from around the country that unless camps were promised for 1933 recruiting would fall off badly. Since the War Office could not commit itself on that question until early in 1933, Stanhope and the DGTA cancelled a projected recruiting tour in the autumn on the advice of several divisional GOC-in-Cs. As the date for the meeting with the Associations drew nearer, Derby became worried that the War Office proposals might be met with a flat rejection unless firm assurances on camps were given. Stanhope shared his anxiety, but though he emphasized that: 'Everyone of us here at the War Office from the Secretary of State downwards and including all the Military Members of the Army Council are all out to get camps for the Territorial Army in 1933', no commitment could be made until January at the earliest. 'It would help us very much if we could', he added wistfully.[33]

As Derby's promises that the War Office would have no trouble in getting from the Associations what it wanted appeared more and more unfounded, the War Office had second thoughts about raising the whole matter of the pledge at this time. Fearing that the Associations might turn the discussion into an airing of real or imagined grievances and manoeuvre the Adjutant-General into accepting an unwieldy compromise that would leave the Territorials from the War Office point of view little more useful than before, Stanhope decided to ask the Associations to accept or reject the case for a general service obligation for all new enlistments after 1 April 1934. The Adjutant-General would address the Associations

---

[32] Derby to Associations, 18 July 1932; Derby to Stanhope, 19 July 1932; War Office press release, 30 July 1932: WO 32/2678.

[33] Stanhope to Derby, 26 August and 12 October 1932; Derby to Stanhope, 6 October 1932: WO 32/2678.

on 15 November, and the next day — to minimise the time in which rumours could spread and opposition to the proposal be whipped up — a vote would be taken. Although the War Office wanted an unequivocal opinion on the abolition of the pledge, it was prepared to agree to a less satisfactory compromise if its main proposal was rejected. Rather than have the Associations offer unacceptable alternatives whose rejection would cast the War Office in a bad light, especially if it was unable to promise camps in 1933, it was prepared to retain the pledge but to make the unit to which it applied the regiment in the case of infantry or the corps for the artillery and engineers. Thus a Territorial serving under the pledge could nevertheless be transferred to a Regular battalion within his regiment. While this did not give the War Office everything it wanted, it made the Territorials much more fluid than they were under the existing pledge.[34]

No sooner had the War Office decided on its tactics than determination all round began to waver. Lord Cobham, an enthusiastic supporter of the abolition of the pledge, told Stanhope that there was a movement among the Associations to barter camps for the pledge, a move which Stanhope said would be a 'disaster' for the War Office. If it became clear that the Associations would press that position, Stanhope thought it better to cancel the meeting and postpone discussion of the pledge until such time as the War Office could promise camps. Both Thwaites, the DGTA, and Paterson, the Director of Finance, rejected that approach, arguing that Cobham did not represent Territorial opinion and that if the War Office backed down now, the Associations would become suspicious of its ultimate intentions and resist changes even more strongly. Thwaites told Stanhope that Cobham's warnings were merely being seized upon by the War Office to shirk the issue, and that they would find that Derby was anxious to go ahead with the meetings. To Stanhope's relief, and to Thwaites' surprise, Derby readily agreed that the meeting should be postponed until the War Office could give firm assurances about camps in 1933.[35]

So the first attempt to change the basic conditions of service had failed. Both Derby and the War Office had completely misread the mood of the Territorial Army and the Associations. For too long

[34] Stanhope to AG, 6 October 1932; Stanhope to Derby, 12 October 1932: WO 32/2678.
[35] Minute by Stanhope, Thwaites to Stanhope, Paterson to Stanhope, Stanhope to Derby, 20 October 1932; Derby to Stanhope, 24 October 1932: WO 32/2678.

they had taken their support for granted. The yearly reductions, the abolition of the bounty, the suspension or cancellation of camps, and the lingering suspicion that the General Staff was somehow 'anti-Territorial' had created an atmosphere of wariness and mistrust with the result that just when the War Office, perhaps for the first time since 1920, was beginning to 'take the Territorials seriously', the accumulated grievances of the previous ten years led the Associations to dig in their heels.

Yet the signs were that the opposition was not so much to the abolition of the pledge as such but to the War Office's timing. While there was stout resistance from the 'die-hards' and 'obscurantists', the War Office had been appallingly inept in its approaches to the Associations. It had failed to offer any convincing reason why the change was necessary at such short notice, and being unable to promise camps for the following year, it virtually invited the Associations to look upon its proposals with the utmost suspicion.

When, in February 1933, the postponed meeting was held, the War Office was in a much better position. On 19 January *The Times* had reported that the Army Estimates included funds for Territorial camps in 1933, and Duff Cooper was able to make the formal announcement that camps would be held that summer just a week before the Associations met to hear the War Office's proposals.[35] Rather than have Derby put the case for the abolition of the pledge — a ploy that had conspicuously failed to draw the light-ning as Derby had hoped — the Adjutant-General, Montgomery-Massingberd (who was soon to succeed Milne as CIGS), addressed the Associations. Unless the Territorial Army was freed of the pledge it could never fulfil the vital role that the War Office assigned to it in the country's mobilization plans. There was no way around the fact that the pledge could not be adhered to in time of war; it was better therefore to face up to that fact and rectify the situation while there was still time for dispassionate discussion. The War Office was fully aware of the importance that many Territorials attached to the pledge, and it had no wish to provoke charges of a 'breach of faith'. There was no intention of altering the rights of any men already enlisted or of those who wished to re-engage. All the War Office wanted was to withdraw the pledge from all men enlisting on or after 1 April 1934. Stanhope added that fears of the Territorial Army being used to supply drafts to Regular units were completely unfounded, for the planned rate of mobilization of the Regular Army was such that although there was

[36] *Parl. Debs.* (Commons), 5th series, vol. 274, col. 12 (7 February 1933).

no longer a Militia or Special Reserve to supply drafts, general service troops — conscript or volunteer — would be available by the time reinforcements were needed. He appealed to the Associations not to listen to the enemies of the Territorial movement or to those self-appointed experts 'calling themselves Military Correspondents' who stirred up mischief by misinterpreting the War Office's intentions. The War Office, he assured them, 'is not going to play the dirty with you'.[37]

The Associations decided to meet again in May, when a formal vote would be taken. The outcome was hardly in doubt, for as the Chairman of the Staffordshire Association wrote to *The Times* on 9 March, 'This change is absolutely and imperatively necessary if the Territorial Army is to continue as the real defensive mainstay of this country in a military sense. Some small changes in details might be considered necessary . . . but the main proposition is unassailable and there is really no alternative — none at all . . . . I cannot think . . . [the Associations] will adopt a course which might almost render necessary the disbandment of the Territorial Army'. He was right. The great majority of the Associations accepted the War Office's case as explained by the Adjutant-General as reasonable and realistic. Some, such as East Lancashire, had done so when Derby first unveiled the plans the previous May; others, including the West Riding, were now reassured that their main objection, which Scarbrough had voiced, namely the protection of the rights of serving men, would be met. The reaction of Nottinghamshire was typical. The Association there voted unanimously to support the abolition of the pledge on the grounds that its acceptance would show that the Territorial Army was at last 'taken seriously' by the War Office. Not all the Associations that voted to accept the Adjutant-General's proposals did so without dissent. Embarrassing for Derby, in view of his constant assurances that the Associations would accept whatever the War Office suggested, was the reaction of his own West Lancashire Association. Although the members voted twenty-one to eight to accept the abolition of the pledge, eight out of fifteen of the COs in the Association rejected the proposal. Similarly in the City of Aberdeen Association, the greatest opposition to the withdrawal of the pledge came from two COs both of whom circulated stinging attacks upon the War Office, whose aim, they charged, was to 'cut at the very root of the whole idea of the Territorial Army'. The abolition of the pledge, they pointed out, would render the

[37] CCTA special meeting, 15 February 1933, Minutes, 1923 – 1933.

Territorials liable to be used as drafts, for although the CIGS and the Adjutant-General had given assurances that this would not be done, the strictly legal effect of the withdrawal of the pledge was to enable the War Office to do just that, and no officer could bind his successors to a particular undertaking.[38]

While most Associations agreed to accept the abolition of the pledge, they also suggested 'some small changes in details' that the Staffordshire Association had admitted might be necessary. Several (including the Gloucestershire, Buckinghamshire, and the City of Aberdeen Associations) wanted the new papers that Territorials would be asked to sign to contain a guarantee that Territorials would not be used as drafts, and an assurance that if transfers were necessary in the extreme circumstances of battle, they should be considered as temporary postings only. Others argued that since the Territorials were accepting increased obligations they deserved additional concessions. Lanarkshire wanted at least the principle of a greater bounty to be accepted, so that when financial circumstances permitted, Territorials liable for general service could be more handsomely rewarded for their peacetime military service with its greater attendant risks. Sussex went further and asked that a whole range of benefits be conferred on non-pledged Territorials: that their exemption from jury service be for life rather than for the length of their engagement in the Force; that pay and allowances ('which in any case seldom covered the cost to individuals of attending annual training and courses') be made tax-free, and that employers be encouraged to support the Territorial Army by being allowed to offset wages paid during annual camp against their income tax.[39]

But the most interesting suggestions were made on the question of the withdrawal of the pledge from serving men. The War Office was desperately anxious to avoid any further charges of 'breach of faith', and though it would have much preferred to see the entire

[38] East Lancashire, 3 March 1933, Minutes, vol. 8; West Riding, 24 April 1933, Acc. 1469/5; Nottinghamshire, 7 April 1933, Acc. 953 TA 1/2; West Lancashire, 21 March 1933, Acc. 2074/2; City of Aberdeen, memoranda by Lieut.-Colonel A. G. Nicol-Smith and Lieut.-Colonel H. J. Butchart, 29 March 1933, MD 4/8.

[39] Gloucestershire, General Purposes Committee, 10 April 1933, D 2388 2/2; Buckinghamshire, 7 July 1932; City of Aberdeen, 10 April 1933, MD 4/8; Lanarkshire, Conditions of Service Sub-Committee, 28 February 1933, MD 2/5; Sussex, Report of Special Committee, 16 March 1933, appended to Association minutes, 10 April 1933, D 912/11.

Territorial Army unpledged after a certain date (preferably as soon as possible) it shrank from suggesting such a drastic course to the Associations. Once they had accepted the Adjutant-General's proposals, however, many Associations realized that it would create an unwieldy situation if the future Territorial Army contained both pledged and unpledged men, the former being those who had been permitted to re-engage on their original pledged status. For some, of course, even this was not enough to shake them from their conviction that the rights of pledged men had to be protected, and these Associations (Cumberland and Westmorland, Lanarkshire and Fife) insisted that serving Territorials be allowed to extend their pledged status after the pledge had otherwise been withdrawn. Most, however, agreed that the anomaly of two classes serving in units together had to be avoided, and they recommended that all Territorial service — whether recruits or re-engagements — be on an unpledged basis from 1 April 1934. This was more than the War Office could have hoped for.[40]

Only a small number of Associations rejected the Adjutant-General's proposals. Cambridgeshire and the City of London (the latter the centre of 'obscurantism' in the War Office's view) feared the effects on recruiting if it became known that friends who had joined in peacetime to soldier together would become liable to be sent to different units in time of war. The greatest opposition came from the County of London. In a poll of its members who were or had been Commanding Officers, thirty-eight wanted the pledge retained, and twenty-eight voted for its abolition. There was an even greater weight of opposition to the proposed general service obligation, which would have made Territorials liable for transfer outside their corps, rather than merely their battalion as in the case of the pledge; only ten favoured it, while fifty-six rejected it.[41]

[40] Cumberland and Westmorland, Joint Recruiting and Equipment Committee, 27 April 1933, Minutes, vol. 6; Lanarkshire, Conditions of Service Sub-Committee, 28 February 1933, MD 2/5; Fife, 5 May 1933, MD 7/25. The Associations that supported the complete withdrawal of the pledge included: Dumfriesshire, 12 April 1933, MD 3/1; Gloucestershire, General Purposes Committee, 10 April 1933, D 2388 2/2; Hampshire, 10 March 1933, 37M69/9; Kirkudbrightshire, 22 April 1933, MD 3/4; Suffolk, 10 April 1933, IA2: 1205/13.

[41] Cambridgeshire, 13 May 1933, Minutes, vol. 4; City of London, 25 April 1933, 12,607/2; County of London, 24 May 1933, A/TA/5. The County of Aberdeen also voted against the War Office's proposals, 31 March 1933, MD 4/47. I cannot identify the fifth dissenting Association.

The final vote at the CCTA meeting in May was almost the exact reverse: fifty-six Associations approved the changes, and five opposed them. Once it was clear that the War Office would go ahead with the abolition of the pledge, the dissenting Associations allowed the vote of approval to be unanimous.[42] The new terms of service were formally announced in July.[43] Despite the indications that the majority of Associations favoured uniform treatment for re-engagements and new recruits, the War Office decided against withdrawing the pledge from serving Territorials when they chose to re-engage. It was clear that most of the pledged Territorials would leave the Army after another four year term, and it was not worth opening up old arguments that were likely to give rise again to charges of a breach of faith for the dwindling number of pledged troops. The date for the withdrawal of the pledge — 1 November 1933 — was a compromise between the desire of the War Office to introduce the new system as early as possible and the wish of some Associations to make the change after annual training. Rather than delay until the end of 1934, it was agreed to push the change back before summer camp in 1934.

The fight over the pledge marked a decisive change in the fortunes of the Territorial Army. The determination of the War Office to effect its abolition was an indication that at least serious thought was being given to the role that the Territorials might realistically be called upon to play. The Associations were forced to recognize that the restrictions placed upon the use of Territorials under the terms of the 1920 reconstitution completely hamstrung the War Office's mobilisation plans. To the extent that the War Office acted to bring the Territorials into the mainstream of military planning and the Associations agreed to surrender rights that had seemed so important in the grievance-ridden days of the immediate post-war years, the abolition of the pledge marked the coming of age of the Territorial Army and the real beginning of its gradual recognition as a serious military force. The fight was not yet over, not even on the pledge itself, but at least the confrontation and hostility between the War Office and the Associations that had been such a feature of their relations in the 1920s had been temporarily laid aside. Increasingly they worked together rather than at loggerheads to make the Territorials into a true 'second line'.

[42] CCTA meeting, 24 May 1933, Minutes, 1923 – 1933.
[43] *The Times*, 19 July 1933.

8

'Saturday Night Soldiers'

While questions of policy were settled at the War Office, the Territorial Army as a whole and the Associations that administered it at the local level carried on a constant struggle to win new recruits and to persuade those already serving to re-engage when their original commitment had expired. The results were never satisfactory, apart from the exhilarating boom of 1938 and 1939. For the most part the Territorials lived a hand-to-mouth existence in the interwar years, battling Government parsimony on the one hand and public indifference and hostility on the other. The obstacles to be overcome were formidable, much more so even than Lord Raglan suggested when he told the House of Lords in 1925 that 'The Territorial Army to-day has three chief enemies — women, trade unions and motor bicycles.'[1]

Recruiting got off to a slow start in 1920. No final decision on the number of units had been reached by the War Office, and the terms of service were not yet finalised. Rumours circulated that the Army Council hoped that poor recruiting would spell the end of the Territorials, or that at best the Territorials would be tolerated but not encouraged by the War Office. Immediately after the war many Associations had established Old Comrades' Associations in an attempt to keep a nucleus of former Territorials in being for the day when units would be reconstituted. But when the new scheme was finally launched and recruiting began, it was a different story. Most Associations found that men with wartime experience had no wish to prolong their service, even in the more relaxed atmosphere of Territorial soldiering. The country was weary of war and of everything associated with it, and wanted for the most part to return unmistakably to civilian life. The London Rifle Brigade encountered the usual difficulties: in nine months it enlisted only 111 men, but unlike the majority of units throughout the country, most

[1]   *Parl. Debs.* (Lords), 5th series, vol. 62, col. 252 (22 July 1925).

of its soldiers had wartime experience. Ninety-one had previously served with the unit; of those twenty-nine had given up wartime commissions to enlist as Riflemen in the ranks, while only twenty men enlisted without any previous military experience. In the country as a whole almost half the recruits who joined up in the first eight months of recruiting in 1920 were without military experience, and two years later over half the recruits were drawn from the under-twenty-one group.[2]

Men who had served in wartime were anxious to re-establish themselves in civilian occupations, and many were reluctant to jeopardise their new jobs by asking for leave to attend camp. Some Associations recognised that problem, and decided not to hold camps in 1920, while those who did tended to make them little more than outdoor holidays, with training almost entirely eliminated and replaced by sports programmes. The first year in the life of the reconstituted Territorial Army was a unique one, and the protestations of Associations that camps in 1920 would be an undue burden on the new units were never heard again.[3] Instead, over the twenty-year period between the wars, the recruiting problems that Associations faced were remarkably constant. Their success in solving them was dependent on changes in policy and attitudes that largely lay outside their power, as they continually told the War Office, pleading for more concessions that were almost always rejected because they involved increased expenditure.

Men joined the Territorial Army for many different reasons. Some, particularly the increasing proportion of lower-paid and unemployed, were attracted by the bounty and the pay during summer camp. Others found the minimal military training a small price to pay for the social attractions of a Territorial unit — the drill hall club, the annual camp, and the comradeship they provided — while others — probably the majority — were undoubtedly motivated by a mixture of patriotism, self-interest and the

[2] For comments on the effects of war weariness, see CCTA, Business and Finance Committee, 26 May 1920, Minutes, 1908 – 1922; Essex, 23 November 1921; Leicestershire and Rutland, 7 February 1922, Acc. 819/3. On the lack of experienced recruits see Devon, 16 March 1921, 1715 c/TA 2; Leicestershire and Rutland, 7 February 1922, ACC. 819/2; Durand and Hastings, *The London Rifle Brigade*, p. 16; Cmd. 1610, 'Annual General Report on the British Army: Year Ending 30 September 1920', p. 127; Cmd. 2114, 'Annual General Report on the British Army: Year Ending 30 September 1922', p. 129.

[3] Surrey, Recruiting Committee, 20 February 1920, Recruiting Minutes, 1908 – 1925.

enjoyment of military life for short periods each year. This made recruiting a difficult business for the Associations and the units: they had to appeal to so many interests that it is hardly surprising that recruiting and its attendant problems took more of their time than any other of their responsibilities.

Undoubtedly the greatest attraction of the Territorial Army was the annual camp. The promise of fifteen days under canvas at full Regular Army rates of pay made the month or so before camp the busiest recruiting season of the year. Men who enlisted in the late spring or early summer were assured of a paid holiday, often by the sea. For the units it was important to have as many men as possible at camp. Apart from regimental pride, large numbers of men meant that more difficult and more interesting manoeuvres could be practised, officers could more realistically learn how to command and lead their men, and the camp functioned more effectively as a whole. But the influx of recruits immediately prior to camp also had its drawbacks. So many of the men at camp each year were new recruits that an inordinate amount of time had to be spent in teaching basic military drill before the recruits were able to move on to more advanced training. For those who had mastered the elements of drill, the constant repetition for the first week of camp was discouraging, and partly accounts for the large wastage rate among engagement-expired men. When in the 1930s Liddell Hart, *The Times* Military Correspondent, criticized the unimaginative training procedures of many units while in camp, he was reminded by one CO that the rapid turnover of men made it all but impossible to undertake the advanced training that Liddell Hart thought necessary if the Territorials were to be taken seriously as a second line force.[4]

The Associations and the units were so concerned to improve their recruiting and strengthen their units, thereby justifying to a supposedly unsympathetic War Office the continued expenditure of scarce funds on the Territorials, that the pursuit of numbers became an end in itself. The greatest concern for every unit, and for the Associations that administered them, was the site of the camp. Experience showed that inland camps, and especially those at Catterick in North Yorkshire, were much less popular than those held by the sea, and preferably within close reach of a medium sized town. One member of the Hertfordshire Association protested in 1923 that recruiting would become very difficult if the artillery had to spend every summer training at ranges; unless they could go

---

[4] *The Times*, 27 August and 3 September 1938.

every second year to an area where there was 'more amusement for the men' numbers would fall off sharply. The argument was not without some force. For many men summer camp was their only holiday, often taken without pay from their civilian job. It was natural that at least some wanted their families to be near them, so that after training was over they could enjoy the attractions of the seaside together. Camps at Catterick and on Salisbury Plain lacked the social amenities that Territorials from urban centres took for granted. The result was that Associations shied away from holding camps there, fearing as Nottinghamshire did in 1934 that their recruiting and retention figures would suffer the following year.[5]

When the War Office tried to economise on the cost of training, it occasionally limited camps to areas within a short distance (fifty miles or so) of unit headquarters. The reaction was predictable. When in 1922 camps were restricted to local sites, the Warwickshire Association protested that the effect on recruiting would be 'disastrous'. It was not, but the protests were duly made whenever units were deprived of 'attractive' (i.e. seaside) camps with the leisure facilities of a resort within handy reach. The GOC 42nd (East Lancashire) Division suggested to his Association that 'popular camp grounds and efficiency were somewhat wide apart', that 'a holiday by the seaside was of no benefit to training', but he was not supported either by the Association as a whole or by COs of the units that made up his Division.[6]

The question of numbers was uppermost in the Associations' minds (not unreasonably, given the War Office scrutiny of strengths and the occasional round of reductions or even the abolition of whole units), while training was not their responsibility. This fixation with numbers to the exclusion of almost everything else produced a nasty situation in 1933–4. In the *Daily Telegraph* Cup competition for the best attendance at camp, two units of Sherwood Foresters reported records of 100 per cent. This unprecedented success aroused suspicion, and the CO of one of the units admitted that he had taken on some men immediately prior to

5   CCTA, 14 February 1923, Minutes, 1923–1933; Nottinghamshire, 31 March 1934, Acc. 953 TA 1/2. The records of virtually every Association consulted contain references to the desirability of seaside camps as a recruiting device. Camps at Catterick were condemned by West Lancashire, 14 August 1930, Minute Book 2; those on Salisbury Plain by Gloucestershire, which preferred that the 5th Battalion should go instead to Weston-Super-Mare (18 January 1926, D 2388 1/3).
6   Warwickshire, 21 November 1922, CR 1141/2; East Lancashire, 10 September 1925, M 73/2/6.

camp who were physically unfit and who had to be sent to hospital once their 'attendance' at camp had been registered. Questionable as that practice was, further investigation turned up even more flagrant abuses. It transpired that some units had inflated their attendance figures by using ex-Territorials or ex-Regulars under false names. Some civilians went to camp as batmen to officers, drew the usual pay and allowances, and were put on the unit strength. The more enterprising of them went from unit to unit, accumulating a tidy sum after several summer camps each year. There was even the case of a Regular Battery Sergeant-Major serving in the north of England who went to camp with a southern Territorial unit under an assumed name and with the rank of Lance Corporal. The whole affair was hushed up, and the word went out to Associations that a much tighter check had to be kept on unit returns.[7]

Once the summer camp was over recruiting fell off, and some units stopped altogether until early spring. For those already in the Territorial Army, training went on throughout the year, always geared towards the two weeks in camp when lessons learned in the drill hall could at last be put into practice. That at least was the intention, but it did not always work out that way. One of the most frequent complaints about training, both at the weekly drill hall sessions and at camp, was the lack of modern equipment. In 1920 the Surrey Recruiting Committee complained bitterly about the poor quality equipment that the infantry was compelled to use, much of it, they claimed, being 'practically unserviceable'. The same year the Essex Association drew attention to the condition of some forty artillery recruits, who were reduced to training on a captured German gun that had been presented to their village as a war trophy. In Derbyshire the CO of an armoured car company warned that obsolete armoured cars and guns did little to attract and retain officers and men (though the position of armoured units was not of course unique to the Territorials; the Regular Army suffered just as badly). The historians of the London Rifle Brigade recalled that only once during the interwar period did the unit see (but not participate in) a tank demonstration, and that exercises with aircraft were 'few and elementary'. Even basic weapons were in short supply, if available at all: 'at camp we trained with wooden Bren guns, our only real one lying preserved like an icon in the

---

[7] The *Daily Telegraph* Cup details can be found in the Derby Papers, Correspondence with Individuals: War Office 1934 (correspondence between Derby and Lord Stanhope, Under-Secretary of State).

store tent'. Clothing was little better, the Territorials being given cast-offs from Regular supplies, which by the 1930s were becoming so depleted and worn that in 1936 *The Times* Military Correspondent wrote that: 'Some of the khaki suits that are issued to Territorials would lower a tramp's self-respect.'[8]

Apart from its training function, the unit drill hall was the centre of Territorial social activities, which were second only to the annual camp in attracting and holding recruits. Those units which had sufficient funds often used them to extend the facilities of their drill halls — to provide bars, billiard and reading rooms, and sometimes the means to prepare simple meals. This was especially important in the 1920s and early 1930s, before the War Office awoke to the importance of the social aspect of the Territorials' appeal and began allotting limited funds to enable all units to start improving their accommodation. Some units had the benefit of spacious and well-endowed buildings dating from the days of the Volunteer movement, and others, such as the London Rifle Brigade, became in effect clubs, charging members an annual subscription (two guineas in the case of the LRB) and a small company subscription. The social life of the unit became the attraction that tided the Territorial Army over from one camp to the next, and for the Associations, concerned as they were with recruiting and everything that affected it, the problem of providing adequate social facilities to induce men to join grew more and more acute as buildings deteriorated through lack of maintenance and as the expectations of Territorials rose. The greatest difficulty was experienced in large cities and towns, where units had to compete with all the other facilities for recreation and leisure that were available to young men. In comparison with new cinemas, pubs and dance halls the cramped and outdated quarters of many Territorial units were a poor inducement to sign up for a four year engagement. In rural areas the situation was quite different: there the drill hall was often the only large building in the village that could be used for social occasions, but that in turn created its own problems.

Clearly many men joined the Territorial Army because of the positive rewards it offered — an annual camp, often in pleasant

---

[8] Surrey, Recruiting Committee, 7 June 1920, Recruiting Minutes 1908 – 1925; Lord O'Hagan (a member of the Essex Association), *Parl. Debs.* (Lords), 5th series, vol. 41, col. 108 (13 July 1920); Derbyshire, General Purposes Committee, 4 June 1928, D 530/5; Durand and Hastings, *The London Rifle Brigade*, pp. 13, 43; *The Times*, 24 August 1936.

surroundings, a yearly bounty and good rates of pay at camp, the comradeship of the unit, and the social activities associated with the Territorials. How far they were also motivated by patriotic feelings is much more difficult to determine. The records of the Associations are replete with affirmations of the Territorials' vital role in the defence of country and empire, though for some years in the late 1920s and early 1930s that was played down and the 'insurance value' of the Territorial Army stressed instead. The Associations constantly complained that the Government did not adequately recognize the value of the Territorials, not only for their military worth but because of their ability to instill order and discipline at a time when society seemed in danger of losing both. These complaints, however, often derived as much from fear that the Army would be abolished either by outright action or by sustained neglect, as they did from a sense that citizen-soldiers were being ignored and slighted.

Except for the years 1938 and 1939, which will be discussed later, there is little evidence that men joined the Territorial Army primarily for patriotic reasons; or if they did, their enthusiasm soon evaporated thus giving rise to the rapid turnover of recruits that was always a feature of the Territorials. Again, except for the last two years before the outbreak of the Second World War, there were no contentious issues of foreign policy with which the individual could identify himself by joining the Territorials. Internally the only time that events appeared to spark a revival of Territorial fortunes was in 1921, when strength temporarily rose as men from the Defence Force transferred into the Territorial Army after the end of the emergency, but it declined almost as quickly as unit COs began weeding out the 'undesirables' who had thereby slipped into the Territorial ranks. Changes in strength were closely connected with concrete issues such as the abolition of the bounty, the suspension of camps, the level of pay and allowances, and — at least according to the Associations — to the more general question of the visible level of Government support.

The Territorial Army had not been very successful in either 1921 or 1926 in its attempts to avoid involvement in political issues that would compromise its standing with the working class from whom it drew most of its strength. It was much more careful in 1936 when Oswald Mosley's British Union of Fascists tried to establish itself within the Territorial ranks. Mosley told the War Office that in response to the recruiting appeal that had been launched in the spring of 1936 the BUF would encourage its members to join the Territorials, if possible in special units. It was a delicate situation for the War Office. It could hardly impose a blanket ban on BUF members joining, but, as it pointed out to Mosley, it was 'impracticable and impolitic' to raise Territorial units solely from the ranks of the BUF. The DGTA warned the Under-Secretary of State that if it became known that numbers of Fascists were using Territorial drill halls, even for legitimate Territorial purposes, the units would be boycotted by other political groups. The BUF members were especially provocative because of their insistence on wearing their fascist uniforms when off duty at Territorial camps and their propensity for publicising their movement's activities at every opportunity.[9] In the mid thirties the Territorial Army faced enough of a recruiting obstacle in public indifference without drawing outright hostility on to itself.

The Associations were rarely at a loss to explain the inability of the Territorial Army to reach its establishment, but they always emphasized that the remedies lay not with them but with the War Office and the Treasury. There was almost no complaint that increased expenditure could not settle, but that of course, through-out the interwar period, was precisely the avenue that was closed. Every year the War Office was implored to raise the level of pay and allowances, and, after 1927, to restore the bounty in some form or another. The fact that Territorials were out-of-pocket as a result of their willingness to undertake military service was held up as the main reason for the poor recruiting figures.

The most notable recruiting failure of the Territorial Army was its inability to attract sufficient officers. Most Associations felt that apart from the psychological factor — men would not volunteer unless they thought their services were wanted and appreciated — there were very real financial obstacles that prevented many men from applying for commissions. The cost of uniforms was high, and was rarely covered by the allowance of £50 given to new officers in the 1920s, a grant that was reduced to £40 in the economy squeezes of the 1930s. Scottish regiments in particular required a heavy outlay by new officers, the average cost of full kit being £67. Those who had served in the Army, Regular or Territorial, were entitled to only £15, even though their new unit still expected them to purchase the appropriate uniforms; and that concession was withdrawn within a year as part of the Geddes economies.

Secondly, only very limited travel expenses were paid. Before the war there had been considerable pressure exerted by rural counties with scattered units to persuade the War Office that some payment

[9]   See WO 32/4608.

for out-of-pocket expenses had to be made if numbers were to be increased. The War Office agreed, but limited the payment to the costs incurred by whole sections to attend company, squadron or section drill, and refused to reimburse the expenses of individual officers or men. When the terms of reconstitution were being discussed in 1919 and 1920, the payment of out-of-pocket expenses had been one of the key issues, but had never been satisfactorily resolved, giving rise to another 'breach of faith' charge. Car expenses were not covered by War Office grants, thus discouraging just the class of young professional and business men that the Associations were anxious to attract. When travel allowances were liberalised in the 1930s they did not go far enough. For example, expenses were only paid for travel within the county where the officer trained, so that those who worked in London but served with units in Sussex or Oxfordshire still found themselves out-of-pocket.

Thirdly, the War Office had promised in 1920 that no officer would have to subsidise his period at camp. This had been one of the strongest Territorial grievances before the war, for most officers, and especially young subalterns, found that their pay during camp came nowhere near covering their expenses. That problem seemed to be solved in 1920 when the War Office announced that henceforth officers would receive a messing allowance of 4s a day as well as full rations, but again it fell victim to the Geddes axe and was replaced by a fixed sum of £1. Another complaint arose out of the taxing of the annual grant of £20 made to officers: a tax rate of 5s in the pound, it was argued, on a grant that was already inadequate to cover costs let alone to provide any sort of reward for an officer, was hardly an incentive to the right type of man to volunteer his services.[10]

For men in the Territorial Army there were also financial obstacles that inhibited recruiting, among them the regulations covering marriage allowance and the inclusion of the bounty and pay during summer camp in the calculation of unemployment benefits and the provision of public assistance. During the war

[10] On uniform allowances see C. T. Kingzett, letter to *The Times*, 13 September 1922; *The Times*, 17 October 1922; Territorial Army Advisory Committee, 5th meeting, 18 May 1936, WO 32/9700. On the problem of poor travelling expenses see: Perth, Executive Committee, 14 July 1919, MD 7/39, CCTA, 13 February 1924; CCTA, Business and Finance Committee, 5 November 1924 and 13 May 1925, Minutes, 1923–1933; *Parl. Debs.* (Commons), 5th series, vol. 309, col. 2416 (12 March 1936). On officers' allowances at camp see *The Times*, 16 July 1920, 10 March 1922.

married men serving in the Territorial Army had received a weekly marriage (or separation) allowance, and much of the work of the Associations had been concerned with its administration. When the reconstitution proposals were being discussed in 1919 and 1920, the Associations had understood that the payment of marriage allowance to Territorials would continue irrespective of age. The War Office decided otherwise, and imposed on the Territorials the same age limit of twenty-six as applied in the Regular Army. It could claim that this was logical since the Territorial Army had always demanded to be treated on an equal footing with the Regular Army; but the Associations pointed out that in this respect, at least, the problem was quite different. The Regular Army took in recruits at seventeen for an eight year term of service, which usually included time overseas. Withholding marriage allowance and married quarters during that period ensured that the maximum number of young Regular soldiers remained unmarried. For the Territorial Army, however, the young married man was precisely the type that the Associations were anxious to recruit: one who had settled in his job and his residence, who had taken on the responsibilities of marriage and who was unlikely to drop out of his unit. Not only was the imposition of the age limit after the war considered yet another breach of faith (especially since the recruiting pamphlets published in 1920 had promised that separation allowances would be continued under the terms of reconstitution), but it was held by many Associations to be a major obstacle to recruiting among young men, and the single greatest reason why men did not renew their engagement after their initial four year term had expired.[11]

When the age limit was imposed on the payment of marriage allowance there was an outcry from the Associations who saw that not only would it discourage enlistment among the youth on whom the Territorials had to rely, given the reluctance of older men with war experience to join, but that in the long term recruiting would become even more difficult if units could not persuade men to re-engage. The War Office based its opposition on two grounds: first that to grant marriage allowance to Territorials under the age of

[11] See Buckinghamshire, 24 March 1921; CCTA, 13 July 1921, Minutes, 1908 – 1922; Northumberland, General Purposes Committee, 5 August 1921, NRO 408/9; CCTA, Business and Finance Committee, 26 October 1921, Minutes, 1908 – 1922; County of London, Press Propaganda Sub-Committee, 23 October 1925, A/TA/3; East Lancashire, 7 March 1930, Minute Book 7; West Lancashire, 14 August 1930, Minute Book 2.

twenty-six would be to make an invidious distinction between the Territorial and Regular Armies, and secondly that it would be too expensive. The first argument was specious, and the second hardly stood up to close examination. The numbers involved were small. The City of Glasgow Association reported that in 1921 only 157 out of 4236 men attending its camp that year were affected by the age restrictions. When the War Office rejected the Associations' pleas on the grounds that to abolish the limit would cost an additional £35,000, the Associations disputed the figure. West Lancashire reported that only 432 men in its units were affected, and that if they had been given marriage allowance the cost would have been only £569. This stirred other Associations to look at the make-up of their units, and eventually it was found by the CCTA that only 6690 soldiers out of a total in 1924 of 134,130 were affected by the age limit. The cost of giving them the marriage allowance was a mere £8,395, and that was based on the unlikely assumption that all the men involved would attend camp for the full fifteen days. Even if the figures were doubled to allow for increased recruiting as a result of removing the age limit, the cost was far from the £35,000 cited by the War Office. Furthermore, there was the indirect cost of not paying marriage allowance incurred through the loss of trained men who did not re-engage.[12]

The sense of grievance that was felt over the age limit was aggravated in 1921 when the Government decided to pay marriage allowance to all men in the Defence Force irrespective of age. This made a mockery of the War Office claim that to abolish the limit for the Territorial Army would be to discriminate against the

---

[12] East Lancashire was the first Association to protest against the age limit for marriage allowance: Recruiting and Discharge Committee, 8 October 1920, M 73/3/26. It was supported by Buckinghamshire, 24 March 1921; City of Glasgow, General Purposes Committee, 12 April 1921; Cornwall, 5 May 1921, DDX 295/12; County of Aberdeen, 24 June 1921, MD 3/45; Derbyshire, General Purposes Committee, 7 February 1921, D 530/4; Durham, 2 November 1920, Minutes, vol. 2; Inverness, 29 March 1921, MD 8/25; Nottinghamshire, General Purposes Committee, 25 October 1921, Acc. 953 TA 1/2; Oxfordshire, 30 April 1921, Minutes, vol. 5; Perth, Executive and Finance Committee, 16 March 1921, MD 7/39. Glamorganshire raised the issue at the CCTA, which resolved to press the War Office to remove the limit: CCTA, 26 January and 9 February 1921, Minutes, 1908 – 1922. The figures on the effect of the age limit come from City of Glasgow, General Purposes Committee, 14 September 1921; and CCTA, 12 November 1924, 4 February 1925 (Business and Finance Committee), Minutes, 1923 – 1933.

Regular Army. As the lean years of recruiting set in the Associations protested regularly to the CCTA and the War Office, urging the former to try yet again to bring about a change of policy. The CCTA approached the War Office in 1924 and 1925 without success, but when the issue was raised once more in 1929 by the Nottinghamshire Association, which attributed its falling recruiting figures to the marriage allowance restrictions, the CCTA decided not to risk another rebuff.[13]

By the early thirties, however, the Associations felt they could not afford to wait any longer. Recruiting was in a critical position, and much of the blame for the Territorials' failure to attract young married men was attributed to the War Office's refusal to grant marriage allowance to those under twenty-six. The War Office adamantly opposed any relaxation of the regulations, even though it admitted in 1931 that some Territorial wives had to go on public assistance while their husbands were in camp since the pay was not sufficient to provide for their upkeep without the marriage allowance. In 1935 the Devon Association reported that during its annual camp that year the wives of four soldiers had to seek parish relief, while another thirty men were granted leave from camp so that their wives would not be forced to turn to the parish authorities. On top of that nineteen men had refused to re-engage because they claimed they could not provide for their wives during camp unless they received marriage allowance. It was an unedifying advertisement for the second-line citizen Army of the country, that it refused to pay its soldiers sufficient to keep them from having to beg for public assistance simply in order to carry out their military duties.[14]

As the evidence grew that this shameful state of affairs was widespread throughout the Territorial Army, the War Office was forced to make concessions. It announced in March 1935 that men serving on a re-engagement would be eligible to receive marriage allowance after their first promotion, but the Associations rejected that as offering too little to persuade young married men to enlist in the first place and as drawing an unfair distinction between men of different ages who volunteered to serve in the Territorial Army. The CCTA unanimously agreed that the new policy would 'neither improve recruiting nor remove the causes for the complaints', and

---

[13] CCTA, 30 April 1924 (Business and Finance Committee), 11 February 1925, 20 November 1929, Minutes, 1923 – 1933.

[14] Duff Cooper, *Parl. Debs.* (Commons), 5th series, vol. 255, cols. 2491 – 2 (30 July 1931); Devon, 25 September 1935, 1715c/TA3.

pressed the War Office, if it was unable to remove the age restrictions altogether, to save the families of young Territorials from the stigma of having to appeal for relief. Not only the Associations but also the Public Assistance Committees protested against the War Office policy, the latter on the grounds that the cost of maintaining soldiers at camp was one that should rightfully be borne by the state. The following year the War Office yielded, and as part of its campaign to revive the long-neglected Territorials announced that marriage allowance would be paid to all married soldiers over the age of twenty-one.[15]

Another group within the Territorial Army that was hard hit by government regulations was the unemployed. Attendance at camp was a costly business. If they were on public assistance they lost that financial support during the camp period because they were then classified as 'employed persons'. Their pay at camp, however, was usually less than they received in assistance, so that they were considerably out-of-pocket. Furthermore when they received their bounty or proficiency grant, which was normally paid in October, that was taken into account in calculating the amount of assistance to which they were entitled. A slight improvement came in 1934 when the bounty was made exempt from the means test, but the grievance over pay during camp remained.

The Ministry of Labour rarely showed much sympathy for the Territorial Army in its interpretation of the regulations. In 1935, for example, the 5th Territorial Battalion, The Welch Regiment, organised a march for its unemployed troops from Wales to Basingstoke, where manoeuvres were to be held. The Ministry ruled that the men were ineligible for unemployment benefits or public assistance while on the march on the grounds that they would thereby by unavailable for employment in their home town. As the CO of the battalion said, 'Of course it is all nonsense, because the bulk of the men have not been employed for about five years, and the prospect of a man getting a job is too problematical for words.' The War Office stepped in quickly, and announced that the men would be given full pay and allowances, both for their time at camp and on the march. The Ministry of Labour was reluctant to make any special concessions to the Territorials for it had refused to

[15] *Parl. Debs.* (Commons), 5th series, vol. 299, cols. 850 – 1 (18 March 1935); vol. 309, cols. 2357 – 9 (18 March 1936). For rejection of the 1935 concessions, see Cumberland and Westmorland, 24 January 1935, Minutes, vol. 6; East Lancashire, 5 April 1935, M73/2/9; CCTA, 29 May 1935, Minutes, 1934 – 35.

make similar payments to unemployed men taking part in hunger marches.[16]

As with the question of marriage allowance the Associations clamoured for changes in the regulations, arguing that recruiting was being harmed. However, although there were cases of unemployed men leaving their unit because they were unable to accept the loss of pay, the Associations were not on particularly strong ground. Hardship undoubtedly was caused by the stringent application of the regulations, but recruiting among the unemployed remained strong. On the basis of his visits to Territorial camps Liddell Hart estimated in 1935 and again in 1937 that many units, especially in the North, Scotland and Wales, found more than half their strength from the ranks of the unemployed. Overall recruiting numbers, of course, declined during the early and mid thirties, but the unemployed do not seem to have been significantly discouraged from enlisting as a result of the application of the means test. No doubt their sense of grievance, such as it was, may have made them less willing to re-engage, but the poor retention rate in all areas of the country was not confined to the unemployed segment of the Territorials and was probably as much to do with general disgust over the prolonged neglect of the army as it was the result of dissatisfaction with specific terms of service. In any case, after constant complaints from the Associations, the War Office was able to announce in 1936 that henceforth unemployed Territorials would not be penalised in the calculation of their benefits because of their pay and allowances at camp.[17]

Ever since the recruiting campaigns of 1920 failed to attract the numbers that had been hoped for, Associations and units had been continually faced with the dilemma: should they sacrifice quality in

---

[16] *The Times*, 28 and 29 August 1935.

[17] For the views of the Associations on the means-testing of Territorial pay, see City of Glasgow, General Purposes Committee, 13 September 1927; County of London, 2 June 1932, A/TA/5; CCTA, Business and Finance Committee, 1 May 1935 and 29 April 1936, Minutes, 1934 – 1945; Cumberland and Westmorland, 30 April 1936, Minutes vol. 6; Lanarkshire, 16 June 1933, MD 2/5; Leicestershire and Rutland, 12 November 1935, Acc. 819/4; Northumberland, 8 February 1935, NRO 408/7; West Riding, 27 April 1936, Acc. 1469/5. Liddell Hart's comments on the composition of the Territorials are in *The Times*, 25 July 1935 and 27 August 1937. The revised regulations on the application of the means test are in War Office to Associations, 14 May 1936, copy in City of Aberdeen, 4/9.

the pursuit of numbers, and later 'weed out' the undesirable element, or should they maintain their standards and accept only those who met them? If the latter approach was taken, what sort of standards should be applied? The CO of the 4th Battalion, The Royal Berkshire Regiment, had a rigid policy of accepting only the 'right sort of man' and that did not include the unemployed. The reason he gave was that after an unemployed man had attended camp and weekly training and had begun to develop a degree of military efficiency, he might obtain employment in another district and hence be lost to his unit. This CO preferred to see his unit remain numerically weak rather than put its strength at the mercy of the vagaries of the employment situation: 'There were many good unemployed and some bad, but they were taking no risks . . . .'[18] Many other units however felt they had no choice but to accept any men who passed the medical examination (which alone caused many applicants to be rejected), but that of course brought its own problems. Recruiting for both the Regular and Territorial Armies suffered considerably because of the appalling medical standards of many of the prospective recruits. In 1922 Leicestershire and Rutland reported that at every recruiting evening held at various drill halls, between 25 and 33 per cent of the men failed to pass the medical examination. Cumberland and Westmorland held a recruiting drive in 1926 where only 16 out of 28 volunteers were found to be medically fit.[19]

Some units that accepted any men who passed the medical test found that their clothing supplies were being subjected to abnormal wear and tear. It seemed that in some areas — Durham and Staffordshire, for example — men were using their Territorial clothes, especially their boots, for civilian purposes, and in Sussex it was suggested that some men joined the Territorials simply to obtain cheap clothing. The Sussex charge was angrily refuted when it was made in 1923, but within a few years there was evidence that the unemployment situation was having a serious effect on the use of Territorial clothing. In 1927 West Lancashire noted the deterioration of its clothing stock and proposed to charge COs for the replacement of unduly worn articles, but dropped the idea when one CO protested that in his battalion alone there were 300 unemployed men who naturally used their Territorial clothes for

[18] *Berkshire Chronicle*, 20 June 1925.
[19] Leicestershire and Rutland, 2 May 1922, Acc. 819/3, vol. 4; Cumberland and Westmorland, Recruiting and Equipment Committee, 22 January 1926, TAA/4.

everyday use since they could afford no others. Similarly Durham found in 1928 that a substantial number of men were coming to camp without a sufficient supply of socks: the War Office refused to approve the spending of Association funds to provide each man with two pairs, and the Association had to be content with buying one pair for each man and charging him for an additional pair. By 1934 the worst-hit areas of the depression found that many of their men were unable to provide for themselves even the most basic items of clothing. Sixteen out of sixty-four Associations told the CCTA that they thought local circumstances warranted the free issue of shirts and socks for men at camp, but the War Office again refused on the grounds that these were normal articles of clothing that every Territorial could be expected to have.[20]

When it tried to draw recruits from those in steady employment, thereby avoiding the problems that arose from having too many unemployed men in the ranks, the Territorial Army came up against other difficulties. In 1924 the War Office established a Supplementary Reserve that could be used in times of emergency to provide technical support — mainly communications and transport — for the Regular Army. Several of the large unions had refused to give their support to the scheme, fearing that men who signed up might be called out during a strike to keep essential services running, but the War Office had gone ahead anyway, and had tried to meet the unions' fears by giving a specific assurance that men in the Supplementary Reserve would not be used in civil disturbances. (See chapter 4.) The Associations had a different fear. They saw in the Supplementary Reserve a rival to the Territorial Army, one that offered marked advantages to the volunteer. Not only was the reservist protected from being called up in aid of the civil power, an assurance that many Territorials had pressed the War Office to grant them, but he was given an extraordinarily high bounty (between £6 and £20 depending on his classification) and had virtually no military duties or training to undertake in return. A Territorial, on the other hand, was liable for overseas service and for duty in aid of the civil power, and had to attend weekly drills and an annual camp — all for a bounty of £3 which was reduced to 30s

[20] Durham, 27 July 1920, Minutes vol. 2; Staffordshire, Transport and Supply Committee, 14 May 1927, D 969/1/3; Sussex, Clothing, Equipment and Recruiting Committee, 19 November 1923, D 912/9; West Lancashire, 18 July 1927, Minute Book 2; Durham, 31 January 1928, Minutes vol. 3; CCTA, Business and Finance Committee, 16 May 1934, Minutes, 1934 – 1945.

in 1927. It is not surprising that the Associations soon found that the Supplementary Reserve was cutting deeply into their own recruiting, not only in numbers but also in terms of the quality of recruits. The 55th West Lancashire Divisional Signals, for example, found in 1929 that it could muster only fifty-seven men out of an establishment of 279, whereas the Supplementary Reserve Signals unit was only twelve short of its assessment of 172. Similar complaints came from Monmouthshire and the West Riding, and the CCTA pressed the War Office to restrict the Supplementary Reserve to those who had already served in the Regular or Territorial Armies. The needs of the Regular Army came first, however — as Staffordshire had admitted when reluctantly giving its blessing to the creation of the Supplementary Reserve — and the War Office refused to intervene on behalf of the Territorial Army.[21]

Most Associations tried to strike a balance between numbers and quality, arguing, as it was put to the Devon Association, that 'the acceptance of a low standard of recruit in a unit will quickly keep the good class from enlisting'. The influx of transfers from the Defence Force in 1921 had burdened many units with men later considered 'undesirables' (though precisely why they were thus labelled was never explained). When the bounty was abolished in 1927 the effect on recruiting was not seen in the enlistment figures but in the rate of re-engagement, although eventually the new recruits under the proficiency grant also showed reluctance to extend their service beyond their first four years. Four years later the War Office ordered units to limit their numbers to ninety-seven per cent of their strength on 1 August 1931. Devon used that economy as the pretext for weeding out the 'undesirable' men who had been taken on following the abolition of the bounty, when most Associations were afraid that recruiting would be dealt a catastrophic blow.[22]

That was the last time there was a deliberate effort to reduce numbers in the Territorial Army. As public interest in the Territorials diminished (and it had never been very great since the war),

[21] CCTA, 6 November (Business and Finance Committee) and 20 November 1929, Minutes, 1923–1933; Staffordshire, 17 May 1924, D 969/1/1. For other complaints about the effect of the Supplementary Reserve on Territorial recruiting, see City of Aberdeen, 13 April 1931, MD 4/7; Devon, 12 March 1924, 1715c/TA3; East Lancashire, Recruiting and Discharge Committee, 18 September 1931, M73/3/34; Staffordshire, General Purposes Committee, 2 November 1929, D 969/1/4; 'Major', letter to The Times, 13 January 1936.

[22] Devon, 13 March 1929, 9 December 1931, 1715c/TA 3.

the Associations could not afford the luxury of rejecting men as 'undesirable' or unemployed. They had to accept any willing man, simply to keep the Territorial Army alive. Yet while they pursued numbers in a vain attempt (for the most part) to reach their peace establishments, they bemoaned the quality of the recruits they were forced to accept. In 1937 the Associations were asked to comment on the difference between the recruits they were taking in and those who had joined before the war. Almost every Association replied that there had been a noticeable decline in standards. 'The better class of man is not so plentiful now', wrote the City of Dundee. 'Generally speaking, not such a good type of man now joins the Territorial Army' was Cornwall's answer. Lanarkshire replied that 'there are practically no recruits of the "black coat" type: and the farmer and the agriculturalist classes have almost disappeared', while Hertfordshire noted that: 'The T.A. is now getting certain of the type that used to join the Militia.' There were many reasons for this change for the worse: the unemployment situation, the continual economies forced on the Territorials by the War Office and Treasury, lack of interest in military service, a decline of patriotic feeling encouraged by virulent anti-war propaganda, and the inability of the Territorials in their state of 'penurious discomfort' to rival the facilities of civilian clubs and entertainments.[23]

Things were very different in 1938 and 1939. Hitler's move against Austria in March 1938 brought a flood of recruits into the Territorial Army, especially into AA units that would provide the first line of home defence. The events of the following September merely added to the rush. The CO of the 70th Searchlight Company in Sussex reported that he had been 'inundated with applications for Commissions' as well as enquiries about joining the ranks. The latter, he added with satisfaction, 'came from men of an entirely different type from those who applied to join the ordinary units and included ex-OTC men and men from banks and offices, which was very encouraging'. In Warwickshire recruiting from May to October 1938 was double what it had been during the same period in 1937, and between August and October increased more than ten-fold. It was the same all over the country: the twin problems of numbers and quality

[23] City of Dundee, 1 February 1938, MD 7/9; Cornwall, 7 February 1938, Acc. DDX 295/12; Lanarkshire, 7 February 1938, MD 2/6; Hertfordshire, 14 January 1938.

disappeared as the sense of impending crisis suddenly emerged.[24]

Apart from those last two years before the war, the Associations had struggled hard to overcome the formidable obstacles that dissuaded men from joining the Territorials. The methods employed by the recruiting committee in each Association varied widely, depending on their location and the type of men to whom their appeal was directed, but until the crises of 1938 and 1939 cast the Territorials and the whole question of national defence in a new and urgent light, the problem of recruiting was always before the Associations. They felt that the War Office and the Government as a whole offered them little real support. The delay in announcing the terms of reconstitution suggested a less than whole-hearted enthusiasm for the Territorial cause, and some of the recruiting material produced by the War Office was ludicrously inappropriate:

> There is one last word to be said about the Territorial System, though in these rather neurasthenic days, when we are suffering from the reaction after the period of strained national effort, it is a word one almost hesitates to utter: patriotism is regarded as a solemn and magnificent thing in war time; in peace time one hardly dares to utter it. One is reminded of that Prodigal Son of the Victorian era, of whom it was said: 'Oh, No! we never mention him, his name is never heard.'

As Esher told the War Office representative at a meeting of Commanding Officers in the County of London Association, what the Territorial Army wanted was more plain speaking and less of that sort of 'rhetorical balderdash'.[25]

Largely left to their own devices most Associations relied on a combination of parades and public displays to make the existence of local units known, publicizing the sporting and social attractions of the Territorials as well as their purely military duties, and approaching local employers of labour to win their cooperation. Their success was mixed. The Associations in Scotland and Wales always had stronger units than in England, especially in the Home

[24] Sussex, 10 October 1938, D 912/12; Warwickshire, Recruiting Committee, 15 February 1939, CR 1141/7.
[25] 'Conference of Officers Commanding Units administered by the Territorial Force Association of the County of London, 9 June 1920.' Copy in the Scarbrough Papers.

Counties, and generally units in rural areas were more popular than those in cities (with the notable exception of the City of Glasgow). In cities and large towns, the Associations relied on posters and newspaper advertisements to attract recruits, and in London, where they felt the keen competition of the cinema, several Associations invaded the new palaces of popular culture with advertising slides and eventually short films. It was an expensive business, as the City of London was forced to conclude in 1922 when it was faced with a bill of £1000 to take the front page of the *Daily Mail* after it had been unable to persuade the County of London Association to share the cost. Most Associations lacked the money even to consider such an extravagance, and preferred instead to feed information to the national and local press in the hope that at least some coverage of Territorial affairs would result. *The Times* consistently championed the Territorial cause, and when Liddell Hart became its Military Correspondent in 1934 it regularly reported in detail on Territorial problems and activities, especially annual camps.

The War Office urged the Associations to use the press to publicize the Territorials as much as possible, but the advice it gave them in 1936 gives cause to doubt that it was any more in tune with the realities of the Territorials at that time than it had been in the 'rather neurasthenic days' of 1920. After cautioning Associations against stressing the patriotism of their units, it suggested that they emphasize 'striking contrasts' between the civil and military occupations of various Territorials. For example Associations could point to the Territorial who was 'driving an out of date car or lorry in the day and an Armoured Car or Rolls Royce in the evening'.[26] The truth was of course that given the parlous state of the Territorials in the 1930s, a soldier was far more likely to be behind the wheel of an obsolete lorry when on duty with his unit.

Posters rarely seemed to have much effect on the number of recruits enlisted, and parades and drill displays were at best a questionable tactic, church parades and 'Territorial Sundays' even more so. When it was suggested in West Lancashire that regular parades would bring in more recruits, the CO of a Territorial unit in Lancaster pointed out that his unit had been on parade every week and yet it was still the weakest in the Division.

Many units experimented at one time or another with the payment of 'bringing-in-money', a reward paid to each Territorial who

[26] City of London, 31 January 1922, 12,606/2; War Office to Associations, 5 March 1936, copy in City of Aberdeen Association Papers, MD 4/9.

persuaded a man to enlist. The War Office disapproved of the practice but since it did not go so far as to forbid it some Associations continued to use it. The amounts paid varied from 2/6 in Cambridgeshire to 1s in Essex in 1920. When the general level of recruiting failed to match expectations the War Office gave in and allowed Associations to pay recruiting rewards, but it refused to provide special funds for the purpose and required Associations to find the money from their own surplus funds. This sometimes created a difficult situation for the Associations. The results tended to show that bringing-in money was simply not worth the expense, that the number of recruits obtained did not significantly increase.

The City of London Association looked at its pre-war records before committing itself to the scheme, and promptly decided against it when it found that when using specially paid recruiters the cost per recruit obtained had been almost 9s, and those recruits had not been especially notable for their quality. When Hampshire launched a recruiting drive in 1929 and offered 5s reward for every man enlisted it drew in 316 men. Yet the previous year, without any financial inducement it had attracted 299 recruits, which meant that the cost to Association funds of the additional seventeen men had been £4.15s each. Within some Associations (Kirkudbrightshire, for example) there were variations: some units paid a reward while others refused on the grounds that it had no appreciable effect on recruiting. Those local variations caused problems: the CO of the 5th King's Own Scottish Borderers asked to be included in the 'bringing-in' scheme even though he doubted its usefulness, simply because he did not want his men to feel they had any grievance when comparing their situation with that of other units within the county that offered recruiting rewards. Similarly when a joint committee meeting of the Kirkudbrightshire, Wigtonshire, and Dumfriesshire Associations rejected the payment of 'bringing-in' money, Kirkudbrightshire kept up the practice anyway, which made Dumfriesshire feel that it had little choice but to fall into line, albeit against its better judgement.[27]

The promise of summer camp was the most powerful attraction that the Territorials could offer. Second only to that was the social

[27] West Lancashire, 10 July 1935, Acc. 2074, Minute Book 3; Cambridgeshire, 14 May 1920, Minutes, vol. 2; Essex, Finance Committee, 19 May 1920; City of London, Recruiting Committee, 13 December 1920, 12,613/1; Hampshire, General Purposes Committee, 15 November 1929, 37M69/8; Kirkudbrightshire, 2 March 1935, MD 3/4; Dumfriesshire, 10 April 1935, MD 3/1.

life centreing on the local drill hall. Units in cities or large towns faced fierce competition from civilian leisure facilities. Many large employers provided sports grounds for their employees, and the spread of cinemas, working men's clubs and dance halls, together with the ubiquitous pub, meant that units had to be prepared to compete for the spare time of the potential recruit. Unless interest could be maintained in the unit in the long months between camps, numbers could not be maintained and the high wastage rate, always a feature of the Territorial Army, could never be reduced. Unfortunately most units had neither the accommodation nor the funds to provide the sorts of facilities that the young urban man had come to expect and enjoy. Dingy drill halls hardly began to compare with the delights of dazzling cinemas. 'Drab' and 'shabby' were the words most often used to describe them by Associations that largely pleaded in vain for money to refurbish and expand their buildings. Individual units were especially angered by a Whitehall ruling that required them to give to the War Office half the proceeds of any income from renting their buildings and the other half to the Association. Not until the mid-thirties, when the evidence of an alarming drop in Territorials numbers and the constant argument that inadequate facilities partly accounted for this could no longer be ignored, did the War Office acknowledge, though very hesitantly, that without attractive headquarters and drill halls the Territorial Army could not appeal to the mass of youth on whom it depended for its strength.

Outside the cities and large towns, the drill halls could more easily attract young men. Sometimes they were the only hall in the town or village available for large gatherings or indoor sports. Most Associations took a stern line and refused to rent their premises to outside bodies unless a sizeable proportion of the membership belonged to the local Territorial unit. In Lanarkshire COs could allow Boy Scouts and the Boys' Brigade to use local drill halls, presumably on the grounds that these uniformed organizations inculcated discipline in the young and were a potential source of Territorial recruits, but badminton clubs were turned away. In Wigan the drill hall of the 5th Battalion The Manchester Regiment was made available to the local badminton club in the hope that it might prove to be a 'profitable source for obtaining a suitable type of officer'. The badminton players in Peterhead, Aberdeenshire, assured their use of the drill hall by offering to assist in recruiting drives. But not all clubs were as cooperative: to show them their duty, Associations such as the City of Glasgow refused to allow any badminton player under the age of thirty to use its facilities unless he was a Territorial, while Denbighshire restricted the use of its drill halls to men who were either in the army or who had been in it. In Hampshire the Association was more direct. When the villages of Swanwick and Totton showed little enthusiasm for the local Territorial unit, the Association ordered that no more public dances or social functions were to be held there. Two months later the CO of the unit reported that recruiting had picked up remarkably, and the drill hall was once more made available to the public.[28]

In addition to the use of drill halls by sporting and social clubs there were more contentious applications that occasionally brought the units into conflict with the community from which they drew their support. Political groups who sought to use the halls for meetings were often refused, especially if they were associated with the Labour Party or any other body that tended to be unsympathetic to the Territorial Army or to the services in general. When the Cumberland and Westmorland Associations were approached by the local branch of the Independent Labour Party for use of the Carlisle drill hall, the request was finally turned down but only after the Associations stressed that they were not making political distinctions, for the Labour Party had previously been allowed use of the hall on condition that they did not sing the 'Red Flag'. What they objected to was the Labour Party's stand on British involvement in China: 'They were not going to send their lads to China and then be insulted in their own Drill Hall.' Several years earlier a similar situation had arisen in Staffordshire when the GOC-in-C, Northern Command, expressed his disapproval of the practice of allowing drill halls to be used for political meetings; on finding that he had no power to prevent it he requested the War Office to change the Territorial Regulations covering the use of halls. The Association reacted angrily, asserting that it was a far better judge of potential 'rowdyism' than the GOC-in-C, and pointing out that 'good recruiting can only be expected when Territorial units, and all connected with them, are able to maintain a sufficient degree of local popularity'. Furthermore, it suggested, it had to be

[28] Lanarkshire, 19 November 1920 (Halls and Ranges Committee), 22 April 1921, MD 2/3; East Lancashire, 1 November 1935, M73/2/9; County of Aberdeen, Ranges and Buildings Committee, 16 October 1925, MD 4/45; City of Glasgow, Property Committee, 13 January 1921; Denbighshire, General Purposes and Finance Committee, 3 September 1920, TA/D/6; Hampshire, 5 January (Finance Committee) and 16 March 1923, 37M69/5.

remembered that many of the drill halls in question had originally belonged to the Volunteers and had been built by public donations. Any move to place unreasonable restrictions on their use would create strong resentment in the community.[29]

The question of whether to allow the unemployed to use drill halls posed the same sorts of problems for the Associations. With many units, especially in Scotland, Wales and the North of England, drawing a sizeable proportion of their men from the unemployed, there was some reason for Associations to consider giving unemployed men access to drill halls. On the other hand, it would not have done to let the Territorial Army become too closely associated in the public mind with the unemployed section of society: that would keep the 'better classes' from enlisting. Most Associations compromised. Men on unemployment 'hunger marches' were refused permission to use drill halls as stop-over places, but local unemployed groups were usually allowed to hold physical training sessions. Encouragement of the latter activity could be construed as an act of patriotism, as Scarbrough reminded the West Riding Association, because it had been endorsed by the Prince of Wales as an effort 'to get young men off the streets and help them to keep physically fit'.[30]

Employers of labour were one section of the community without whose cooperation the Territorial Army could not function. Unless men could obtain the necessary leave from work to attend summer camp (for many were not entitled to two weeks' holidays each year) and could be assured that they would not suffer penalties, even dismissal, for joining the Territorials, it was unlikely that units would be able to attract sufficient recruits. The decision to enlist in the Territorial Army was therefore often conditioned by the attitude of employers and the Associations worked hard to convince employers of the need to support local units by giving their men any extra leave that was needed and, if possible, by supplementing their Army pay so that they would not be out-of-pocket during

---

[29] Cumberland and Westmorland, 28 January 1927, TAA/3; Staffordshire, Organization Committee and General Purposes Committee, 10 January 1925, D 969/1/2.

[30] Among Associations denying their drill halls to unemployed marchers were Dumfriesshire, 11 November 1936, MD 3/1; Staffordshire, General Purposes Committee, 12 November 1932, D 969/1/5. Associations that permitted physical training classes in their halls included Kent, General Purposes Committee, 30 November 1933, MD/TA 3/6; Kirkudbrightshire, 11 February 1933, MD 3/4; West Riding, 30 January 1933, Acc. 1469/5.

camp. Not only would employers be contributing to a 'national insurance scheme for peace at a very low premium', but they would find that the Territorial Army had an immediate impact upon their employees: it inculcated useful habits of discipline into the workforce and it acted as a 'renewer of the tired worker's health and strength', thereby increasing his productive capacity.[31]

When the reconstitution proposals were under discussion in 1919 and 1920 several Associations blamed their slow recruiting before the war on the lack of cooperation from employers, and argued that the only way to avoid a repetition of that experience was to impose some sort of legal obligation on them. That had also been the conclusion of a War Office committee, but when the CCTA discussed the idea it was found that opinion was almost evenly divided. The main drawback was the practical question of how the requirement would be enforced. Clearly large employers could afford to be much more flexible than smaller firms, yet to oblige them alone to make concessions to their employees was hardly the way to win their enthusiastic support.[32] Instead the Associations chose to rely on moral suasion, and tried to appeal to the employers' sense of patriotism (and self-interest).

Each year Associations reported that numbers of men had been refused leave from their employment to attend the annual camp. In 1924 twenty-one men of the Leicester squadron of the Leicestershire Yeomanry had to miss camp because they could not get leave, and this was repeated across the country. Those men who took leave sometimes found that they had no job to go back to once camp had ended: West Lancashire reported such a case in 1922, and Derbyshire had four instances in 1924. The numbers were quite insignificant in themselves, but they helped spread the impression that men would jeopardise their jobs by joining the Territorial Army. When recruiting began in 1920 some Associations found that men who had recently been demobilised and had found new jobs were unwilling to join the Territorials or, if they did enlist, were afraid to ask for leave to go to camp for fear of being dismissed. As the unemployment rate rose steadily throughout the 1920s and 1930s recruiting became even more difficult because of men's reluctance to endanger their jobs. Sometimes men found jobs in other districts, or they emigrated, and were thus lost to their unit. Several Associations tried to place their unemployed Territorials in local jobs, only to find that in some cases these men withdrew from their

[31] DGTA to Chairman, Essex Association. Essex, 24 September 1923.
[32] See chapter three.

units rather than risk dismissal or even displeasure by asking their employer for leave to attend camp.[33]

Each year most Associations were faced with a significant rate of absenteeism from camp, much of which was directly related to the attitude of employers. Some men undoubtedly had no intention of fulfilling their Territorial obligations, but most who did not go to camp were prevented from doing so by circumstances over which they had little control. With most units below establishment, the Associations felt they had no choice but to prosecute men who failed to go to camp or to carry out the prescribed number of drills. Some were untraceable: they had left the district to look for work elsewhere. Others had been unable to get the necessary leave or were too afraid to ask for it. The Associations tried to adopt a uniform policy of prosecuting defaulters, but it was not easy to bring charges against a man who had just found a job after being unemployed and who was unwilling to risk losing it. If the Territorial Army was to win local support, it could not afford to appear in such an unfavourable light.

Most Associations therefore tried to prosecute only those men who had failed to attend drills as well as camp, for the former required no time off work and absence from them could be taken as a sign of wilful neglect of duty. Otherwise units were reluctant to bring men to court. In 1923 West Lancashire decided against any prosecutions 'owing to the labour difficulties, and to the impecunious condition of the men'. Two years later in Caernarvonshire, when the 6th Battalion, Royal Welch Fusiliers, had twenty-one men absent without leave from camp, the Associations thought it impolitic to prosecute the ten who remained in the regiment (the rest having emigrated, gone to sea or simply disappeared) on the grounds that they might have been at the Royal National Eisteddford during the camp period. The CO of a West Lancashire unit in 1933 had a more direct solution to the problem of absenteeism and prosecution: any men who had not been excused were rounded up by the local police and brought to camp.[34]

---

[33] Leicestershire and Rutland, 8 July 1924, Acc. 819/3; West Lancashire, 10 October 1922, Acc. 2074, Minute Book 1908 – 22; Derbyshire, 5 October, 1925, D 530/4.

[34] West Lancashire, Recruiting and Discharge Committee, 5 January 1923, 6 October 1933, Acc. 2074, R&D Minutes, Books 2 & 3; Caernarvonshire, 4 September 1925. For the effect of employment on camp attendance, see Essex, 4 October 1922; Hertfordshire, 22 October 1926; Northumberland, 9 January 1925, NRO 408/9.

Employers who dismissed men because they belonged to the Territorial Army were few, but the problems of employing Territorials were real enough. In many areas, those near the sea for example, much of the work was seasonal, and demand for labour was at its height just at the time when units were holding their summer camps. Large companies might make special arrangements, but for smaller firms it was virtually impossible to let two or three men leave at the busiest time of the year. In 1923 the CO of the 5th Battalion, The Royal Sussex Regiment, attributed the poor attendance at camp (54 per cent) to the fact that his men were drawn from those who worked in hotels and boarding houses, or who came from rural areas where the harvest tended to coincide with camp. In Cambridgeshire the Association pointed out that the timing of camps was very difficult because of the large numbers of college servants involved. Throughout the interwar period it was suggested several times that training be staggered so that leave could more easily be given to Territorials, but there were serious objections to this alternative. Divisional Commanders preferred to have as many units as possible concentrated in a single location, not least because it made cooperation with Regular units much easier. Those men who took their families to be near them during camp were bound to protest that moving camps from August to September interfered with their holiday plans, while for the Associations the extra work and expenses involved in staggered camp periods was not appealing.[35]

Apart from the employers themselves much of the opposition to the Territorial Army came from their other employees. When Associations approached local firms for support they often found that the problem lay not with management but with foremen and staff supervisors, who resented the leave privileges that some firms gave Territorials, especially where the men's pay was supplemented by their employer. When engineering companies in Manchester were asked in 1920 to cover any financial losses that Territorials might suffer while at camp, the Engineering Trades employers' Association refused for fear of causing labour unrest by making a distinction between those of its employees who belonged

---

[35] Sussex, 19 November 1923, D 912/9; Cambridgeshire, 12 February 1938, Minutes, vol. 2. For proposals to stagger camps see Essex, 21 January 1925; Oxfordshire, 26 April 1919, Minutes, vol. 5; Territorial Army Advisory Committee, 6th meeting, 14 October 1936, WO 32/9700; Brigadier-General F. S. Thackeray, letters, *JRUSI*, LXXXIII (August 1938), pp. 631–2.

to the Territorials and the great majority who did not. Another grievance that non-Territorial employees had was over leave for camp. As one employer told a conference in London in 1920, 'the difficulty was that the training was usually in August, when the senior members usually took their holidays. They resented the juniors having an advantage over them in having their holidays in that month.'[36]

In an attempt to win the support of employers, most Associations formed liaison committees that visited local businessmen and explained to them the value of the Territorial Army and the duties of the individual soldier. Occasionally the local Chamber of Commerce threw its weight behind Territorial recruiting schemes — the Brighton and Hove Chamber in 1925, the Leicester Chamber in 1926, for example — but for the most part it was left to the Associations and often to commanding officers to approach employers and appeal for their cooperation. In Caernarvonshire, one Association member took it upon himself to obtain from the managers of local quarries an assurance that men would not be dismissed for attending camp. In the City of Aberdeen Association, the Recruiting Committee wrote to all major employers within its boundaries to ask if they would agree to have their name included on a confidential list that would be made available to COs of firms that not only encouraged their men to join the Territorial Army but did not discriminate against them when they went to camp. Cambridgeshire tried a similar approach, but its list was to be published in the form of an 'Employers' Roll of Honour'. It was not successful: after a month only forty favourable replies had been received in answer to 160 letters. Suffolk did rather better when it sent out almost 300 letters to local employers, but it had not proposed to publish the list and it was careful to follow up each letter with a personal visit by a member of the Association.[37]

When they came to discuss the question of employer cooperation, there was general agreement throughout the Associations that the Government had to offer some sort of reward to those employers who supported the Territorial Army. In 1920 Denbighshire

---

[36] *The Times*, 22 February 1921; East Lancashire, Recruiting and Discharge Committee, 21 May 1920, M73/3/26; West Lancashire, 18 July 1927, Minute book 2.

[37] Sussex, 29 April 1925, D 912/9; Leicestershire and Rutland, 9 February 1926, Acc. 819/3; Caernarvonshire, 14 June 1929; City of Aberdeen, Recruiting Committee, 28 April 1936, MD, 4/9; Cambridgeshire, 8 January 1921, Minutes, vol. 3; Suffolk, General Purpose Committee, 10 July 1933, IA2: 1205/13.

suggested that uncooperative firms should be assessed an additional penny in National Insurance contributions for each employee — and that the money should be given to the Associations! A scheme that was only slightly more sensible, and one that was discussed by several Associations, came from Devon in 1937, when it proposed that a tax concession of £4 be given to employers for each of their employees who went to camp for the full fifteen days and who had their Army pay supplemented by their employer. By far the most favoured form of reward was the institution of an equivalent of the 'King's Roll', a list of all businesses that employed a minimum of 5 per cent of their workers from the ranks of disabled servicemen. In return these firms were allowed to bid for Government contracts. Opinion was widespread among the Associations that unless a similar concession — and honour — was extended to patriotic employers, the Territorial Army would never get the support that it needed from business and industry to build up its strength. The situations, however, were quite different. As Bromley-Davenport told the CCTA in 1925 when the issue came to a head, there was general public sympathy for the plight of the war disabled, but it was very doubtful whether the Territorials enjoyed the same sympathy. In any case the difficulty that most Associations encountered was not with the large firms but in small businesses and shops where a quota system could hardly be applied.[38]

The proposal got nowhere in the twenties, but was revived in the mid-1930s as the Associations watched their strengths decline year by year. This time it was not simply the Associations who backed the idea. The Quarter-Master General favoured a system of contract preference for those employers who supported the Territorials, but the Government was not about to interfere with normal business in such a blatant manner, and the Under-Secretary of State decided to make the appeal to business entirely on grounds of patriotism. The President of the Board of Trade, Walter Runciman, readily gave his approval to a Territorial version of the 'King's Roll', with cooperative employers being entitled to display a

---

[38] Denbighshire, 8 July 1920, TA/D/6; Devon, 10 March 1937, 1715c/TA3; CCTA, 18 November 1925, Minutes 1923–1933. Support for a Territorial 'King's Roll' came from the President of the London Chamber of Commerce, *The Times*, 9 December 1920; Derbyshire, General Purposes Committee, 4 May 1925, D 530/4; Devon, 15 July 1925, 1715c/TA3; Inverness, 21 July 1925, MD 8/25; Leicestershire and Rutland, 12 May 1925, Acc. 819/3; Middlesex, Recruiting Committee, 1 October 1925, Acc. 994/4.

badge indicating their support of the Territorial movement. This, Runciman thought, was the only way that recruiting would recover from the slump that had set in after the withdrawal of the bounty and the cancellation of camps. Even this mild proposal, however, met with objections from the Ministry of Labour, which argued that the promise of a badge might cause some firms to pressure their employees into joining the Territorials as a condition of employment, thus giving rise to charges of indirect Government compulsion. Nothing could be done that might hinder the rearmament programme, in which the cooperation of labour was such a vital element. The Territorials had to fend for themselves.[39]

In other sections of the community the Territorial Army faced outright hostility. Many Associations felt that Lord Raglan had not been too wide of the mark when he pointed to women as among the main enemies of the Territorials. Wives, it was thought, discouraged their husbands from joining the local unit because it took them away from home too much (which may, of course, have been why the men thought of joining in the first place). Those who had lost husbands or brothers in the war were understandably reluctant to see their sons enlist in the Territorial Army, the more so since its supporters insisted that the Territorials were the second line behind the Regular Army and might at any moment find itself involved in battle. Others discounted the social benefits that were said to come from belonging to the Territorials, and instead looked on drill halls as little more than drinking centres. 'Mothers had an idea', said the GOC-in-C of the 42nd (East Lancashire) Division in 1925, 'that if their boys went to the Drill Halls they would learn to drink.' All the recruiting problems of the Territorials could be solved, the Chairman of the Suffolk Association argued in 1936, if women would 'give the cradle ever such a gentle push'.[40]

Much of the anti-war sentiment that the Associations felt was such an obstacle to recruiting came from the League of Nations Union, which was assiduous in arguing that the existence of large armies nurtured an international atmosphere in which the resort to

[39] Note by QMG, 30 January 1936, WO 32/2679; Strathcona to Ministry of Labour, 10 July 1936; Runciman to Strathcona, 18 July 1936; Ministry of Labour to Strathcona, 24 July 1936; WO 32/4646.

[40] East Lancashire, 18 September 1925, M 73/2/6; Lieut.-Colonel F. Garrett, letter to *The Times*, 2 June 1936; Cumberland and Westmorland, 30 October 1925, Minutes vol. 4; Nottinghamshire, 14 December 1934, Acc. 953 TA 1/2; West Lancashire, 10 July 1935, Minute book 3.

arms was inevitable. The Associations chafed under the constant denunciation of war and its evils, even though in 1932 the League insisted that its opposition to war did not mean that it condemned those who belonged to the Territorial Army. The distinction was lost on Sussex, which demanded the right to 'counter false views' such as those propagated by the League in schools throughout the country and in talks to local branches of the Women's Institute.[41]

The greatest opposition, however, came from the Labour Party, which consistently attacked defence expenditure and the arms mentality as contributing to international tension and perpetuating the internecine national rivalries that had clashed so bloodily in the Great War. The maintenance of standing armies to defend an embattled world order diverted scarce resources away from social reform and reconstruction at home. The use of armed forces in aid of the civil power was the last resort of those who sought to uphold the inequities of the *status quo*, to defend political and economic privilege and the social influence that they bestowed. Recruiting for the Regular Army traditionally picked up in times of high unemployment so that its ranks were filled with the poor while its officer corps was drawn from the privileged classes.

The Territorial Army was no less a target of Labour hostility. The uncertainty over its liability to serve in aid of the civil power deepened the fears of those who suspected that its real purpose was to act as a strike-breaking body; and its none too covert involvement in the strikes of 1921 and 1926 did little to suggest otherwise. The Associations' own insistence that the Territorial Army was the second line behind the Regular Army and the sole means of expansion of the country's military forces in time of war simply linked it unmistakably to the militaristic attitude towards world affairs that Labour so distrusted. Socially, with its faint air of feudal military service and its strength in rural districts, the Territorial Army perpetuated the very social attitudes and sense of hierarchy that were anathema to Labour.

In 1920 the Labour MP, George Barnes, told a recruiting rally in Glasgow that a strong and efficient Territorial Army — a true 'citizens' Army' — was the best safeguard against the dangers of large standing armies, and that it could serve a useful social function in bringing different classes of men together in a common purpose. That argument was rarely heard in Labour circles. Instead Labour was haunted by the experience of conscription during the

[41] *The Times*, 27 December 1932; Sussex, 10 April and 10 July 1933, D 912/ 11.

Great War; its preoccupation with preventing the reintroduction of conscription blinded it to the possibility that support for the Territorial Army might forestall that necessity, even when several Secretaries of State argued that if recruiting for the Territorials did not improve the state might have to turn to compulsion.[42]

Labour's disapproval was mainly expressed at the local level. In large and small business firms and industries there was evidence that men tried to dissuade their fellow workers from enlisting, a situation that Essex tried to rectify by inviting businessmen to bring their foremen and other employee representatives to a meeting in the hope that Labour's suspicions of the Territorial Army could be allayed. The main centre of Labour opposition to the Territorials, however, lay in Labour-controlled councils. When recruiting opened in London in 1920 Churchill stressed that the Associations had to spread their appeal as widely as possible. Half the coopted members of the County of London Association were the mayors of London municipalities, who had been asked to form local committees to assist in the recruiting drive. Of the twenty-eight mayors involved, twelve had not replied to the Association's invitation; the eight who had refused came from Labour-controlled councils in working class areas. When the Mayor of Warrington defied Labour opinion in 1928 and called for men to join the local Territorial unit, he was bitterly criticised by the local branch of the Labour Party for 'prostituting' his office 'in so ignoble a cause'. In 1920 three Councils in East Lancashire (Salford, Padiham, and Middleton) declined to offer their employees any concessions, and two years later the Labour majority on the St Pancras Council rescinded the regulation passed in 1908 that gave Territorial employees an additional week's holiday on full pay to attend camp.[43]

For the most part during the twenties and early thirties the Territorials encountered either indifference or outright hostility from local authorities. A notable exception was the Middlesex County Council, which from 1920 on gave all its Territorial employees an extra two weeks' leave on full pay to encourage them to go to

[42] *Glasgow Herald*, 26 February 1921.
[43] *The Times*, 27 October 1920; *Parl. Debs.* (Commons), 5th series, vol. 130, col. 1073 (15 June 1920); *The Times*, 17 April 1928; East Lancashire, Recruiting and Discharge Committee, 21 May 1920, M73/3/26; *The Times*, 22 February 1922. The refusals came from the Mayors of Battersea, Bermondsey, Camberwell, Fulham, Greenwich, Poplar, St. Pancras, and Stepney. The Mayor of Bermondsey later explained that although he was unable to form a committee he would personally do all he could to assist the recruiting appeal.

camp. From the middle of the 1930s, however, the response was much more favourable, a reflection of the deterioration of the international outlook and the growing concern over the dangers of air attacks. In 1936 Cambridge and Worthing Town Councils gave their employees an extra week's leave with full pay, in the former case despite the objections of the Labour members of the Council. The following year the Government announced that all civil servants would have fully paid leave to go to camp, thus answering a long-standing plea from the Associations that Whitehall set an example to the rest of the country. The City Corporation and Westminster City Council followed suit, and by the time of the 1938 summer camp the Territorial Army had little complaint to make about the lack of support from most local authorities.

There were still those councils that refused to make any concessions: Southwark withdrew its extra leave in 1936 at the behest of the local Labour Party, on the grounds that it had put Territorial employees in a privileged position and that if Army rates of pay had to be supplemented then the cost should fall upon the state. Salford Council claimed that if it gave leave and pay concessions to its employees so many would join the Territorials that the normal work of the various municipal departments would be seriously disrupted. Glasgow Corporation refused to grant any extra leave or to supplement pay during attendance at camp, despite the fact that in 1938 100 of its 407 employees who attended camp had done so during their unpaid holidays, while another 106 were paid by the Corporation for only one week of their annual holidays. Experience in Westminster seemed to indicate that the combination of leave and pay concessions had a direct bearing on recruiting. When that Council gave its employees an additional week's paid leave, the Territorial strength jumped from 24 in 1936 to 62 in 1937.[44]

For the most part during the interwar years the Territorials attracted little enough attention from the public. There was a constant struggle to keep numbers up, and while the Territorials never suffered the ridicule that befell their predecessors, the Volunteers, they never won the wide public support that the Volunteers had enjoyed. The picture we have of the Territorial Army in the twenties and thirties is curiously lacking in the human element. The records of the Associations and of the War Office deal with issues and

---

[44] *The Times*, 7 May 1936, 16 October 1937; East Lancashire, 6 May 1938, M73/2/10; City of Glasgow, General Purposes Committee, 17 May and 6 September 1938.

problems, but rarely with the groups of individuals who made up the units. Very few units produced histories that deal in any satisfactory way with these years; understandably enough, perhaps, since the two wars naturally loom large in the records of any military unit. Those unit histories that do give some space to the interwar years paradoxically reinforce the 'official' picture: lists of officers' names and company achievements on the sports field do nothing to fill in the missing dimension.

Even more notable is the lack of Territorial memoirs. One of the few exceptions, and a brilliant one at that, is John Verney's *Going to the Wars*. Only the first chapter deals with the pre-war Territorials (in this case the North Somerset Yeomanry, disguised in the book as the 'Barsetshire Yeomanry'), but it is an invaluable pen sketch. Why did John Verney join the Territorials in 1936? His case was not untypical of that of many young men. Verney explains his decision to take a commission in terms of a mixture of patriotism and self-interest. 'To join the Territorial Army was the easiest and most obvious course open to anyone who felt he should make some effort to avert it [the impending world war]', and it allowed one to get in 'on the ground floor of an expanding racket'. But to Verney, more important than either of these, at least in retrospect, was the challenge that the Territorials offered: the prospect of two weeks' riding was one of 'those self-imposed ordeals, imposed for the good of my "soul" ', that he felt he could not shirk. In this sense Verney unwittingly came close to ascribing to the Territorial Army a role of which Haldane would have heartily approved.[45]

The struggles of the twenties and early thirties were largely forgotten by 1938 and 1939. Hitler's moves against Austria and especially against Czechoslovakia made the question of home defence against air attack a much more pressing one than it had been for years. The Territorial Army was the key to the anti-aircraft defence system, and it experienced a surge of interest the like of which it had never seen before. Most of the old difficulties disappeared, and units faced new and unexpected problems. Where was the equipment to train so many men? How could small and cramped buildings accommodate the flood of recruits that poured in as each successive crisis brought the prospect of war closer? The solution to these problems was not easy, but at least the Territorials had won the battle of numbers.

[45] John Verney, *Going to the Wars: A Journey in Various Directions* (London, 1955), pp. 24 – 5.

It was undoubtedly the fear of aerial attack on families, homes and properties that gave rise to the great surge in recruiting in the late thirties. As early as 1937 Football League Clubs in London had approached the War Office with the suggestion that AA batteries could be established drawing on clubs and their supporters. The scheme spread to Lancashire, and eventually to most parts of Britain that were involved in AA defence. The football success encouraged a number of Old Boys' Associations of London grammar and secondary schools to form their own AA batteries, and rugby clubs took up the challenge. Soon business firms and corporations, beyond those that had traditionally supported the Territorials, followed suit. In mid-1938 London Transport received permission to form an AA brigade in north and north-west London.[46] Long before field units of the Territorial Army, particularly the infantry, were up to strength, anti-aircraft units were virtually complete. Even after the announcement of a continental strategy in March 1939, infantry units were rarely deluged with applications to join in the way that anti-aircraft units were. The home defence role of the Territorials, which they had carried with them from their Volunteer antecedents, proved to have a remarkably durable, if at times dormant, appeal. Only the announcement at the end of March that the strength of the Territorials would be doubled brought a new wave of recruits to infantry units, but many of them were no doubt impelled to join by the wish to beat conscription which appeared almost inevitable, or, as John Verney put it, to 'get in on the ground floor of an expanding racket'.

The new sense of urgency in national life provided the stimulus to recruiting that normal peacetime never could. Yet despite the atmosphere of mounting crisis it would be wrong to think that patriotism was the only factor in the dramatic rise in recruiting. Rather we should look to the combination of motives that had attracted many Territorials during the earlier years, even if the balance between them had changed. The historians of the London Rifle Brigade spoke for much of the Territorial Army when they wrote that 'the great majority of those who . . . [enlisted] in the lean years before 1938 did so . . . because they had a friend there already who told them that they would find good company, a good club, and a job worth doing'.[47] That was no less true in 1938 and 1939.

---

[46] *The Times*, 28 January, 27 February, 8 April 1937, 27 August 1938; East Lancashire, 1 October 1937, M 73/2/10; West Lancashire, Recruiting and Discharge Committee, 1 October 1937, R&D Minutes Book 4.

[47] Durand and Hastings, *The London Rifle Brigade*, p. 6.

9

Rearmament

While the War Office, the Associations and the Territorial Army were embroiled in the struggle over the pledge, much broader questions of defence were coming under increasingly critical scrutiny. The 'ten year rule', adopted in the flush of success in 1919, had imposed severe limitations on the armed services. These could be accepted during the 1920s, but by 1932 the Chiefs of Staff could claim that none of the assumptions on which the rule rested any longer held true. The requirement that in planning the services assume that there would be no major war for ten years, and especially a war in which Britain would need an expeditionary force, had produced alarming deficiencies in essential items, the more so since the surplus stocks held over from the war had now been depleted. If Britain's military position were not to decline beyond an acceptable point, the ten year rule would have to be scrapped in favour of a more realistic appraisal of the world situation. The Committee of Imperial Defence concurred, and in recommending to the Cabinet that the rule be abolished, warned: 'We cannot ignore the writing on the wall.'[1]

The Cabinet agreed that the situation in Europe and Asia had so changed as to render invalid the basic tenets of the rule. But while it was prepared to accept the Chiefs of Staff's and the CID's

---

[1] COS, 'Imperial Defence Policy: Annual Review for 1932', 23 February 1932, CP 104(32), CAB 24/299. The question of rearmament and the debate over the role of the Army is treated extensively in N. H. Gibbs, *Grand Strategy*, vol. 1 (*History of the Second World War: United Kingdom Military Series*, J. R. M. Butler, ed.) (London, 1976); G. C. Peden, *British Rearmament and the Treasury 1932 – 9* (Edinburgh, 1979): Robert Paul Shay Jr., *British Rearmament in the Thirties: Politics and Profits* (Princeton, 1977); and Peter Dennis, *Decision by Default: Peacetime Conscription and British Defence, 1919 – 1939* (London, 1972). The most useful synthesis is provided by Brian Bond, *British Military Policy between the Two World Wars* (Oxford, 1980).

arguments, and withdraw the rule, it stressed that this was not to be interpreted as ready approval for any large increases in defence expenditure.[2] The depression remained the major concern of the Government for some years to come. For the Chancellor of the Exchequer, Neville Chamberlain, in particular, the struggle for economic and social recovery and the maintenance of financial stability were of more immediate concern than the requirements of the services. Almost alone among his colleagues he opposed the abolition of the ten year rule. He bowed to the Cabinet decision only after it agreed that abolition was not necessarily grounds for ignoring the domestic economic situation or the long-term financial stability on which the future of the country rested.[3] More than anyone else in the Cabinet, Chamberlain despaired over the growing expenditure on defence over the next seven years. It offended his social conscience and priorities, and threatened the country's financial stability, or, as he later called it when thinking about the possibility of war, its 'staying power'. As Chancellor of the Exchequer and later as Prime Minister, he was powerfully placed to resist the claims of the services, to question their strategic assumptions, and to initiate a vigorous attack upon the whole direction of Army thinking.

Developments in Europe and Asia in 1932 and 1933 underlined the Chiefs of Staff's warning. Japanese aggression in Manchuria continued unabated, and in March 1933, in the face of western disapproval of its actions, Japan withdrew from the League of Nations. The coming to power of Hitler in Germany in January 1933 merely speeded up German rearmament, which, as the Chiefs of Staff warned, would continue regardless of the outcome of the Disarmament Conference. Hopes that the talks at Geneva might find a way to stop an incipient arms build-up were destroyed when the Conference collapsed in October 1933 and Hitler announced his intention of withdrawing Germany from the League. In their review of imperial defence for 1933 the Chiefs of Staff understandably sounded a gloomy note. The alarming trends in German policy, coming on top of a rapidly deteriorating situation in the Far East, underlined the sorry state of Britain's military forces. As long as the threats were basically imperial ones, a slow rate of mobilization leading to a small expeditionary force was acceptable. That was not the case if Britain was required to fulfil its European obligations under the Locarno Treaty. Then it would be

---

2 Cabinet 19(32)2, 23 March 1932, CAB 23/70.
3 Cabinet 12(32)5, 10 February 1932, CAB 23/70.

facing not an 'undeveloped' aggressor but a modern European army. All that Britain could send would be a poorly-equipped expeditionary force of two divisions, with little hope that rein-forcements would be forthcoming. The Chiefs of Staff cautioned:

> To launch so small a force into war on the continent would be of value from the moral point of view, but most dangerous from every other aspect, since if it became involved in serious fighting we should be unable to reinforce it with adequate units and formations for many months. One of the great lessons of the last war is that it is impossible to limit the liability once we are committed to any theatre of operations.

The Foreign Office advised that 'the more the nations of Europe are convinced of our readiness to fulfil our guarantee, the less likelihood will there be that we shall be called upon to do so'. A mere two divisions were hardly likely to convince anyone — either to hearten a potential ally or deter a potential aggressor, especially when it was clear that whatever the pressures to reinforce the original commitment, there were simply not the reserves available if the Empire was to be kept secure. As a result of these depressing realities, the Cabinet directed the Chiefs of Staff, together with the Treasury and the Foreign Office, to prepare a programme to make good the worst of the deficiencies that had accumulated under the ten year rule. This was the origin of the Defence Requirements Sub-Committee of the CID (the DRC).[4]

The DRC deliberated for three months, and presented its report to the Cabinet in February 1934. It stressed that in the face of the world-wide nature of Britain's responsibilities and the financial impossibility of providing for every contingency, it was imperative to reduce by diplomatic means the likelihood that Britain would become involved in a major war, especially one in which it would face both Germany and Japan. While the Far East was the more immediate danger, the DRC emphasized that Germany was 'the ultimate enemy against whom our "long range" defence policy must be directed'. It recommended a five year rearmament programme that would repair most, but by no means all, of the deficiencies arising out of the neglect inspired by the ten year rule.

The costs involved in the five year programme were enormous:

---

[4]   COS, 'Imperial Defence Policy: Annual Review for 1933', 12 October 1933, CP 264(33), CAB 24/244; Cabinet 62(33)5, 15 November 1933, CAB 23/77.

the capital expenditure would amount to just over £61 millions, with another £10 millions for additional personnel and maintenance. For the Navy, the completion of the Singapore base and the modernization of part of the fleet for operations there would provide a sufficient show of strength to keep Japan under control. The building programme that the Admiralty wanted would cost £67 millions, far beyond anything that the Treasury was prepared to consider within the initial five year period. The RAF was to be brought up to a full fifty-five squadrons, which was merely the figure agreed upon as far back as 1923 but never achieved because of financial restrictions. Anti-aircraft defence, which had been even more neglected, was to be improved with additional searchlights and guns, but the expenditure of £2.23 millions in five years would still leave the Midlands and north of England totally devoid of protection.

The most controversial recommendation of the DRC was that concerning the Army. Even though coastal defences were completely out of date and anti-aircraft measures hopelessly inadequate (London was best protected, and it had less than half the necessary guns, lights and troops), the DRC fixed upon the Army's lack of real ability to send an expeditionary force to the continent as its greatest weakness. The development of air power had reinforced the vital connection between the security of the Low Countries and the security of Britain. If a hostile power could establish bases just across the Channel, not only London but the industrial Midlands and north of England would be exposed to air attack. It was essential that Britain be able to forestall such a threat, and the only means of doing so, the DRC argued, was to have an expeditionary force available for immediate despatch to the continent, so that within one month of the outbreak of war at least four infantry divisions, one cavalry division, one tank brigade, and two air defence brigades could be landed to secure these vital areas. A force of this size was the 'absolute minimum' which could be expected to have 'any hope of operating effectively in conjunction with Allies.' It would also, 'as a deterrent to an aggressor, exercise an influence for peace out of all proportion to its size'. It was a cleverly worded argument, implying that if Britian could demonstrate its ability to send such a force quickly, its deterrent effect might be such that the question of an unlimited liability might never arise.

If reinforcements were required within several months (after which time conscripts would presumably be available), they would have to come from the Territorial Army. The Regular Army had many deficiencies, but the Territorial Army was in a much worse way. Important though the Territorials were, however, to the ability of the Regular Army to maintain an expeditionary force in the field, the needs of the Regular Army had to come first. Until those were satisfied, little could be done for the Territorial Army beyond allocating an annual sum of £250,000 to begin the process of modernization. Eventually though, the DRC warned, large sums would be required to bring the Territorials up to an acceptable level.[5]

The emphasis placed in the DRC report on a continental role for the Army raised fears in the Cabinet that Britain was about to prepare for a repetition of the experiences of 1914 – 18. A military alliance with France would put Britain under French strategic control, and any commitment to the continent would inevitably turn into one of unlimited liability. This was not a prospect that could be contemplated with equanimity. There was widespread feeling in the Cabinet that the DRC proposals rested upon strategic assumptions that had to be scrutinised just as carefully as the recommendations that followed from them. Ironically perhaps, the DRC's recommendations for a rearmament programme were referred to the Ministerial Committee on the Disarmament Conference.[6]

Again, much of the Ministerial Committee's time was taken up with the question of a continental role for the army, described by Chamberlain as a 'fresh and, perhaps a controversial point'. Controversial it certainly became, as Chamberlain and others attacked the Chiefs of Staff's line of reasoning. What guarantee was there, they asked, that a British expeditionary force would be able to land in Europe and secure the Low Countries before a German attack? Even if the Germans did establish bases there, could they not be neutralised by air attacks from Britain? Was it necessarily true that France looked to Britain for a significant land contribution: perhaps it would prefer a larger air commitment or financial help in building fortifications along the Franco-Belgian border? In reply the Chiefs of Staff insisted that German possession of the Low Countries would enable them to increase their initial attacks upon Britain by a full eighty per cent. A threat of that magnitude could not be guarded against by air power alone, nor could France undertake the defence of Belgium without substantial British assistance on land. Military and political imperatives demanded that Britain be able to send an expeditionary force to Europe to fight alongside her continental allies.

[5]   DRC, 'Report', 28 February 1934. CP 64(34), CAB 24/247.
[6]   Cabinet 18(34), 30 April 1934, CAB 23/79.

Assistance on the sea and in the air will always appear to Continental peoples threatened by land invasion to be but indirect assistance. Refusal on our part to provide direct assistance would be interpreted by our allies as equivalent to abandoning them to their fate.

The corollary to this argument was that without the demonstrable willingness and capacity to send an expeditionary force to the continent, Britain might have no allies on whom she could rely to do the fighting on land while she concentrated on the war at sea and in the air.[7]

Chamberlain was not convinced and remained unmoved by the Chiefs of Staff's demands. Others in the Ministerial Committee, however, were not inclined to disagree with the stated case for a continental capability, even if they were not prepared to accept its logical consequences. Once it was apparent that the Ministerial Committee would approve the rationale behind the DRC's proposals for the Army, Chamberlain switched to the financial argument.

The DRC programme, Chamberlain declared, was 'impossible to carry out'. Not only that, but there was a grave imbalance between the sum recommended for the Army, 'which bulks so largely in the total as to give rise to the most alarmist ideas of future intentions or commitments', and that for the Air Force. It proposed to do no more than complete a programme for home defence that had been drawn up more than ten years before, even though public attention was being increasingly focused on the problems of defence against air attack. Chamberlain wanted the allocation reversed. Britain should build up a massive air deterrent, and cut down on the expenditure allocated to the Army. The Ministerial Committee shied away from Chamberlain's proposal to create a deterrent that lacked depth behind its impressive facade, and settled on a compromise that would enable the RAF to establish forty and a half new squadrons while the aircraft industry built new plants that would eventually be able to supply the reserves that were necessary if the deterrent was to have any long-term substance. The Army fared much worse. Chamberlain wanted an overall cut of 30.5 per cent in the expenditure levels recommended by the DRC, and

---

7   DCM(32), 41st meeting, 3 May 1934, CAB 16/110; COS, 'The position of the Low Countries: Summary of Information obtained from the Chiefs of Staff Sub-Committee', Appendix II of CP 205(34), CAB 24/250.

though that was more than the Ministerial Committee was prepared to accept, he had his way on the Army. The DRC's figures of £40 millions, which had been reached by determining what was possible, given the run-down in industrial capacity, rather than of what was actually required (one estimate put the latter figure at an 'impossible' £145 millions over five years[8]), was cut by half, and even then Chamberlain refused to commit himself to maintaining the projected level of expenditure in the future.[9]

The Territorial Army was left with the crumbs. Even the DRC had not seen its way clear to recommending more than £250,000 annually over a five year period, and this was to be cut to a derisory annual sum of £50,000. At the end of five years, the Territorial Army would be virtually without any modern equipment or war reserves, and there was no guarantee that the enormous sums that would be required to bring the Territorial Army up to an acceptable level would be forthcoming. It was a gloomy prospect: little enough money, no modern equipment, and few prospects of getting any, and in all likelihood fewer and fewer citizens willing to volunteer for a second line that might well collapse through sheer government neglect.

Any hopes the Territorials had that the War Office's revival of interest in them, demonstrated by the Army Council's anxiety to have the pledge removed, might lead to greater concessions in the 1934 Army Estimates were disappointed. Apart from a few minor adjustments to grants, the War Office offered the Territorials nothing that might stimulate sagging recruiting. Increasingly the Territorial Army felt that it was being asked not only to devote its spare time to volunteer soldiering, but to pay for the privilege of doing so. Requests for a lowering of the age for marriage allowance were again turned down in the 1934 Estimates, despite the relatively small sum — put at £20,000 in 1935 for its complete abolition[10] — involved. Even that amount was for the moment apparently beyond the means of the War Office, though Commanding Officers around the country bemoaned the loss of young men who could not afford to support their families without a marriage allowance while they went to camp. *The Times* endorsed the

[8] Colonel Henry Pownall (Assistant Secretary, CID), quoted in Bond, *British Military Policy*, p. 199.
[9] Ministerial Committee on Defence Requirements, 'Report', 31 July 1934, CP 205(34), CAB 24/250.
[10] Captain Douglas Hacking (Financial Secretary to the War Office), *Parl. Debs.* (Commons), 5th series, vol. 299, col. 916 (18 March 1935).

Territorial claims for better allowances, both for officers and men, and added in a leader on 16 August 1934:

> The voluntary principle is one deeply rooted in the social structure of the British nation. But the possibility that any man should be financially handicapped as a result of voluntary service in its military forces is one which no self-respecting nation can face with equanimity.

The Parliamentary Territorial Army Committee added its voice to the campaign, pressing the War Office for the reimbursement of travelling expenses to and from drills, better pay for specialists, and the abolition of the age limit for the marriage allowance.[11]

There was nothing new in these pleas, for they had been made ever since the economy cuts of the 1920s. What gave them added weight was the coincidence of the steady decline in recruiting and in the retention of four-year men, the evident lack of interest in a commission shown by potential officers, and the growing importance of the Territorial Army in the long-term plans of the DRC and the Cabinet. The Territorial Army was closely involved in the programme to improve anti-aircraft defence, especially around London. The War Office proposed to man those defences with Territorials converted from other — mainly infantry — units, yet it was precisely in London and the Home Counties that recruiting was weakest. Unlike conversions from cavalry to other arms, which could be spread around the country, anti-aircraft troops had to be raised near their war stations so that they could man the defences at short notice for extended periods. If these men were to be found, concessions had to be made to the Territorials.

They were made in the 1935 Estimates. The War Office announced that at least some progress had been made towards meeting the strongest of the objections that had been voiced over the years. Travel costs to and from drills would be paid at the rate of one shilling for all compulsory drills and for half the voluntary drills that a Territorial attended. NCOs who acted as instructors would be paid up to £1 extra per year, while the bounty for specialists (such as range-finders) would be increased from 30s to £2. Most welcome of all was the decision to widen the eligibility for the marriage allowance. Henceforth NCOs under 26 would receive the allowance when they re-engaged, while men who re-engaged would qualify on their first promotion.[12]

[11] *The Times*, 9 November 1934.
[12] Army Estimates speech by Hacking, *Parl. Debs.* (Commons), 5th series, vol. 299, cols. 850 – 1 (18 March 1935).

This it was hoped would help units retain the best men, those who hitherto had been unable to carry the extra financial burden. The Associations had hoped for a complete abolition of all restrictions, but at least it was an improvement on the old rule. In December 1934 the bounty had been ruled exempt from calculations of unemployment assistance — a practice that had also discouraged recruiting. Now the War Office showed signs of appreciating the Territorial point of view. The CIGS, Sir Archibald Montgomery-Massingberd, admitted as much when he said that he 'felt very strongly that the Territorial Army deserved more encouragement and more sympathy from the country at large . . .. But sympathy was cheap if there was nothing behind it . . .'.[13] Even if the concessions announced in the 1935 Estimates had not gone as far as the Territorials had hoped, they were for the Associations a long-overdue sign that at last the period of economy was over, however slowly the purse strings might be loosened.

Newly sympathetic as it was the to claims of the Territorial Army, the War Office was not reconciled to the greater emphasis on a home defence (i.e. anti-aircraft) role that the Ministerial Committee had projected for the Territorials. The Home Defence Sub-Committee of the CID pointed out in 1935 that the provision of the required 43,500 anti-aircraft men would have to come from converted Territorial units, since with only about 100,000 Regular troops in Britain, it would be 'quite out of the question' to raise that number from the Regular Army. It went on to stress that such a conversion would mean a substantial reduction in the number of Territorial troops earmarked for service with the Expeditionary Force. Montgomery-Massingberd was reluctant to see so many troops diverted to home defence. He told the DRC that two divisions formerly allotted to later contingents of the Expeditionary Force could be converted to provide about 18,000 men, but beyond that the War Office would not go. He insisted that the needs of the Field Force came before those of the anti-aircraft defences of Britain, with the exception of defences around London.[14]

The War Office was not without allies in its fight to retain a continental role for the Army, a role which was based on the assumption that reinforcement contingents would be provided by the Territorial Army. In an interim report the DRC warned that 'without additional expenditure the Field Force will not be able to

[13] Speech at the Royal Academy: *The Times*, 6 May 1935.
[14] 'Memorandum by the Home Defence Sub-Committee', 11 April 1935, COS 375, CAB 53/24; DRC 14th meeting, 19 July 1935, CAB 16/112.

fulfil its responsibilities for many years', and added, 'this is even more true of the Territorial Army for which a less than meagre pittance has been provided'. Sir Robert Vansittart, Permanent Under-Secretary at the Foreign Office, had been one of the strongest supporters of a continental role for the Army when the DRC drew up its first report. When the final draft was being prepared he had objected to the inadequate measures proposed to remedy the deficiencies of the Territorial Army. Now, in 1935, he returned to the charge, and insisted that in the eyes of her allies, Britain's intentions to fulfil her obligations would be gauged by her ability to carry them out. 'In particular', he said, the allies 'would regard money spent on a Territorial Army as being a clear indication that we meant to bring all our defence forces into proper condition'.[15]

The strengthening of the country's armed forces was no longer a matter that could be postponed or prolonged unduly. In 1933 the Cabinet had directed the DRC to submit proposals aimed at repairing the worse deficiencies that had accumulated as a result of the ten year rule. By mid 1935 it was no longer simply a question of making up lost ground. The evident and alarming rearmament programme of Germany, the continuing hostility of Japan, and now the deterioration of relations with Italy over the Abyssinian question impelled the Defence Policy and Requirements Committee to adopt a much more urgent approach. The DRC was told to prepare a programme of rearmament so that by early 1939 each service 'should have advanced its state of readiness to the widest necessary extent in relation to the military needs of national defence and within the limits of practicability'.[16]

The third DRC report, presented in November, again argued the case for a continental role for the Army in fulfilment of Britain's obligations under the Treaty of Locarno and to deny air bases in the Low Countries to a hostile power. This required a Field Force of some four infantry divisions and one cavalry division, with air forces and support troops, all of which could, if possible, be dispatched to the Continent within two weeks of the outbreak of war. This was not significantly different from the original recommendations of the DRC in 1934, but it was no longer considered sufficient. The DRC now proposed that the Territorial Army, as well as undertaking an anti-aircraft defence role at home, should also

[15] 'Programme of the Defence Services: Interim Report by the Defence Requirements Sub-Committee', 24 July 1935, DRC 25, CAB 16/138; DRC 15th meeting, 3 October 1935, CAB 16/112.
[16] DRC, 'Third Report', 21 November 1935, CP 26(36), CAB 24/259.

reinforce the Regular Field Force at intervals of four, six and eight months after the outbreak of war with contingents of four divisions each. To bring the Territorial Army up to the required standard the DRC asked for an expenditure of £26 millions, in addition to the annual £250,000 that had been recommended in 1934 but cut down to £50,000. This would enable the Territorial Army to come near to completing its requirements within five years, whereas within the period envisaged by the DPR — 1936 – 9 — it would reach only about eighty per cent of the level of the Regular Army Field Force.[17]

But although the DRC's reasoning was accepted, the Ministerial Committee was unwilling to face up to the full implications of a continental role for the Army. Without full and effective Territorial reinforcements, there was little point in making plans to equip the Regular Field Force. On the other hand, the Ministerial Committee argued that since a three year period would be insufficient to repair the deficiencies of the Territorial Army and bring it up to the required standard for operations on the continent, there was no reason to push ahead with such a programme. There was simply no need to commit the Army to a policy of continental deployment when the Government did not accept it was unavoidable in the event of war. The Ministerial Committee preferred to postpone a decision on the provision of equipment for the Territorial Army, rejecting the DRC's recommendation for spending £26 millions in favour of an annual £250,000 that would help to improve training and provide some modern equipment without irrevocably tying the Territorials to a continental role. The Cabinet agreed with this approach. It endorsed the DRC programme for improving the Regular Field Force, but decided to do nothing about the Territorial Army for the time being, apart from emphasizing publicly that if the Territorial Army was sent abroad in time of war it would proceed in its own units and would not be used as drafts for the Regular Army.[18]

This, of course, simply avoided the all-important question: if the Territorial Army was not to be made ready for a continental role and if, when required to fight on the continent it would do so in its own units, how was the Regular Field Force to be reinforced? That question had not yet to be answered, because the Cabinet was not yet resigned to a British continental military role. It did agree that the whole question of the Territorial Army could be reconsidered before the end of three years if it became possible to make a start on

[17] *Ibid.*
[18] Cabinet 13(36)2, 2 March 1936, CAB 23/83.

its re-equipment, but that was not — as it seemed at the time — a sign that the Cabinet had accepted the basic DRC premise that the Territorial Army should be modernised and trained to provide the second, third and fourth contingents for the Field Force. Chamberlain in particular had not been convinced by the DRC's reasoning, and for the next three years fought against the automatic assumption that Britain should think in terms of a continental role for her Armies, Regular and Territorial.

Meanwhile, within the War Office, the condition of the Territorial Army was being closely scrutinised. In a report submitted in October 1935, the DGTA, General Sir Charles Bonham Carter, concluded: 'At the present time it is quite clear that the Territorial Army is quite incapable of undertaking its duties.' The single most important factor undermining the efficiency of the Territorials was its declining numbers. Apart from short-lived improvements in 1931 and 1933 as a result of special recruiting campaigns, there had been a continuing decline since 1926. Every year the proportion of officers with war experience fell, and the Territorials were finding it increasingly difficult to attract the right sort of man to take a commission or to serve in the ranks. The reasons were not hard to find: 'The Territorial Army was neglected for 15 years by successive Governments; the men serving know it and so does the mass of the general public. So by the majority of people it is not thought really essential to our plans for defence.' The Territorials felt that their efforts were not appreciated, and 'deeply resented' having to make financial sacrifices on top of giving up their free time. They were apprehensive that under the 1920 terms of enlistment they could be called out for service in circumstances short of a war requiring a national mobilization, and feared that their jobs would be snatched by less patriotic men unless the Government made a public pledge to protect their rights.

On a day-to-day basis, there was a 'very general feeling of resentment among serving officers and members of associations of the War Office', which had all too often been high-handed and unsympathetic in its interpretation of the regulations. As he later wrote to Scarbrough, ' "F" [Finance] deals with papers and cases and forgets men — and the naturally sensitive feelings of a man who is giving service voluntarily to his country.' It was essential that the War Office give in to the 'unanimous and insistent demand' for marriage allowance and that pay be given for extra drills. Eventually there would have to be a full-scale recruiting drive, but until the proposals for the Territorial Army had been finalised, the War Office should concentrate on a public education campaign aimed at raising the esteem in which the Territorial Army was held. The most important change had to come within the War Office and Government, for without their support the public would never respond. He concluded:

> We must avoid pinpricks. Territorial soldiers give so much to the state that the state should treat them with generosity and consideration. Frequently it does not do so now . . . . What they demand is just treatment and a real opportunity to prove themselves fitted to face the tasks allotted to them. If they receive only small concessions which do not seriously tackle their difficulties or remove their sense of injustice, the feeling will remain of neglect, lack of sympathy and unjust treatment, resentment and articulate complaint will continue to grow and in time we shall be forced to spend far more in the face of agitation than the sum which if expended now would bring great results.[19]

The Under-Secretary of State, Lord Stanhope, endorsed the report, adding that the War Office would no longer pursue quality at the expense of quantity, since the fall in numbers seriously impaired training. The 'most immediate' need was for the Territorial Army to be able to fulfil its role as the second line in the Field Force, but before additional burdens could be imposed on the Territorials, the War Office would have to make some substantial concessions, such as granting marriage allowance at twenty-one. A parsimonious attitude now would only compound the problem, just as the 'really very false economy' of cancelling camps in 1931 was still harming recruiting.[20]

Further pressure for more sympathetic treatment came from the GOC of the 47th (2nd London) Division (Territorial Army), Major-General G. C. Liddell. A 'cheese-paring' approach simply disheartened those who were serving, and was directly responsible for the lack of senior officers. Recruiting would never improve, nor would efficiency be increased, until service with the Territorials was made a more attractive prospect. The Government had to overcome the apathy (rather than hostility) of the country, and launch a major campaign to inform the public of the importance of the Territorials. Employers had to be encouraged to cooperate with

[19] DGTA, 'Report on the Territorial Army', October 1935, WO 32/2679.
[20] Stanhope, minute on DGTA Report, 18 October 1935, WO 32/2679.

the War Office and, with their frequently obstructive foremen, won over to the Territorial cause. More than anything else, the Government had to provide the necessary funds to enable Territorial units to offer the military and social facilities that would attract the right sort of men. In the large cities such as London the Territorials had to compete with all the diversions of modern urban life. They were put at an enormous disadvantage in doing so, he wrote, when the 'general character of the majority of [Territorial] premises at present is one of penurious discomfort'. If substantial improvements were made, the recruiting problem could be solved, as was demonstrated by the 56th Divisional Signals, whose numbers tripled to 300 after the drill hall was rebuilt.[21]

Reports by Bonham Carter and Liddell were well received by the military members of the War Office. To a very great extent the efficiency of the Territorial Army was the key to the viability of a continental role for the Field Force, and calls to improve that efficiency added weight to the DRC's proposals concerning the vital role that the Territorial Army played in providing reinforcements for the first contingent of the Field Force. Montgomery-Massingberd agreed that all too often the Territorials had been unsympathetically treated, sloughed off with out of date equipment, and administered by officials preoccupied with the financial implications of decisions to the exclusion of everything else. Until there were real improvements in the lot of the Territorials — modern equipment in sufficient quantity, adequate pay and allowances, more 'human and reasonable' regulations, and above all a firm commitment by Government actions rather than words — he warned that 'We shall get no forwarder and the sooner that is realized the better'. The Territorial Army Advisory Committee produced a string of recommendations, ranging from extra allowances to a restoration of the 2½ per cent cut in Associations' grants and eligibility for old age pensions at sixty. The Master-General of the Ordnance, Sir Hugh Elles, was particularly enthusiastic about the proposals to rewrite the Territorial regulations: 'This is a ghastly book which no one can understand except the author, and I have some doubts whether he does.'[22]

The ultimate target of many of these criticisms, Sir Herbert

---

21 Liddell, 'Organization and Administration of the Territorial Army', 4 November 1935, WO 32/2680.
22 CIGS, minutes, 19 and 29 November 1935; MGO, minute, 25 February 1936: WO 32/2679; Territorial Army Advisory Committee, 3rd meeting, 20 November 1935, WO 32/9700.

Creedy, the Permanent Under-Secretary at the War Office, was stung by what was really an unfair attack. If there had been cases of unfair treatment, that was the fault of the regulations, not their application. Financial considerations did loom large in the War Office view of the Territorial Army: how could they do otherwise, given the severe restraints under which the War Office had laboured since the end of the war? In any case, was it true that the Associations were suffering unduly? At the end of 1934, forty-nine Associations had reported a profit in the previous year, thirty-five had made a loss, and seventy-seven accumulated reserves totalling £497,000. The 2½ per cent cut could be restored for 'psychological reasons', Creedy conceded, 'but it is rather [a] waste of £22,000'.[23]

Creedy was basically right, even if he was defending his own position. The neglect of the Territorial Army since the war had in part derived from financial restraint, but even more from the hostility or indifference of the General Staff which had never accepted the reconstitution of the Territorial Army with anything other than reluctance. Now, in 1935, when the revival of the Territorials was essential to the continental strategy propounded by the War Office and adopted by the DRC, the General Staff suddenly awoke to the fact that the policy of neglect had to be reversed, and quickly. The Cabinet also agreed that the Territorial plight could no longer be ignored, but for quite different reasons. Although it was reluctant to accept fully the implications for the Territorial Army of a continental role for the Regular Field Force, it did appreciate that the Territorial Army was the key to the anti-aircraft defence system in Britain. The improvement and eventual expansion of that system depended in the first instance on bringing the Territorial Army up to establishment.

The first signs of change came in the Army Estimates presented in March 1936. Duff Cooper, now Secretary of State for War, admitted to the House that, 'Frankly we have not encouraged the Territorial Army. In fact I am afraid we have done a great deal to discourage it.' A 'wild demand for economy' in 1922 had led to savage cuts in expenditure on the Territorial Army, which had then suffered from successive reductions. Times had changed, and now the Territorials were so integral a part of the defence scheme that if they collapsed through neglect 'the whole should fall to pieces and we should not have a defence scheme at all'! To prevent that from happening, the War Office and the Government had decided upon a wide range of concessions that would not only put a brake on the

[23] Creedy, minute, 6 November 1935, WO 32/9700.

slide in enlistments but would ensure a significant increase in numbers. The bounty would be restored to its original 1920 figure of £5, made up of a proficiency grant of £3, a weapons training allowance of 10s, and 30s for extra drills. Grants to specialists and instructors would be continued so that a specialist who also instructed could earn £6.10s a year. Travelling money for all drills up to a maximum of fifty per year would be paid. Marriage allowance would be granted to all married Territorials over the age of 21, whether newly enlisted or not, and the camp allowance for officers, which had been set at £1 in 1922, would be raised to £5, so that 'the young officer will not have to pay for the privilege of serving his country'.[24] Together with these concessions to individuals, which were aimed at removing the most strongly-felt grievances, the Government had allotted £250,000 a year to modernise the equipment of the Territorial Army gradually without inhibiting the rearmament of the Regular Army.

Welcome as these measures were, it was doubtful whether they would suffice to stem the decline in recruiting, both in the Regular and the Territorial Armies. The Adjutant-General, Sir Harry Knox, warned that the average intake of the Territorial Army over the previous ten years had been only 66 per cent of the numbers required to reach full peace establishment, and there was no reason to think that voluntary enlistment would ever be able to produce the necessary numbers.[25] Duff Cooper blamed the general mood of the country, and in particular the uncooperative attitude of the Ministry of Labour, which had consistently refused to handle recruiting material at employment exchanges or to suggest the Army to those looking for work.[26] Ernest Brown, the Minister of Labour, rejected this criticism, and rightly pointed to the fact that in a rearmament programme on the scale envisaged by the Government the cooperation of organized labour was absolutely essential. Any hint of conscription, or any actions by the Government that could be interpreted by Labour as a form of pressure to get men to enlist, would produce an uproar in union circles, and the resultant disruption to industry would have far more serious effects than a temporary shortage of men.[27]

24 *Parl. Debs.* (Commons), 5th series, vol. 309, cols. 2357 – 9 (12 March 1936).
25 Knox, memorandum on recruiting, 30 April 1936, WO 32/4246.
26 Duff Cooper, 'Recruiting for the Army', 16 October 1936, CP 322(35), CAB 24/265.
27 Brown, 'Recruiting for the Army and the Ministry of Labour', 30 November 1936, CP 327(35), CAB 24/265.

In any case, as Duff Cooper himself admitted, hostility towards service in the Army had a much wider origin. He tended to put the blame on the pacifist sentiment in the country, and especially on academics, intellectuals and non-conformist churches who preached against militarism and military forces.[28] This was a symptom of a much deeper hostility and fear, a reaction against the horrors of trench warfare on the Western Front and the determination that never again should Britain become involved in such a seemingly futile campaign. But Duff Cooper, as perhaps befitted a man who had written a basically uncritical biography of Field Marshal Earl Haig and his performance in the Great War, was not attuned to these sorts of sentiments. Nor would he have had much sympathy with Liddell Hart's explanation of the decline in Territorial recruiting: one commanding officer had been told by his NCOs, 'What can you expect, the boys now growing up are the sons of the infantry in the last war.'[29]

Nor was Duff Cooper alone in his thinking. The Army's obsession with a continental role was made apparent in the answers it gave to questions put to Baldwin and Sir Thomas Inskip, Minister for Co-ordination of Defence, by a deputation of Conservative MPs and peers. In reply to the criticism that the fear of being dragged into a continental war was the greatest single deterrent to Army recruiting, the War Office simply referred to the arguments that had been put to the DRC in 1934, adding that while it was essential that Britain have a continental capability that did not mean that she was automatically committed to intervene on the continent with military forces. Nevertheless, although it could be argued that Britain's contribution could best be made on the sea and in the air, a national war would require the total mobilisation of the country's man-power. The War Office calculated that once all the needs of the Navy, the RAF and industry had been satisfied, there would remain a 'residuum' of about five million men. Where else could they go other than the Army? The country would demand it. Yet in the short run this huge mass of men would be of no use to the Army, and especially not in reinforcing the first contingent of the Field Force. The Territorials would not be ready for at least four months after the outbreak of war (and that would be possible only if the Cabinet reversed itself and accepted the DRC's re-equipment proposals) and even then the Government had

---

[28] See Duff Cooper's speech reported in *The Times*, 24 March 1936.
[29] Liddell Hart to Deverell, 25 November 1936, quoted in Dennis, *Decision by Default*, p. 78.

promised that they would proceed overseas and where possible serve in their own units. For up to six months, therefore, the Regular Field Force would be without reinforcements, for the Regular and Special Reserves would be unable to satisfy the demand. Neither Inskip nor Baldwin could solve the problem. Inskip merely repeated the Government's pledge to respect the integrity of Territorial units, and Baldwin concluded, 'It is an extraordinarily difficult subject.'[30]

For Duff Cooper, however, the proper course of action was clear. Since Britain could not enter any great war on the basis of limited liability, it was foolish to think that a Field Force of five Regular divisions would be sufficient. The Cabinet itself, the previous February, had accepted in principle that twelve Territorial divisions should be equipped on a scale suitable for first class warfare, and had postponed the implementation of that decision only when it seemed unlikely that substantial progress on the Territorials could be made before the re-equipment of the Regular Army had been completed. That forecast had been unduly pessimistic, and Duff Cooper had been advised that a start could be made on re-equipping the Territorials at the same time as efforts to upgrade the Regular Army. A seventeen division (five Regular and twelve Territorial) Field Force was the *minimum* that Britain could put into the field, and he asked the Cabinet in December to approve his proposals to begin the modernisation of the Territorial Army.[31]

This reopened the whole question of the role of the Army, and especially of the Territorial Army. Although the Cabinet had indeed accepted in principle the modernisation of the Territorials to enable them to provide the second, third and fourth contingents of the Field Force, it had never faced up to the implications of that decision nor embraced with any degree of certainty the notion of a large scale continental role for the British Army. Chamberlain in particular was alarmed by Duff Cooper's request, for despite the latter's assurance that the modernisation of the Territorials could be undertaken without unduly straining the resources of the country, Chamberlain saw it as a threat to the guideline adopted by the Cabinet in March, namely that the rearmament programme should

---

[30] See CAB 21/437, which contains an account of the deputation's meetings and the briefs provided Baldwin by the War Office; also Dennis, *Decision by Default*, pp. 69–75.

[31] Duff Cooper, 'The Role of the British Army', 3 December 1936, CP 326(36); 'The Organization, Armament, and Equipment of the Army', 4 December 1936, CP 325(36), CAB 24/265.

be carried out without interference with social services or with the recovery of business and industry. Already there were signs of strain, and if the Cabinet were to approve Duff Cooper's proposals there was a danger that the whole rearmament scheme might break down.

Furthermore, Chamberlain was not convinced that the modernisation of the Territorial Army for a continental role was by any means the best use of Britain's resources. Some months before he had decided that Britain's most valuable contribution in a future war could be made through powerful naval and air forces rather than by 'building up great armies'. Now, in answer to Duff Cooper, he argued that a policy of limited liability on land (although he did not call it that) was not only the most practicable but also the wisest course open to Britain.[32]

The Cabinet was now confronted with two diametrically opposed view-points. When the Chiefs of Staff were asked to comment on the question of a continental role for the Army, they argued their case along much the same lines as they had to the DRC: while a commitment was to be avoided, the ability to intervene was desirable if not essential. That intervention could be sustained only if there was a substantial number of Territorial divisions — at least twelve — to reinforce the first Regular contingent of the Field Force. Since the Territorial Army had to be able to support the Regular Army anywhere in the world, whether in imperial theatres or on the continent, it had to be provided with the same equipment as the Regular Army. If industrial capacity was not sufficient to complete that in the short term, what equipment there was had to be spread throughout the twelve divisions for training purposes, and efforts made to increase industrial output so that the deficiency could be repaired as quickly as possible. The Minister for Co-ordination of Defence, Sir Thomas Inskip, accepted the basic argument of the Chiefs of Staff, but he recommended to Cabinet that the provision of equipment to the Territorial Army be on a scale such that in an emergency it could be pooled to equip fully one or two divisions for intervention in a major European war.[33] This was a significant departure from the proposals of both the Chiefs of Staff and Duff Cooper, all of whom had talked in terms of a second

---

[32] Chamberlain, 'The Role of the British Army', 11 December 1936, CP 334(36), CAB 24/265.

[33] COS, 'The Role of the British Army', 28 January 1937, CP 41(37), CAB 24/267; Inskip, 'The Role of the Army', 2 February 1937, CP 46(37), CAB 24/268.

contingent of four Territorial divisions, within four months of the outbreak of war, followed by third and fourth contingents of th same size.

The Cabinet was quite prepared to approve expenditure for the equipment of the Regular Army and the two Territorial anti-aircraft divisions (£208 millions) and for the provision of training equipment for the rest of the Territorial Army (£9.25 millions), but it baulked at Duff Cooper's additional request that it should also approve the sum of £43.5 millions to provide full equipment for a Territorial Field Force contingent of four divisions, and that the necessary steps should be taken to ensure there would be sufficient industrial capacity to enable the remaining eight Territorial divisions to be dispatched overseas within eight months of the outbreak of war. The objections to this proposal were mainly voiced by Chamberlain, who again argued that on both financial and military grounds it would be unwise to adopt a course aimed at developing a full scale continental capability. He rejected the so-called 'expert' advice as being self-interested and narrowly based, and suggested that Britain's inability to maintain a large Army as well as a powerful Navy and Air Force was counter-balanced by the need of her continental allies to maintain huge land forces. Chamberlain's resistance was strong enough to persuade the Cabinet to withhold its approval of Duff Cooper's proposals to equip the twelve Territorial divisions on a scale suitable for continental warfare. Instead it called for yet another review of the role of the Territorial Army, this time by the Defence Plans (Policy) committee of the Cabinet.[34] Duff Cooper interpreted this as a failure to agree upon a policy for the Army, but it was a major victory for Chamberlain. The Cabinet's unwillingness to endorse Duff Cooper's Territorial package and to override the Chancellor's objections left Chamberlain in a strong position. Without the Territorial programme the continental role proposed by the DRC and implicitly (though reluctantly) accepted by the Cabinet made little sense. If that was not entirely clear to all the Cabinet, Chamberlain understood the position well. He had firm ideas about the Army, Regular and Territorial, and when in May 1937 he succeeded Baldwin as Prime Minister he was able to bring the Cabinet around to accepting a policy of limited liability, with all that it involved for the Territorial Army.

---

[34] Cabinet 20(37)4, 5 May 1937, CAB 23/88.

10

Limited Liability

When he became Prime Minister in May 1937 Chamberlain pressed even more strongly for the adoption of a limited liability role for the Army. Increasingly the Territorial Army became the key to the overall role of the Army, and of its ability to carry out that role. Under Sir John Simon as Chancellor of the Exchequer, the financial argument continued to hold sway, the more so since the growing demands of all the services threatened to undermine the all-important 'staying power' of the country. Chamberlain was determined to have his way on the matter of army policy. Duff Cooper, who had argued vigorously for a continental military strategy, went to the Admiralty for his efforts in resisting Chamberlain's limited liability proposal.[1] In his place as Secretary of State for War, Chamberlain appointed Leslie Hore-Belisha, formerly the Minister of Transport. He told Hore-Belisha that he wanted to see 'drastic changes', adding that 'the obstinacy of some of the Army heads in sticking to obsolete methods is incredible'. He might well have added 'and obsolete policies':[2] it was these that Chamberlain was determined to reverse.

The choice of Hore-Belisha was an inspired one, and was largely greeted as such in the press. His period at the Transport Ministry had shown that he was a man who got things done, even at the expense of appearing unorthodox and sensational. Hore-Belisha had a keen sense of the value and power of publicity and propaganda, and exploited his connections with the press to the full. His

---

[1] Chamberlain's attitude to Duff Cooper was a curious one. He was clearly irked by Duff Cooper's support of a continental role for the Army, yet at the same time he felt that he had been 'lazy' in presenting the Army's case. See Bond, *British Military Policy*, p. 242. Shay (*British Rearmament in the Thirties*, p. 158) suggests that Duff Cooper's promotion to the senior service ministry was an attempt to muzzle his criticism by keeping him within the Cabinet.

[2] Quoted in B. H. Liddell Hart, *Memoirs* (London, 1966), II, p. 2.

receptiveness to new ideas, whatever their source, his enthusiasm, energy, and obvious enjoyment in tackling new problems brought him widespread admiration and praise. It also, as perhaps is inevitable in the case of such success, aroused considerable unease and ill-feeling, even hatred. Popular as they were in the country at large, his methods were considered by many in public life to be vulgar and demeaning, his passion for publicity to be an unwholesome attachment to personal advancement, and his appreciation of his own talents and the talents of others to be laughable if not dangerous on the one hand and insensitive and uncharitable on the other.

Two comments illustrate the hostile views of some of those who worked with Hore-Belisha. In February 1938, Colonel Henry Pownall, Director of Military Operations and Intelligence at the War Office, recorded in his diary:

> He has an amazing conceit, thinking himself in the direct line of descent with Cardwell and Haldane in matters of Army organization. He knows nothing about it . . . and he doesn't seem to listen and he will not read what is put before him. Impossible to educate, thinking he knows when he doesn't know, subject to a lot of improper outside influence [especially from Liddell Hart, who became his unofficial adviser], ambitious, an advertiser and self-seeker — what can we do with him?[3]

Shortly after the war broke out, Derby wrote to Creedy:

> Everyone tells me that the team in the War Office is working extraordinarily well. I rather gather that the only fly in the ointment is the Secretary of State himself, who seems to vie with Greta Garbo in his desire to be photographed in all sorts of positions and in all sorts of characters.[4]

In 1937 however, even among those who looked with some apprehension on Hore-Belisha's appointment, there was a hope that somehow he might be able to pull the Army out of the neglect in which it had languished for so long as the 'Cinderella of the Services'. Major-General Sir Edmund Ironside, GOC-in-C, Eastern

---

[3] Brian Bond (ed.), *Chief of Staff: The Diaries of Lieutenant-General Sir Henry Pownall* (London, 1972), I, p. 136.
[4] Derby to Creedy, 6 October 1939, Derby Papers, Correspondence with Individuals: War Office 1939 – 1944.

Command, bemoaned the indecision over the role of the Army, and after discussing the problem with the CIGS in May wrote in his diary: 'Once again I came home profoundly sad at the state to which the Army has been brought.' Shortly afterwards he added:

> I cannot say what Hore-Belisha will do or what I think of it. He is 41 and full of energy . . . . We are at our lowest ebb in the Army and the Jew may resuscitate us.[5]

But even the energies of a Hore-Belisha could not reverse the trend of military policy, and in any case he was far from being the captive of the continental mentality that permeated the War Office. He did do much to improve recruiting, and fought vigorously for the Army, but he was increasingly at odds with his military advisers over fundamental issues.

Early in 1937, while still Chancellor of the Exchequer, Chamberlain had initiated a detailed study of the cost of Britain's military needs. Simon continued this review until the middle of 1937, and while it was under way rejected any proposals by the services for piecemeal financial commitments. Thus Hore-Belisha's request in July 1937 that the War Office be authorised to proceed with equipping the four Territorial divisions that would make up the second contingent of the Field Force was turned down. When the War Office submitted its forecast to the Treasury in August, it included the cost of providing the Territorial Army with the same equipment as the Regular Army to enable the former to train in peacetime at the same level as the Regulars, but it made no provision for war equipment and reserves for the second Field Force contingent of four Territorial divisions, let alone the Territorial divisions of the third and fourth contingents. If those costs had been included the War Office estimate would have been increased by an extra £100 millions on top of the base figure of £467.5 millions.[6]

These sums and the strain they threatened to put on Britain's financial stability underlined the need to reach a firm decision on the role of the Army and a clear and accepted order of priorities. The Cabinet's reluctance to endorse a continental strategy was reinforced by growing anxiety over the inadequate nature of Britain's

---

5   Roderick Macleod and Denis Kelly (eds.), *Time Unguarded: The Ironside Diaries 1937 – 1940* (New York, 1962), pp. 213, diary entries, 13 and 23 May 1937.

6   Gibbs, *Grand Strategy*, I, p. 465; R. J. Minney, *The Private Papers of Hore-Belisha* (London, 1960), p. 35.

defences against attacks from the air. Those defences had originally been planned to provide protection against attacks from France, i.e. to defend London and the southeast of England. The rise of Germany as the greatest threat to Britain in the 1930s exposed the Midlands and the north to enemy bombardment, and made the provision of air defences a matter of considerable urgency.

It was a complex question, one that involved difficult choices between priorities. The basic responsibility for AA ground defence had been given to the Territorial Army in 1923, but the Territorial Air Defence Brigades had found it difficult to attract recruits. By 1935 Territorial AA units had less than half their peace establishment, despite the attention that was increasingly focused on the dangers of air attack. The War Office was unwilling to convert more than two of the fourteen Territorial infantry divisions to AA duties; it would go no further on the grounds that the second, third and fourth contingents of the Field Force would be unable to reinforce the Regular Field Force if stripped of troops. In any case almost all the Territorial divisions were well below their peace establishments, so that even if the War Office had been willing to switch more divisions to anti-aircraft roles, there were simply not the troops to effect the change, except on paper. For the War Office, of course, the continental capability came first, an order of priorities it defended by arguing that unless the Low Countries were prevented from falling into enemy hands the German potential for bombing Britain would be increased by 80 per cent.

It was generally accepted, however, that a declaration of war by Germany would be followed by an immediate heavy air offensive against Britain, from whatever bases Germany possessed, and, as Colonel Hastings Ismay, Assistant Secretary of the CID, pointed out, the denial of air bases in the Low Countries to Germany was only a means to the vital end, the security of Britain. Ismay was critical of the War Office's persistent concentration on the Field Force to the detriment of the AA defences of Britain, which it regarded, he claimed, as being of only 'secondary importance'. He went on to draw attention to another weakness in the War Office's approach to the provision of AA defences. If the Field Force was dispatched overseas as the War Office planned, the only Regular AA troops (the two Regular Air Defence Brigades) would go with it, leaving Britain entirely denuded of full-time anti-aircraft specialists. Just as many of Haldane's critics had charged that the Territorials would be unable to master the skills of gunnery, so Ismay was sceptical of the Territorial AA units' ability to provide the necessary protection, especially in the opening stages of a war (even assuming that their units could by then have been brought up to full strength). Furthermore, total reliance on Territorial units left a critical gap in the country's defences. If it was accepted that an air attack would be launched immediately after the declaration of war, the air defences had to be working at full efficiency when war broke out. 'It is unlikely', wrote Ismay, 'that those parts of the system which are to be manned by Territorials will be able to fulfil this condition.' Hankey supported Ismay's conclusions, but left it to Inskip to raise the matter, fearing that if Ismay's paper was circulated as written the CID would be drawn into an open confrontation with the War Office.[7]

Through the winter of 1936 and 1937 an intensive study was made of Britain's air defence requirements. The 'ideal' scheme that evolved projected an increase of almost 100 per cent in the number of anti-aircraft batteries and searchlight companies (as well as substantial increases in the strength of the RAF). These provisions were not considered to be excessive by the CID, but their implications in terms of manpower and equipment were far-reaching. No real progress towards meeting the 'ideal' requirements could be made unless top priority was given to anti-aircraft production, which a Ministerial meeting chaired by Chamberlain decided on in November 1937.[8]

Hore-Belisha too was gradually distancing himself from the General Staff's insistence on a continental strategy. He had attended the French military manoeuvres in September and came away convinced that the French had sufficient land forces both to man the Maginot Line and to have a reserve army for field operations without having to rely on a large British Field Force. Chamberlain pressed him to read Liddell Hart's chapter on 'The Role of the British Army' in his book, *Europe in Arms*, in which Liddell Hart wrote that 'the balance seems to be heavily against the hope that a British field force might have a military effect commensurate with the expense and the risk.' After studying the book, Hore-Belisha told Chamberlain that he was 'impressed' by Liddell Hart's theories. He saw in Liddell Hart the willingness to question orthodox positions that was so lacking in the senior advisers who surrounded him at the War Office, obsessed as they were with the continental strategy. At the end of November he again wrote to Chamberlain:

[7] Ismay, 'Home Defence: Part II — The Present Situation as Regards Air Defence', 17 September 1936; Hankey to Inskip, 21 September 1936: CAB 21/622.
[8] Gibbs, *Grand Strategy*, I, pp. 466 – 7.

My view, after the fullest survey, including a visit to France, is that our Army should be organised to defend this country and the Empire, that to organise it with a military prepossession in favour of a Continental commitment, is wrong. The C.I.G.S., although he may overtly accept this view, does not accept it in fact or practice, and he has told me that he is unable to advise any modification in our organization.

The CIGS and the Adjutant-General had consistently opposed Hore-Belisha's proposals and innovations since he became Secretary of State for War. Now that he had decided on a fundamental shift in military policy, Deverell and Knox had to go. On 1 December their resignations were requested. In their place Hore-Belisha appointed two men he hoped would be more receptive to change, Lord Gort as CIGS and Major-General G. C. Liddell as Adjutant-General.[9]

He had made several other changes in October. He announced that in view of the growing responsibilities of the Territorial Army, the DGTA would be made a member of the Army Council, thus satisfying a long-standing request by many of the Territorial Associations. Secondly he created the post of Deputy DGTA, and laid down that it should be held by a Territorial Officer. Colonel Sir John Brown, who had formerly commanded the 162nd (East Midland) Infantry Brigade (TA), was appointed. Another Territorial, Colonel C. F. Liardet, was given command of a Territorial division. This at last fulfilled the promise made by Haldane which had been blocked by the military members of the War Office on the grounds that such a policy would deprive Regular officers of commands and that no Territorials could be found who had the confidence of the Territorial Army as a whole. Hore-Belisha also appointed a Territorial, Lieut.-Colonel J. K. Dunlop, to be the Assistant Adjutant-General of the Territorial Army, in the hope that the Territorials would feel more sympathetically represented at the War Office.[10]

The indecision and uncertainty over the role of the Army, and especially of the Territorial Army, was finally ended in December. The demands of the services were so great, Inskip told the Cabinet, that a strict order of priorities had to be established. What had emerged most clearly from the recent studies had been the

[9] Minney, *Private Papers of Hore-Belisha*, pp. 54–76 *passim*.
[10] *The Times*, 21 October 1937.

paramount importance of the defence of Britain itself, particularly against the ever-growing threat of air attack. All other needs had to be subordinated to the maintenance of the security of Britain, the metropolitan centre of the Empire. The 'ideal' scheme of anti-aircraft defence was no more than an acceptable level, and Inskip recommended that the Cabinet approve an extension of the scheme as soon as practicable. In general, the rearmament programme had to be based on four main requirements: the security of Britain (including its productive capacity and economic prosperity); the defence of imperial communications; the protection of the Empire; and lastly, and only after the first three requirements had been met, 'co-operation in the defence of the territories of any allies Britain might have in war'. Both internal and external factors justified the relegation of the continental hypothesis to the fourth priority. The heavy burdens placed on British industry and man-power by the demands of an accelerated and expanded anti-aircraft programme, on top of the costs of maintaining a large navy and air force, threatened to overwhelm the British economy and weaken the country's 'staying power'. Externally there was evidence (not least from Hore-Belisha) that France no longer relied on Britain for massive land assistance, which in any event Britain would be hard put to give, for the provision of garrisons for the Empire would absorb a large proportion of her forces. Germany had guaranteed the integrity of Belgium, and Inskip felt that it was probably in her best interest to uphold that pledge. Logical as the limited liability policy might thus seem to be, Inskip nevertheless added:

> I must, however, warn my colleagues of the possible conse-quences of this proposal in order that they may share my responsibilities for the decision to be taken with their eyes open. Notwithstanding recent developments in mechanised warfare on land and in the air, there is no sign of the displacement of infantry. If France were again to be in danger of being overrun by land armies, a situation might arise when, as in the last war, we had to improvise an army to assist her. Should this happen, the Government of the day would most certainly be criticised for having neglected to provide against so obvious a contingency.[11]

For the Territorial Army the proposed policy involved

[11] 'Defence Expenditure in Future Years: Interim Report by the Minister for Co-ordination of Defence', 15 December 1937, CP 316(37), CAB 24/ 273.

considerable changes. Inskip recommended that in place of the three Territorial contingents earmarked for the Field Force, three or four divisions should be converted to anti-aircraft duties, while others should be used to maintain civil order and essential services which might otherwise collapse during air attacks. The remainder of the Territorial Army should be available to proceed overseas as soon as possible after the outbreak of war to assist the Regular Army in defending the Empire.

Inskip's case was clearly strengthened by Hore-Belisha's agreement. He told the Cabinet that he had no doubts at all that it was completely correct to give the continental role the lowest priority. The French had sufficient troops for a large field army, and if they were told that they could not count on a British land commitment, they would be persuaded of the need to complete the Maginot Line along the Franco-Belgian border. Together with Chamberlain and Simon, he saw in the new order of priorities a means of saving considerable sums in the Army Estimates and, more important, of concentrating available resources more effectively on repairing the appalling deficiencies in the system of anti-aircraft defence (which the new commander of the 1st AA Division (Territorial Army) had described as a 'fool's paradise').[12]

The only serious reservations were voiced by Anthony Eden, the Secretary of State for Foreign Affairs, who admitted that on balance Inskip's arguments were irresistible, although he had 'some apprehensions' over the defensive posture that Britain was apparently adopting. If the Channel ports were captured by German forces, France would be gravely threatened: how then could Britain refrain from sending land forces to the continent? If it was decided in advance that Britain should limit its commitment to a force of two divisions, then staff talks should be held with the French to inform them of this new turn in British policy and to enable the allies to plan a joint defence.

Inskip's recommendations were accepted by the Cabinet. The continental role was subordinated to the needs of home and imperial defence, with additional Territorial divisions being converted to an anti-aircraft role or possibly used to maintain order if air attacks caused a breakdown of public order in beleaguered cities.[13] Two months later, in February, Inskip laid before the

---

[12] Cabinet 49(37), 22 December 1937, CAB 23/90A; Major-General T. A. Pile, 'Anti-Aircraft Defence of London', 13 December 1937, CAB 21/622.

[13] Cabinet 49(37), CAB 23/90A.

Cabinet the details of Army expenditure based upon the new order of priorities. The Field Force was now to be organised on the assumption that it would operate in an 'eastern' theatre, probably for the defence of Egypt, a reorientation that would enable its cost to be reduced by £14 millions, even after provision had been made for additional mechanical transport. These savings, however, were to be more than offset by the increased cost of the expanded anti-aircraft scheme, which would add almost 20 per cent to the total Army budget for the five year period.[14]

The policy of limited liability marked a sharp break from the strategic assumptions that had been the basis of the original DRC report and from the Cabinet's acceptance, albeit a reluctant one, of those general assumptions. In the years since the DRC had first spoken strongly in support of a continental role for the Army, for both military and political reasons, there had been a telling shift in the balance of opinion. The unanimity of the DRC recommendations did nothing to resolve deep differences between the three services, whose strategic views increasingly diverged during the mid-1930s, and whose relations were marked by mounting rivalry over access to the limited funds for rearmament. By 1937 unanimity no longer existed. Given that in 1934 the Government had taken the decision to begin a programme of rearmament, the services should have presented a united front to the Government but this had given way to competition for a greater share of the nation's resources within the ceiling imposed by the Treasury.

Secondly, in explaining why the continental hypothesis was so readily dropped in 1937, its original supporters must be recalled. They included, on the DRC itself, the three main non-service members — Vansittart, Fisher and Hankey. Once Chamberlain became Prime Minister, Vansittart, with his uncompromising anti-German and pro-French attitude, began to be pushed out. By the end of 1937 his days were already numbered, and several months later he was shunted off into the ineffective post of Chief Diplomatic Adviser. By 1936 Fisher had concluded that air defence had to have absolute priority, and senior officials within the Treasury were concerned lest piecemeal additions to the rearmament programme lead to a situation in which 'money and effort would be wasted in building isolated parts of a structure planned

[14] Inskip, 'Defence Expenditure in Future Year: Further Report by the Minister for Co-ordination of Defence', 8 February 1938, CP 24(38), CAB 24/274.

on so gigantic a scale that it could not be completed', and which, in the process, might destroy the all-important staying power of the country in time of war.[15] Most critical of all, perhaps, was the defection of Hankey, who had become Inskip's closest adviser. Hankey had been one of the strongest supporters of a continental capability for both military and political reasons, but faced with the apparently incontrovertible evidence from the Treasury that financial disaster stared Britain in the face unless the Government made some tough choices between the claims of the various services, he changed his position and pressed for the scrapping of a continental role for the Regular Army and the abandonment of the plan to use the Territorial Army as reinforcements in Europe.[16]

Lastly, Chamberlain, whose opposition to the continental role envisaged by the DRC had been made clear from the beginning, was in a position of great strength. He had the backing of the Treasury, he increasingly dominated foreign policy, he was supported by the chairman of the Chiefs of Staff (the First Sea Lord, Admiral Sir Ernle Chatfield), and his appointee to the War Office, Hore-Belisha, had himself been persuaded to oppose the continental hypothesis espoused by the Army. The result was that, as one historian has written, 'by the time Inskip's momentous reappraisal of defence priorities came before the Cabinet on 22 December 1937 the Army's European role had virtually no supporters'.[17]

When Hore-Belisha told the Cabinet of the new priorities for the organization of the Army, he stressed that Britain's allies 'should be left in no doubt of the possibilities of direct assistance on our part'. No one criticized the severely restricted role that was posited for the Army: on the contrary, there was some feeling that even the mention of an 'eastern' theatre was undesirably specific. The Cabinet decided that such a reference might complicate negotiations with Italy, whose neutrality was highly desirable as the threat from Germany increased, and instead substituted the term 'for general purposes'.[18]

Under the new proposals the greater part of the Territorial Army, that is those divisions not converted to anti-aircraft duties,

---

[15] Peden, *British Rearmament and the Treasury 1932–9*, p. 127.

[16] *Ibid.*, p. 138.

[17] Bond, *British Military Policy*, p. 257.

[18] Hore-Belisha, 'The Organization of the Army for its Role in War', 10 February 1938, CP 26(38), CAB 24/274; Cabinet 5(38), 16 February 1938, CAB 23/92.

would not be able to reinforce the Field Force until at least eight or ten months after the outbreak of war. With this delay in mind, and in view of the reduced priority for continental ventures, it was suggested to Hore-Belisha that there was no reason to maintain so many Territorial units, especially when the question of costs played such an important part in defence policy. Hore-Belisha agreed but added that 'unfortunately public sentiment' would react unfavourably to any move to reduce the country's small armed forces. There was the added (but unvoiced) consideration that at a time when there was growing concern over the state of Territorial recruiting, upon which the success of the anti-aircraft defence scheme depended, there would undoubtedly be an outcry over Territorial reductions, even if it was infantry or cavalry units that were disbanded.

Desirable as it was to switch more units to an anti-aircraft role, which would have been more in line with the new order of Army priorities laid down by the Cabinet, Hore-Belisha argued that by not converting a third Territorial division, he had been able to make substantial savings.[19] Anti-aircraft defence was important, but it was not to be pursued at the expense of financial stability which, as Chamberlain told the Commons when introducing a White Paper on Defence in March, 'is recognized to be a powerful deterrent against attack'.[20] Hore-Belisha made much the same point when explaining the new limited liability policy in his Army Estimates speech: 'It must be remembered that support on land is not the only support we can offer.'[21]

Although the Cabinet had readily accepted the policy of limited liability it had never completely faced up to the possibility that it might still become necessary to send land forces to the continent. Inskip had warned his colleagues of the implications of a grave threat to France which the French Army was unable to resist, but nothing was done to provide reinforcements on a realistic timetable for the small Field Force that was henceforth relegated to the lowest of the Army's priorities. Yet so long as there was a possiblity that a British Field Force might be dispatched to the continent, there had to be some provision made to reinforce it. Whatever the Cabinet said, a strict policy of limited liability simply could not be followed once the first contingent of the Field Force had landed. Gort for one was convinced that if war broke out in 1938 or 1939 Britain would

[19] Cabinet 5(38), CAB 23/92.
[20] *Parl. Debs.* (Commons), 5th series, vol. 332, col. 1561 (7 March 1938).
[21] *Ibid.*, col. 2138 (10 March 1938).

have no choice but to create a large army as it had in 1914: this was the justification, he told Hankey, for what appeared to be the attempt by the War Office to go back on policies previously accepted by the Cabinet.[22] Gort was not alone. Ismay, who had earlier criticised the War Office for promoting the needs of the Field Force to the detriment of the anti-aircraft defences in Britain, felt by the end of 1937 that the pendulum had swung too far and that the Field Force had been unduly neglected. He wrote to Hankey: 'It is impossible to wage national war on a principle of limited liability', and Hankey, after listening to Gort's arguments, agreed.[23]

In his Army Estimates speech on 10 March, Hore-Belisha had argued that 'the assumptions of an unforgettable past are not always the surest guide to an unpredictable future'.[24] Two days later German troops cross the Austrian border and Austria was absorbed into Hitler's Third Reich. Chamberlain was moved to write that 'force is the only argument that Germany understands', and that only 'collective security' backed by 'a visible force of overwhelming strength . . . [and the] determination to use it' would deter Hitler from further aggressive ventures.[25] That show of force, however, added up to very little. The Cabinet decided that 'non-interference with trade' should be dropped as the basis of the rearmament programme, but ruled out any compulsion or government dictation to industry.[26]

The Anschluss crisis occurred while the Cabinet and CID were discussing Hore-Belisha's paper on the role of the Army. Hore-Belisha had accepted the priorities laid down by the Cabinet, namely that anti-aircraft defence in Britain came first and that continental commitments came last. But he asked that two points be borne in mind. The first was that with limited industrial capacity, all stages of the 'ideal' anti-aircraft scheme could not be completed without straining and ultimately distorting the entire rearmament programme. Secondly he argued that the scheme could only be completed at the expense of providing new artillery for the Field Army. Only five days before, he had told the CID that a mere seven out of the required 352 3.7-inch guns for the ADGB scheme had been delivered, although they had been ordered almost a year

---

[22] Hankey to Inskip, 7 March 1938, CAB 21/510.
[23] Ismay to Hankey, 1 December 1937, CAB 21/510.
[24] *Parl. Debs.* (Commons), 5th series, vol. 332, col. 2138.
[25] Keith Feiling, *The Life of Neville Chamberlain* (London, 1946), p. 342.
[26] Cabinet 16(38), 22 March 1938, CAB 23/93. See also Chamberlain's comments in *Parl. Debs.* (Commons), 5th series, vol. 333, cols. 1410–11 (24 March 1938).

earlier.[27] Even though the CIGS had warned that without the new field guns 'it would be murder' to send the Field Force overseas against a first class enemy (which included the Italians in North Africa), the Cabinet was more concerned about the alarming deficiencies in the anti-aircraft programme. Not surprisingly Hore-Belisha's plea for a diversion of artillery towards fulfilling the needs of the Field Force was held to be a blatant departure from the recently accepted order of priorities. Nevertheless, while rejecting the War Office proposals as they stood, the Cabinet agreed that once the immediate needs of the ADGB scheme had been met, any new capacity for producing guns could be diverted to the re-equipment of the Field Force. However, the CID and the Cabinet also reinforced the limited liability role of the Army by deciding that the second (Regular) and third (Territorial) contingents of the Field Force were to be equipped with only half the scale of war reserves and ammunition.[28]

Financial considerations continued to dominate discussions on defence. Much of the burden for additional cuts fell on the Army, but this time not only the Field Force suffered. In April the Cabinet accepted Hore-Belisha's suggestions for saving some £70 millions over a five year period. No provision would be made for war reserves or equipment for the Territorial Army, which previously had been designated as the third and subsequent contingents of the Field Force. Now it would be at least a year after the outbreak of war before any divisions of the Territorial Army could reinforce the first and second Regular contingents of the Field Force. At a time when the War Office was appealing for recruits for the Territorials, this was unlikely to commend enlistment to those holding back until they could be sure that their services were needed. Hore-Belisha proposed to side-step that problem by simply keeping the new policy secret, at least for the time being. Secondly, the number of guns for the ADGB scheme would be reduced from the level envisaged under the 'ideal' scheme of 1937, and of these a greater proportion would be of the obsolescent 3-inch variety. Again, when greater public emphasis was being placed on the anti-aircraft programme, the proposed cut-back in the provision of equipment, both in its quality and quantity, was hardly evidence to the man in the street that the Government was serious about the threat from the air.[29]

[27] Cabinet 16(38), 22 March 1938, CAB 23/93.
[28] CID, 313th meeting, 17 March 1938, CAB 2/7.
[29] Inskip, 'Defence Expenditure in Future Years — the War Office Programme. Further Report by the Minister for Co-ordination of Defence', 22 April 1938, CP 99(38), CAB 24/276; Cabinet 21(38), 27 April 1938, CAB 23/93.

The competing claims of the services and the need to balance short-term threats against long-term prospects were studied carefully by the Cabinet. Its decision was not an easy one to reach. 'But', as the official historian writes, 'whatever the criticism and dissatisfaction, one thing is clear. The further limitations on the performance of the Army were accepted by the Cabinet and they were accepted mainly for financial reasons.'[30]

The decisions taken in 1937 and the first half of 1938 had a profound effect on the Territorial Army. The virtual abandonment of the continental hypothesis and indeed the swingeing attack on the ability of the Territorial Army to operate in any overseas role during the first year of war, and the slowing down in the provision of equipment for the anti-aircraft units left the War Office in an awkward position. Hore-Belisha had admitted to the Cabinet that under the new order of military priorities there was no military justification for maintaining twelve Territorial divisions. Public opinion, however, would demand not only their retention but their expansion. The concessions announced in the Army Estimates in 1937 and 1938, coupled with an official drive for recruits, had resulted in an enormous influx of men. Many units were all but swamped, their training and social accommodation and scanty equipment hopelessly inadequate after years of neglect. Gripped by a sense of urgency, which the Government's own appeals had helped to instil, the new recruits often showed an enthusiasm for training that was positively embarrassing. Many of them, wrote the DGTA with an almost audible sigh, 'want to drill 4 or 5 nights a week, a condition which the scale of training equipment never contemplated'.[31]

The new men were also, especially in London and the home counties, of a markedly different sort than had usually enlisted in the Territorial Army. Whereas in the late 1920s and the 1930s, the Territorials had drawn their strength from the working classes, and particularly from the unemployed, the majority of those who enlisted in anti-aircraft units were from the middle, and often professional classes. City firms, Old Boys' Associations, and Government departments formed anti-aircraft batteries at a rate that threatened to overwhelm industry's limited capacity to provide even minimal training equipment.

After years of living in what seemed to be a state of almost

---

[30] Gibbs, *Grand Strategy*, I, p. 482.
[31] DGTA to DCIGS, 31 May 1938, WO 32/4610.

permanent financial stringency, with little more than lip-service support from the Government and apathy from the public, the Territorial Army had learned to survive and to adapt itself to its meagre circumstances. It was ill-prepared to cope with the sudden change in its fortunes in 1938. A hand-to-mouth existence during the late 1920s and 1930s had instilled in the Territorials an appreciation of the need to widen their appeal beyond their purely military activities. Sports programmes and a busy social life, topped off by the annual camp — at the seaside if possible — were the Territorial Army's answer to the competitive attractions of civilian leisure. Not for nothing were they called 'Saturday night soldiers', even if they never met with the public ridicule that had been the lot of the nineteenth century Volunteers. Interest — and attendance — was often kept up by stressing the social side of unit life at the expense of hard military training. The War Office's inability to meet the constant demands for better social facilities was often as much a source of grievance as its failure to supply modern equipment. Sometimes it was even more so. In 1937 the Commanding Officer of the 32nd (7th City of London) AA Battalion complained that the new equipment his unit had just received as part of the ADGB modernisation and expansion programme took up too much space and interfered with dances and other social activities.[32]

Recruiting, especially for anti-aircraft units around London, picked up in 1937, and surged ahead after the Anschluss in March 1938. It was not long before the strains between the 'old' Territorial Army and the new class of recruits began to show. In June the War Office circulated to all Commands a memorandum submitted by a group of men who had enlisted in an anti-aircraft unit in March, and who were, in their own words, 'dissatisfied and (as citizens) alarmed' by the level of instruction they had received. In sending out their trenchant criticisms, the War Office added that the Army Council 'had reason to believe' they were 'not exaggerated'.[33] The picture they painted was a gloomy one. 'The original keenness of recruits which caused them to enlist', they wrote, 'to persuade their friends to enlist and to sacrifice a considerable amount of time each week to regular parades, is fast evaporating as a result of their feeling that most of their time is merely being wasted . . ..' Too much

---

[32] Territorial Army Advisory Committee, 9th meeting, 23 September 1937, WO 32/9700.

[33] War Office to all English and Scottish Commands, enclosing 'Memorandum on the Territorial Army' (n.d.), 24 June 1938, WO 32/4610.

time was taken up in 'barely relevant' activities such as calling roll, making social announcements, and falling in, so that after four years, a Territorial would have spent less than forty hours out of a minimum of 100 in actual training and instruction. What instruction was given was incompetent:

> The instructors, almost without exception, lack general intelligence; they have learnt their lesson parrot-fashion and can only teach in that fashion; they cannot answer questions which are not 'in the drill book', and finally their method and speed of instruction is entirely ill-suited to their audience. They take in fact an hour to teach what their hearers can all grasp in five minutes.

This was the result, the writers suggested, of the system of training having been devised 'to suit the stupidest class of recruit, e.g. the rural ploughman': it was entirely inappropriate to the general level of recruits, and especially to the 'intelligence of City recruits'. No account was taken of the fact that men from the City had proven managerial abilities that were frustrated by the 'business inefficiency' so obviously displayed by the officers of many units, that many of them had specialised technical knowledge which far outstripped that of their so-called 'instructors'.

The results of this clash between the 'old' Territorial Army and its new recruits inevitably showed the Territorial Army in a bad light. The examples of wasted time that the writers produced would perhaps come as no surprise to any student of military history, but they underlined the lack of preparation and apparent inability to adapt that struck so many new recruits. One member of an anti-aircraft unit who had joined after four years with the OTC, spent twenty-five hours of instruction (the equivalent under normal circumstances of three months training) on sloping, ordering and presenting arms and tying clove-hitch knots. One man in a searchlight unit who took a special course designed to train NCOs, spent only two hours of a total of thirty-seven studying the searchlight and sound apparatus: the rest was given over to lectures on the correct placement of latrines, and on the theory of electricity that failed to reach even the elementary level because of the instructor's ignorance. In a mechanized cavalry unit training with light tanks, men had first to master sword drill designed for mounted troops: until they had done so they were forbidden to attend the lectures on technical subjects. Another unit devoted two days of a three-day Easter camp to drill and kit inspection. The message was clear: the

Territorial Army had appealed for additional recruits, but then short-changed those who volunteered their services.

The Times Military Correspondent, Liddell Hart, made much the same criticisms when writing about Territorial infantry units. 'The Territorials should no longer be treated as holiday soldiers', he wrote, 'but as men who are preparing for a test that may be imminent.' Many officers of the Territorial Army were of the 'old Volunteer type': for them training was a 'necessary evil' that simply interfered with the more attractive sport and unit competitions. Their enthusiasm had been useful in keeping the Territorial movement alive during the years of neglect, but it was misplaced in a modern Army that claimed a serious role. The non-essential aspects of Territorial training, claimed Liddell Hart, 'appeal both to the county gentlemen who takes it up from a sense of duty that has its roots far back in feudal days, and to others who cherish the prestige that a commission conveys'. Their mistaken order of priorities exerted its most pernicious influence at camp. By the time men were paraded, inspected and marched out to the exercise area, very little in the way of proper training could be done if they were to be marched back to camp for a midday meal, as was the normal practice. The afternoon was usually given over to sport, so that the men were rarely if ever exposed to extended training.[34] One former Territorial wrote to *The Times* to support Liddell Hart: 'Since the War', he complained, 'there have been 17 camps and, generally speaking, the work has been dull, unimaginative and unilluminating: "platoon in attack", "company in attack", and so on *ad nauseam* from 9 a.m. to 1 p.m. Training on these lines may be vital but is it to continue for ever?'[35]

Although these criticisms, and particularly those dealing with anti-aircraft units were by and large endorsed by the War Office,[36] the old methods had their supporters. One retired Territorial officer wrote in *The Times* that Liddell Hart had unrealistic expectations. Far from commanding officers doing too little with their men, he argued, they tried to do too much. All too often it was forgotten that the average unit had a yearly turnover of between 20 and 25 per cent, so that a great deal of time had to be spent at every drill, and even more at each summer camp, learning

---

[34] 'Territorials in 1938: A Year of Progress', *The Times*, 27 August 1938.

[35] F. H. Turner, letter to *The Times*, 1 September 1938.

[36] DGTA to DCIGS, 31 May; DCIGS to PS, Secretary of State, 9 June 1938: WO 32/4610.

very basic military skills.[37] The GOC-in-C, Scottish Command, replied to the War Office that the criticisms that had been circulated were not typical of the great majority of non anti-aircraft Territorial units. In his own Command, for example, most soldiers were drawn from the manual labouring class, so that there were not the wide divergences in mental capacity that created problems in London units. The difficulty he faced was not of selecting the most qualified from among those who were suitable NCO material, but of providing any NCOs at all. Those who did become instructors were not necessarily chosen because of their educational qualifications but simply because they were available to take the appropriate course. With unemployment still high, many men were unwilling to jeopardise their jobs by applying for leave to attend military courses. The result was that it was often the unemployed man, sometimes with the lowest educational level, who was sent on instructional courses. Much of the so-called 'barely relevant' activity — the keeping of proper records, the inculcation of elementary military discipline, and an active social programme — was in fact essential to the maintenance and well-being of units. The key to remedying any defects in the Territorial Army lay in the much greater provision of equipment, accommodation and Regular instructors.[38]

The extant records on this particular exchange are very slight, but there can be little doubt that while many other officers agreed that improvements could be made in the Territorial Army, they shared the feelings of Scottish Command. A sense of grievance and resentment towards the London memorandum clearly emerges from the Scottish reply. The satisfaction that long-time Territorials must have felt when recruiting began to pick up after so many years of decline was tinged with a sense of anger, perhaps even bitterness, that those who now were so free with their criticisms had done nothing to help the Territorials during the years of neglect. Where had been their willingness to serve then? What support had they given the volunteers they now so readily disparaged? It must have been galling for those who had trained themselves before the crisis arose, when there was little public interest or government support, to have not only new recruits (whatever their civilian background) but also the Army Council circulate such denigrating reports.

It was in fact symptomatic of a much wider problem: what was

---

[37] Lt-Col. E. D. Jackson (ret.), letter to *The Times*, 3 September 1938.
[38] GOC-in-C, Scottish Command, to War Office, 25 November 1938, WO 32/4610.

the Territorial Army for? The adoption of the limited liability thesis by the end of 1937 and the decision to restrict the non anti-aircraft units of the Territorial Army to peacetime levels of equipment and reserves had not provided a clear answer to the question, since political considerations made it necessary to maintain far more units than could be justified under the new order of priorities. It was no solution to the problem, the DGTA stressed in May, to single out some units for early employment while putting others at the end of the line, with only a remote chance that they might be required to serve in an active role. The Territorial Army was 'very sensitive to shocks' and such a policy would so divide it that all but the favoured units might wither away. Yet the military situation might suddenly change, as it had several times during the previous year, and make it necessary to maintain a large Army for roles which had formerly been rejected. The only solution was to raise and administer the Territorial Army on a 'general purpose' basis, so that when an emergency arose it would be flexible enough to fulfil whatever role was assigned to it.[39]

So long as the roles which the Army might be called upon to fulfil remained subject to change, there was no need to disband or convert those units for which there was no immediate justification. Here Kirke was thinking of yeomanry regiments, the number of which in the Territorial Army the Army Council had always considered excessive since the reconstitution period. They should be retained, he argued, on two grounds. First that the imperial role, especially policing work, assigned to the Territorial Army made them invaluable should the Territorials ever be called upon to assist the Regular Army in the Empire; and second that they were cheap to maintain and very popular. Whereas the majority of infantry units were unable to fill even their peacetime quotas, most yeomanry regiments had long waiting lists, mainly drawn from the rural gentry who would not take to conversion to a mechanized unit, or, conversely, drawn from the urban population (and sometimes from the industrial working class) that joined the yeomanry as a welcome distraction from the preoccupations of city life. Underlying these considerations, of course, was the bald political fact that the government dared not disband any units, no matter how irrelevant they appeared to Britain's military requirements, at a time when the country was demanding a greater and greater emphasis on defence. The Army Council agreed with Kirke's proposal to convert the Territorials to a general purpose

[39] DGTA to CIGS, 20 May 1938, WO 32/4611.

Army, and to maintain the existing number of yeomanry regiments,
rather than risk public displeasure and a setback to the encouraging
recruiting figures.[40] These decisions, however, raised more difficult
questions.

If the Territorial Army was to be raised for 'general purposes' and
if the Army Council rejected the policy of earmarking some units for
early deployment there had to be some method of bringing those
units required for active service up to full war establishment with
qualified men so that they could be dispatched overseas as soon as
possible. One solution was to pool the man-power of several
selected units to form complete composite units. However the great
stumbling block was — yet again — the pledge. In 1932 and 1933 the
War Office had tried to disentangle itself from the undertakings
given to the Territorials both in the original Territorial Act of 1907
and in the terms of reconstitution in 1920. These had been to the
effect that no Territorial would be required to serve overseas except
in his own unit or in a Territorial unit of the same corps and
furthermore, that he would proceed overseas in his own unit. After
a long wrangle with the Associations, general agreement to remove
these restrictions had been reached. Territorials were made liable
for general service, with the proviso that the War Office would try
to return transferred men to their own Corps if possible and that
Territorials would not be used to supply drafts for Regular units.
(This point was discussed in chapter seven.) However, when the
regulations were rewritten, the paragraph that contained the
undertaking that men would proceed overseas in their own units
was, by something of an oversight, allowed to remain. It seems
from the very sketchy records available that after the meeting with
the Associations in May 1933, when they had agreed to accept a
general service liability, the War Office wrote to one Association
that had not been represented at the CCTA meeting (since
membership was at the discretion of the individual Associations)
and said that there was no intention to abolish the pledge to send
men overseas only in their own units. Having given that undertaking to one Association, it had to formalise the pledge in the
Territorial Regulations, despite the fact that almost all the other
Associations had agreed to its abolition. The result was that when
the War Office began to think of creating 'first-line' composite
units, it found to its embarrassment that it could not do so before

40 DGTA to DCIGS, 25 February 1938: DCIGS to DGTA 20 May 1938; War
Office, 'Note on the Reorganization of the Territorial Army', September
1938: WO 32/4611.

the troops had arrived at their overseas destination, the negotiations over the pledge in the early 1930s notwithstanding.

It was intolerable, Kirke advised in November 1937, that the mobilization plans of the Territorial Army should be hamstrung by such a pledge. By the following May, as the War Office sought to provide some military justification for the maintenance of an Army that political pressures demanded be increased rather than reduced, it had become 'urgently necessary' to remove the pledge.[41] Again, as in 1933, the War Office had to go to the Associations and ask for their agreement. When the CCTA summoned representatives of the Associations in June, Kirke explained that unless the pledge was removed, the War Office would be prevented from fulfilling its undertaking that the Territorial Army would be the sole vehicle for the expansion of the country's forces in the event of an emergency. The War Office had to be free to use men as necessity demanded, rather than have them tied up in units that could not take to the field without a considerable intake of post-embodiment recruits. It was precisely that sort of difficulty that had driven Kitchener in 1914 to bypass the Territorials and create his own 'New Armies'.

Dubious as this argument may have been, it was enough to convince the Associations to accept what many of them had long since recognised, that — in Kirke's words — 'in the case of a National Emergency . . . it is morally certain that the existing Pledge could not possibly be maintained'. The representatives of the Associations unanimously agreed that all restrictions on the use of Territorials be removed, as long as the War Office undertook not to use them as drafts for Regular units (except where absolutely necessary), and that the small number of men still serving on the pre-1933 terms (i.e. the 'double-pledged' men) should be invited to re-engage on the new terms of service. It seemed a very satisfactory solution, 'a great step forward', as Kirke wrote to Derby.[42]

It was not quite so simple however. Creedy pointed out that the pledge could not be abolished without consultations with all the Associations, and especially not without some testing of the reactions of the Territorial soldiers themselves. The 'vested rights' of individuals could not be withdrawn unless they were individually consulted. The Judge Advocate General confirmed that the War

---

[41] DGTA to DRO, 8 October 1937, WO 32/4527; DGTA to Under-Secretary of State, 31 May 1938, WO 32/4526.

[42] CCTA, special meeting, 8 June 1938, Minutes, 1933 – 39; Kirke to Derby, 8 June 1938, Derby Papers, Correspondence with Individuals: War Office 1938.

Office's proposed course was not as easy as it had assumed, and Kirke admitted in despair that the only way out of the situation was to create three classes of Territorials, those who had engaged before and after the regulations had been changed in 1933, and those who would enlist on the basis of the new (i.e. 1938) regulations. The first two classes would be invited to re-engage on the basis of the new regulations, but if they refused to do so, the War Office would have no choice but to allow them to continue serving on their old, 'pledged' basis: if it tried to release them from the Territorial Army, there would be a public outcry, and recruiting might well be harmed if potential recruits thought that the War Office could afford to pick and choose.[43] But this 'solution', of course, was no solution at all. The majority of Territorials would still be enlisted under restricted terms of service, which cut across the concept of a general purpose Army. The matter rested there uneasily until the crisis of September 1938 forced the War Office to confront the problem squarely.

Another issue that had to be settled related to recruiting. The War Office was anxious to avoid a repetition of the experiences of the Great War, when the acceptance of any and every man into the Army had wreaked havoc with industrial production and ultimately with military efficiency when the inevitable 'weeding out' process took place and industry reclaimed vital workers. When the rearmament programme began (albeit hesitantly) in 1936 and 1937, the question of the division of manpower became one of considerable importance. On the one hand the War Office was hardly in a position to choose who would and who would not be accepted into the Army — Regular or Territorial, yet it did not want to recruit men only to find that when a crisis arose they were pulled out and returned to their industrial jobs. On the other hand neither Government nor industry relished the prospect of having large numbers of workers, who had been encouraged by their firms to join the Territorials in response to the Government's plea, pulled out of production and kept in the Territorial Army for several months in the critical opening phases of the war.[44]

One solution was to suggest or even require that firms put a maximum quota on the number of its employees who could join the Territorial Army, so that when the Territorials were embodied, industrial disruption would be minimized. In 1937 this idea was

43 Memorandum by Creedy, 24 June; by JAG, 20 July; by DGTA, 4 August 1938: WO 32/4526.
44 Note by Secretary, DP(R), and enclosure, 18 February 1937, DP(R), 175, CAB 16/141.

studied, but finally dropped. The Government was unwilling to do anything that could be interpreted as hindering Territorial recruiting, and it was found to be almost impossible to formulate precise instructions that would enable industry to divide its manpower in peacetime along lines that would prove the most useful in wartime. In addition industry was afraid that any measures it might take to channel some men into the Territorials while restricting others might be interpreted as pressure on its workforce, thereby angering the unions. Anxious as both the Government and industry were to assist in Territorial recruiting, industrial harmony was even more important if the rearmament programme was to meet its production targets.[45]

A new twist to the manpower question arose in 1938. The German move against Austria in March sparked enormous public interest in defence matters. The Territorials were gratified to find that suddenly they were being flooded with recruits. But so were other auxiliary bodies. Thousands joined up as Air Raid Wardens and Auxiliary Police, much to the chagrin of the War Office, which saw fit young men absorbed into duties that could be equally well performed by those too old for active service with the Territorials. Thirteen Territorial Associations appealed to the War Office to protect Territorial recruiting against these inroads, arguing that the low age limits — ARP wardens could be recruited as young as thirty — encouraged men to join the ARP service instead of serving where they were most useful, in the Territorial Army, especially in anti-aircraft units. In response to pressure from the War Office, the Home Office quickly raised the lower age limit to thirty-five and promised to coordinate appeals for recruits more closely between the competing claims of the various services.[46]

Within a month of that decision, however, recruiting for the ARP service began to fall off. To its dismay, the War Office found that the Man-Power Sub-Committee of the CID recommended lowering the age for joining certain categories of the ARP Service down as far as eighteen. Yet, as the Adjutant-General noted, the War Office was in no position to complain. Clearly the needs of anti-aircraft and coastal defence units took precedence over those of the ARP service, but that accounted for only 60,000 out of a Territorial establishment of 200,000. Since the decision to abandon the continental thesis was taken at the end of 1937, 'the remaining 140,000 have had no place in

---

[45] See the discussions on industrial quotas for the Territorial Army in CAB 21/683; also DGTA to AG, 3 April 1937, WO 32/4646.
[46] Hore-Belisha to Hoare, 13 May; note by DRO, 27 May 1938: WO 32/4648.

our war plans and their role, seven months later, is still undecided'. The Territorial Army entirely lacked the equipment and reserves that were necessary for it to carry out an imperial role, and there was no likelihood that these would become available until well after the outbreak of war. In those circumstances it was difficult to argue that the Territorial Army should have a prior claim over the ARP service, when men who enrolled in the latter would be on active duty months before the bulk of the Territorial Army was ready to go overseas. Nevertheless, as long as there were deficiencies in the establishment of anti-aircraft units, and as long as the possibility existed that field units might have to be dispatched overseas, the War Office felt that the Territorial Army should have first call at least on the eighteen – twenty-five age group.[47] The only way to solve the dilemma of the patriotic citizen, faced as he was by conflicting appeals for his time and energy, argued Hore-Belisha, was to make a 'clear cut decision on the age limit . . . [thus] indicating where a man's duty lies'.[48] The CID agreed, and decided that since it was 'of the first importance to preserve the prestige of the fighting services' any recruiting drives in the future should emphasize that the Territorial Army should have the first claim on the youngest and fittest age group.[49]

The War Office found that in practice, however, the decision did not go as far as it had hoped. Shortly after the boom in recruiting for the Territorial Army began, the War Office was authorised by the Treasury to accept recruits up to 10 per cent in excess of the peace establishment for infantry units and 30 per cent for yeomanry regiments. Even this was not enough, and some units such as the London Scottish were having to turn men away, or put them on waiting lists, which often meant that they became discouraged and were lost to the Territorials. Associations tried to divert them to units that still had vacancies but this was not very successful because men usually applied to join a specific unit, often one where they had friends. The War Office hoped that the interest in the Territorials would be stimulated further by the annual summer camp, and it therefore asked the Treasury for permission to recruit in infantry units up to 30 per cent in excess of the peace establishment. The answer was a qualified 'no'. The Treasury appreciated the problem, but it was prepared to do no more than allow individual units to recruit up to the 30 per cent excess level,

---

[47] AG to Secretary of State, 24 June 1938, WO 32/4649.
[48] Hore-Belisha to Inskip, 25 July 1938, WO 32/4649.
[49] CID, 331st meeting, 27 July 1938, CAB 2/7.

as long as the overall strength of the Territorial Army did not exceed the peace establishment together with 10 per cent excess agreed to in May.[50] Even though the War Office had insisted that it was not asking for additional accommodation, the Treasury was unwilling to countenance any suggestion that might open the door to increased expenditure and strain on industrial capacity in the way of extra equipment.

At the end of the summer of 1938, the strength of the Territorial Army was greater than it had been since its reconstitution after the Great War. Recruits were streaming in, equipment was at last beginning to trickle into units, and new buildings were being opened at an astonishing rate. But the situation was not as healthy as it looked. The rejection of the continental thesis had not been accompanied by a careful consideration of alternative roles for the Territorial Army. As long as an overseas role had any priority, the Territorials had to have the capability to carry out that role, however it was defined. That they did not have, nor were there signs that they would have it in the foreseeable future. Furthermore the growing emphasis on the anti-aircraft role threatened to distort the overall alignment of the Territorial Army and to deprive it of that flexibility which the War Office and the Army itself continued to believe was the only sound basis on which to recruit and train.

---

[50] War Office to Treasury, 12 July; Treasury to War Office, 20 August 1938: WO 32/4650.

11

Towards the Continent

The first real test of the post-reconstitution Territorial Army came in the early autumn of 1938. Tensions between Germany and Czechoslovakia over the future of the German minority within Czechoslovakia brought Europe to the brink of war. The events of September 1938 are well known, and will not be repeated here. But for the Territorial Army the Munich crisis had a double significance. It pointed up the difficulty the Territorial Army would have in fulfilling the vital anti-aircraft role assigned to it, and it ultimately, though not immediately, cast into doubt the policy of limited liability which for the past year had been the basis of the Army's role.

On 22 September, Chamberlain met Hitler at Godesberg to work out the details of the general agreement they had reached a week before in talks at Berchtesgaden. To Chamberlain's dismay and anger, Hitler rejected his proposals and insisted instead that Czechoslovakia make new and far-reaching concessions. Chamberlain flew back to London where the Cabinet turned down Hitler's demands, even though by then Chamberlain had resigned himself to accepting them as the price of preventing war.

The tense situation required that the Government take preliminary steps to get Britain's defences in order in case war did break out. The most important line of defence was the ADGB system, especially its anti-aircraft component. When the Chiefs of Staff were asked 'as a matter of urgency' what had to be done to prepare the country's defences, they replied that a period of between twelve and forty-eight hours would elapse before the ADGB system would be fully operational. Within twelve hours 75 per cent of the anti-aircraft guns and searchlights could be deployed, while the remainder would be ready within forty-eight hours. This could be done without embodying the Territorial Army as a whole, a step which might be considered unnecessarily provocative and alarmist.[1]

---

[1]   COS, 'The Czechoslovak Crisis', 23 September 1938, COS 770, CAB 53/41.

So grave was the threat that at 2.30 on the afternoon of 26 September orders were given to deploy the anti-aircraft units of the Territorial Army in case Germany should launch a surprise air attack on Britain. By the following morning twenty-four anti-aircraft regiments and thirty searchlight batteries had been manned. Eventually 58,000 Territorials were called out for temporary duty. Although the Government tried to impress on the public that this measure was quite distinct from general mobilisation or even embodiment of the Territorial Army, the sight of gun emplacements being manned and the presence of the Territorial Army in and around London brought hundreds of new recruits to Territorial headquarters. At Lloyds of London, one of the first firms of the City to form its own anti-aircraft battery (the 159th Lloyds Battery), appeals for volunteers to form a second battery were so successful that within several hours under-writers, brokers and clerks had filled the 150 places, and there were still almost enough volunteers for a third battery. So great was the interest that the War Office tried again to get the Treasury to agree to lift the restrictions on recruiting. This time, with the situation so critical, the Treasury could hardly refuse: Territorial units were authorised to recruit up to 30 per cent over establishment in the case of AA and yeomanry units, and 10 per cent for field units, on condition that if the crisis was resolved satisfactorily, the War Office would try to absorb the excess men into existing units, especially Field Force (i.e. mainly infantry) units.[2]

The crisis passed when Chamberlain flew to Munich and on 29 September with Hitler, Mussolini, and Daladier of France, signed the Munich agreement, in effect giving Hitler everything he wanted. The Territorial troops that had been called out when war seemed imminent were kept on duty until 14 October, when they stood down. Then it was time to assess the effectiveness of the anti-aircraft defence scheme. The reassurance that came from the knowledge that the defences had been deployed quickly soon evaporated as the stories of inadequacy and incompetence became public knowledge. Within a week of the call-up of the Territorials, and only days after Chamberlain's triumphant return from Munich, Inskip told the Commons that 'nobody who has seen this most valuable test of our arrangements can be unaware of the fact that there have been gaps, serious gaps, and defects

---

[2] War Office to Treasury, 26 September; Treasury to War Office, 29 September 1938: WO 32/4650.

which must be remedied in our preparations'.[3] From the Home
Office came the frank admission that: 'We were not prepared; we
had hardly begun to prepare.'[4] The Government survived a
censure vote in November, but in the course of the debate
conceded that many of the worst stories were true. Some guns
were deployed without dials or predictors; in others batteries had
been allowed to run down. Several units did not draw the
necessary stores to enable them to make their guns operational;
some were issued the wrong sort of ammunition. Distribution of
stores was chaotic, resulting in long delays before even a nominal
cover could be provided.[5]

The Commander of the 1st Anti-Aircraft Division, General Pile,
knew that the position was even worse. He had previously
described the state of the anti-aircraft defences around London as a
'fool's paradise': the 3.7-and 4-inch guns were unavailable, and
even the number of obsolescent 3-inch guns did not meet
requirements. Ammunition was in short supply, and there was a
'crying necessity' for all types of training equipment to enable the
troops to practise under more realistic conditions. Exercises in
August had shown that the accuracy of fire was depressingly poor,
as was the ability of troops to distinguish between hostile and
friendly aircraft. When the crisis came in September, there were
only 126 guns ready for action between London and the Medway
despite the fact that defence against air attack had been given a
high priority for several years.[6]

The alarming picture of the state of the anti-aircraft defences as
revealed by the September crisis led to a public outcry and a firm
commitment by the Government to improve the system. So great
was the public unease, warned the War Office in January 1939, that
it had led to 'widespread and even excessive demands for local and
visible protection in terms of AA guns'.[7] The DGTA publicly cautioned against an overemphasis on the 'purely passive' anti-aircraft

3 *Parl. Debs.* (Commons), 5th series, vol. 339, col. 308 (4 October 1938).
4 C. W. G. Eady (Deputy Secretary of State at the Home Office), 'The
   Progress of Air Raid Precautions' (lecture, 26 October 1938), *JRUSI*,
   LXXXIV (February 1939), 1 – 23.
5 For the debate on the censure motion see *Parl. Debs.* (Commons), 5th
   series, vol. 340, cols. 411 – 530 (3 November 1938).
6 Pile, 'Anti-Aircraft Defence of London', 13 December 1937, CAB 21/622.
   See also Pile's memoirs, *Ack-Ack: Britain's Defence Against Air Attack during
   the Second World War* (London, 1949), pp. 80 – 5.
7 War Office memorandum, 'Anti-Aircraft Defence', January 1939, CAB
   21/623.

defence to the exclusion of the active role of the Field Force.[8] When the Home Defence Committee noted that by relying on the Territorial Army to man the anti-aircraft defences, there was a delay of between twelve and forty-eight hours before the system became operational (and even then not fully), Inskip pressed Hore-Belisha to reverse the policy whereby the new 3.7-inch guns were made available first to the Territorial Army and then to Regular AA units. Since Regular units alone would be able to provide protection in the event of a surprise attack, i.e. within the twelve hour period before the first Territorials took up their positions, was it not right that they should be given priority over Territorial units in the provision of the new guns?[9]

Hore-Belisha replied that as well as undermining the accepted policy of relying on the Territorials to provide anti-aircraft cover — and the damage that such a policy might do to recruiting — there were practical difficulties in switching priority to the Regular Army. The Regular anti-aircraft units had to be available to go overseas with the Field Force, and therefore required full war reserves and equipment. If the new guns were to be provided on that scale for the Regular troops the whole programme of re-equipping the Territorials would be distorted. Nevertheless Hore-Belisha agreed that some Regular troops could be trained to man fixed guns (as opposed to the Territorials' mobile guns), which would enable some measure of protection to be given within three or four hours. Within a further two hours the system could be almost fully operational, but only if the Territorial anti-aircraft troops were called out well in advance of the rest of the Army.[10] That was a difficult political decision, for both domestic and international reasons. As a result of these pressures, Hore-Belisha announced in February that two Regular regiments of anti-aircraft artillery would be stationed in London to provide additional cover, but he added that this was not to be interpreted as any qualification of the Government's reliance on the Territorial Army to man the bulk of AA defences.

There were equally difficult political decisions facing the Cabinet on the fundamental question of British military policy. For a year

[8] Kirke, speech at a dinner of the 349th (Royal Bucks. Yeomanry) Field Battery, Royal Artillery (TA), reported in *The Times*, 23 January 1939.
[9] HDC, 'Air Defence of Great Britain. Conspectus of Arrangements as at 1st January 1939: Arrangements for the higher direction of the A.A. defences', 21 December 1938, HDC 48-M, CAB 21/263; Inskip to Hore-Belisha, 7 January 1939, CAB 21/263.
[10] Hore-Belisha to Inskip, 12 January 1939, CAB 21/263.

preceding the crisis over Czechoslovakia that policy rested on the assumption that Britain would not be required to send large land forces to Europe in the event of war. The Regular Army was being equipped for general purposes and the Territorial Army field divisions were not intended to be dispatched overseas until many months after the outbreak of war. Hore-Belisha's visit to France in the late summer of 1937 had convinced him that the French Army had sufficient troops to hold the Maginot Line and man a large field army. That reassuring picture, and the ramifications it had for Britain, changed after the signing of the Munich Agreement.

The annexation by Germany of the western areas of Czechoslovakia effectively destroyed Czechoslovakia's ability to defend itself. Its frontier fortifications and all the equipment that went with them were lost, and the centre of its formidable armaments industry now lay within minutes of German airfields. For the French the outcome was a disaster. The destruction of Czechoslovakia's military base removed the equivalent of thirty-five to forty first line divisions from any anti-German and anti-Italian alliance that might be constructed. The forces that Germany could throw into battle against France were that much greater, and the French increasingly looked to Britain to make good the losses which had resulted from the Munich Agreement. Throughout the autumn and winter of 1938 and 1939 the French put mounting pressure on Britain to reconsider its military priorities and to abandon the limited liability hypothesis that had been adopted as the basis of British defence policy barely a year before.

When Anglo-French talks were held in Paris on 24 November, Chamberlain and Halifax found themselves pressed by Daladier to make a more realistic commitment of British forces, to go far beyond the paltry two divisions that had been promised within three weeks of the outbreak of war. What was needed, the French argued, was a much larger Field Force dispatched more quickly. Chamberlain replied by stressing that the paramount consideration of his Government was the security of Britain itself: anti-aircraft defence had to continue to have priority over the needs of field artillery, while the whole accelerated programme of rearmament had to be carefully balanced and distributed between the needs of all the services. The most urgent need was for more equipment, not more men. As Chamberlain told Daladier, 'it seemed to be of no use to increase the number of troops which would be ready to be sent abroad, if it were not possible to equip them properly'.[11]

[11] E. L. Woodward and Rohan Butler (eds.), *Documents on British Foreign Policy, 1919–1945*, Third Series, 1938–9 (London, 1949–55), III, pp. 285–94.

This was cold comfort for the French. Much as Daladier admitted the logic of the British position it was not enough to counter the growing feeling in France that Britain was unwilling to carry her fair share of the burden of defending western Europe. One French officer told the British Military Attaché in Paris that what was required from Britain was an *effort du sang*; that it was not enough for Britain to argue that she was already maintaining a large navy and air force together with a growing armaments industry. As the Military Attaché told the British Ambassador in Paris:

> I think we must recognise that there is always latent in France the idea that Great Britain is very willing to fight her battles in Europe with French soldiers, and if this idea gains ground and she realises that British help on land is to be so limited that it can have no decisive effect, she may lose heart, with results that might eventually be disastrous to ourselves.

If the French needed any proof of Britain's willingness to fight to the last French soldier, the Attaché added several weeks later, they had only to read the correspondence columns of *The Times*, which had been filled in November with letters from Liddell Hart and others supporting a policy of limited liability on land.[12]

The gravity of these warnings, which were repeated throughout December and January, were not lost on the Foreign Secretary, Lord Halifax, who, unlike Chamberlain, had been impressed by French pleas in the November talks. The growing and alarming possibility that the French would be unable to withstand a German attack through Belgium and Holland unless much greater assistance on land was forthcoming from Britain led him to urge the Cabinet to reconsider the limited liability policy, and to take steps that would enable Britain to dispatch far more divisions much earlier to the continent. Even if there could be no immediate improvement in Britain's military position, he said, the moral effect of such an undertaking would be immense, and would avoid the danger 'that a section of opinion [in France], appalled at the prospect of being left unaided to fight a land war on two or three fronts, may slowly swing over to a policy of complete surrender'.[13]

---

[12] Col. W. Fraser to Col. W. E. van Cutson (War Office), 18 October 1938, FO 371/21592, C 14067/13/17; Fraser to Sir Eric Phipps, 5 December 1938, CAB 21/555, enclosure no. 1. The letters to *The Times* were published on November 8, 16, 19, 22 and 28.

[13] Gibbs, *Grand Strategy*, I, pp. 500 – 1.

Halifax was not alone in realising that Britain's military posture no longer suited the developing situation. In December Hore-Belisha submitted proposals to the CID for a major change in the rearmament programme as it applied to the role of the Army. He asked that the two divisions that made up the first contingent of the Field Force be equipped for counter-offensive operations rather than for a merely defensive role; that the third and fourth divisions be provided with reserves and ammunition on the full scale for defensive operations; that colonial units be fully equipped so that the Field Force would not have to be stripped of essential equipment to keep these units at an operational level; and that war equipment and reserves be made avilable for the four Territorial divisions that would make up the third and fourth contingents of the Field Force, with the remainder of the Territorial divisions being issued training equipment on a realistic scale. Much as he stressed that this was not a fundamental change in the role of the Army but merely the provision of the means to enable it to carry out the roles already assigned to it, he had in fact virtually abandoned the limited liability policy which he had supported so strongly only a year before.[14]

The Chiefs of Staff endorsed Hore-Belisha's proposals, arguing that Britain needed the ability to employ a flexible response in the first year of the war, which might well prove the critical period. As plans then stood, Britain would only be able to send four infantry divisions and one mobile division — equipped for defensive warfare only — to the continent, or wherever they were most needed. Just as Hore-Belisha had disclaimed any intention of challenging the order of priorities in the role of the Army, so the Chiefs of Staff denied that they were recommending a fundamental change. Yet they referred to Halifax's anxiety about French demands for British assistance, and they added: 'It is difficult to avoid the conclusion that such assistance may have to include support by land forces if only for the moral effect which would thereby be produced on the French nation.'[15] Significantly, the War Office position was strongly supported by the First Sea Lord, Admiral Sir Roger Backhouse, who agreed that it would be impossible to wage a war of limited liability against Germany. The contrast with the Army's position in 1937 could not have been more striking. Then it had

---

[14] Hore-Belisha, 'The State of Preparedness of the Army in Relation to its Role', 13 December 1938, COS 809, CAB 53/43.

[15] COS, 'State of the Army in Relation to its Role', 25 January 1939, COS 827, CAB 53/44.

been alone in its pressure for a continental capability, unsupported even by its own minister. Now it had that, together with strong backing from the Foreign Secretary and the First Sea Lord.[16]

After several months of discussion, Chamberlain accepted Hore-Belisha's basic proposals, though with extreme reluctance. He still hoped that the French might be persuaded to agree to the British position enunciated in the November talks. But, as he told the Cabinet in February 1939, while the proposed changes would impose additional and serious burdens on the country, they could not be avoided given the deterioration of the allied position since September and the growing French demand for a significant military contribution on land from Britain. The Chiefs of Staff recommended that efforts be made to speed up the dispatch of the Field Force to the continent. That was agreed to by the Cabinet, but following the approach taken by a preliminary Ministerial study of the question, it hedged its position. It decided that while Britain should be in a position to send four Territorial divisions to the continent within six months of the outbreak of war (as opposed to the twelve months' delay previously determined), the second contingent of the Field Force should be dispatched after six weeks instead of the four weeks originally planned.[17]

Throughout these discussions, reference was continually made to the demands of public opinion, both in France and Britain. Halifax hoped that the plans for the accelerated dispatch of the first contingent might satisfy the French, while Hore-Belisha added that the changes would go some way towards meeting growing demands in Parliament which argued that Britain's ties with France had to be cemented by the promise of substantial forces for the continent.[18] There was also the clamour for action to repair the gaps in British defences that had been exposed but mercifully not put to the test by the September crisis. Calls for action ranged from the introduction of compulsory military service (usually called 'national service' to avoid the emotive term 'conscription') to the establishment of a compulsory national manpower register and the scheduling of occupations.

The enormous surge in Territorial recruiting after the September crisis was evidence of the public's concern over defence matters. By 1 December the War Office was able to announce that the Territorials had reached a strength of 200,190, only a few hundred

[16] Bond, *British Military Policy between the Two World Wars*, p. 297.
[17] Cabinet 9(39), 22 February 1939, CAB 23/97.
[18] *Ibid.*

below their newly-raised peace establishment and by far the highest level reached since the 1921 reconstitution.[19] There were two drawbacks to this startling success. The first was that the sheer numbers of Territorials would overwhelm the meagre supplies of equipment and exacerbate the dissatisfaction voiced in the wake of the March flood of recruits. The solution to that seemed to lie in the establishment of a Ministry of Supply, charged with coordinating industrial capacity to the various needs of the services, and especially to the needs of the branches within the Army. Hore-Belisha urged Chamberlain to take that step, but Chamberlain resisted, fearing that the use of compulsory powers against industry and labour would hamper production and create unrest among the unions. The second problem was that the Territorial Army was undoubtedly recruiting men who in wartime would be in restricted occupations. Unless some sort of manpower register was established in peacetime, the chaos that had disrupted Britain's war effort in the Great War would inevitably recur. Chamberlain opposed this suggestion, again on the grounds that compulsion was both unnecessary and divisive. In any case, as he told the Commons on 1 November, a Ministry of Supply and a national manpower register compiled on a compulsory basis were irrelevant to Britain's position, since the Government was not 'contemplating the equipment of an army on a continental scale'.[20]

By January 1939, however, the Government could no longer resist the pressures for some sort of positive lead. There was widespread public demand for guidance on the duties of individual citizens and how they could best serve the country in the various auxiliary forces. On 23 January Chamberlain broadcast a National Service Appeal, calling on those who were able to enrol in the special forces for which they were most suited. Once again he stressed the voluntary system, saying that: 'We are confident that we shall get all the volunteers we want without recourse to compulsion.' The following night, at an all-party rally at Albert Hall, Labour promised its support for the campaign whose success would surely silence the calls for conscription.[21]

The *Daily Mail* (24 January) welcomed the Government's initiative as a chance to 'see some real action', but its enthusiasm, largely shared by the rest of the London press, was soon tempered with dismay. There had been plans to release twenty million

[19] *The Times*, 9 December 1938.
[20] Dennis, *Decision by Default*, pp. 144 – 50.
[21] *The Times*, 24 and 25 January 1939.

National Service Appeal Handbooks to coincide with the launching of the campaign, but many were not delivered to individual households until days after the broadcast and rally. Their design was uninspiring and the order of priorities set down by the Government hardly corresponded to the sense of urgency that was increasingly felt throughout the country. The needs of the Regular Army — still suffering a severe shortage of recruits — were dealt with only very briefly and were not given the prominence that many felt the situation both in Britain and in France warranted. In his broadcast to the nation Chamberlain had announced that: 'A schedule has been prepared of all the occupations which are so essential to the war effort that persons engaged in them should not bind themselves to undertake any other form of full-time service.' Yet when the reserved list was published, it was found that *chefs de cuisine* and sleeve link makers were among those 'essential to the war effort'.

As the weeks passed the Territorial Associations chafed over the arbitrary and apparently cavalier approach to the scheduling of occupations, and pressed the War Office to draw up a more realistic list. Derby protested to Kirke, 'really, when one hears of ice-cream merchants being exempted from National Service it does make one angry'. Kirke replied that he entirely agreed, and had been fighting against the details of the schedule since it was first drawn up. Hore-Belisha, he added, had asked the Minister of Civilian Defence, Sir John Anderson, to exempt the Territorial Army from the restrictions of the schedule, but the decision did not rest with him: the War Office was up against a Cabinet policy which in Kirke's opinion was 'quite one of the most fatuous that has even been promulgated by any Cabinet'.[22] The *Daily Mirror* (26 January) summed up the widespread bewilderment arising out of the apparent contradiction between Chamberlain's reference to essential war work and the occupations that were actually on the schedule: 'Either it's all got something to do with mystery armaments, or else the authorities want "business as usual" — as they did last time; though they didn't get it.'

By the middle of February the National Service Appeal showed signs of slowing down. It was rarely mentioned in the press, apart from reports of one or two speeches by Government ministers. There was some pointed criticism of the Government's lackadaisical handling of the appeal in the *Daily Telegraph*, which contrasted the note of urgency sounded in Chamberlain's broadcast with the

[22] Derby to Kirke, 30 March; Kirke to Derby, 31 March 1939: Derby Papers, Correspondence with Individuals: War Office 1939.

situation that many would-be recruits had encountered: they turned up at enlistment posts only to be told that their services were not needed at that time.[23] The Labour movement saw in the fortunes of the appeal a test of the voluntary system. As the campaign began to falter the threat of conscription, whether for the services or for industry, became ever more real, and some Labour supporters suggested that the Government had tricked Labour into supporting the appeal as a means of identifying it with the failure of the voluntary system, thereby eventually leaving Labour no option but to support some sort of compulsion.[24]

In launching the appeal Chamberlain had said that the Government would wait two months before deciding whether the results justified its determination to avoid compulsory powers. The mounting criticism of its performance was partly offset by Hore-Belisha's presentation of his second Army Estimates in early March. With consummate skill he outlined a military posture that marked a radical departure from the policy of limited liability while reinforcing the vital role of home defence that had been one of the *raisons d'être* of that policy. The number of anti-aircraft divisions in the Territorial Army would be increased from five to seven, and the Deputy CIGS would be appointed to head the new Anti-Aircraft and Coast Defence Command. Immediate steps would be taken to increase the number of batteries by between 50 and 100 per cent, and by the autumn a new factory would be producing the 3.7-inch guns that had been in such short supply in the September crisis. Additional accommodation, administrative and maintenance staff would be provided, and extra training camps would be established to handle the expansion. It was an impressive testament to the Government's renewed emphasis on home defence and something of an answer to those who claimed that not enough was being done to repair the deficiencies exposed when the Territorial anti-aircraft units had been called out in September.

These changes however were overshadowed by Hore-Belisha's statement on the continental role of the Army. The Government now planned a Field Force of more than nineteen divisions, including nine infantry divisions, one motorized division, one armoured division, and two cavalry brigades from the Territorial Army. While there had been no commitments made to the French that this Force would be sent to the continent, Hore-Belisha added that 'prudent minds should be ready for any eventuality. If we are

[23] *Daily Telegraph*, 13 and 17 February 1939.
[24] *Daily Herald*, 14 and 15 February 1939.

involved in war, our contribution and the ways in which we can best make it will not be half-hearted nor upon any theory of limited liability'.[25]

It was a stunning reversal of policy, even if for the moment (and indeed, for many months, if not several years) it was little more than a bold statement of intent with no real means of implementation. The next day the *Daily Telegraph* reported that Hore-Belisha's announcement that limited liability had been abandoned was greeted with 'general cheering', and in a leader stated that 'it will be a relief to the mass of informed opinion in this country, as well as to our friends in France' to know that Britain was prepared to send *at least* 19 divisions' to the continent. Much of the rest of the London press, however, was less sure. *The Times* gave a grudging and reluctant approval to Hore-Belisha's new policy, but the *Daily Mirror* pulled no punches: it suggested that 'the best Expeditionary Force for another Western front would be a corps of mental experts to examine the brains . . . of the high command'.[26]

The reaction in France was much more positive. The *Daily Telegraph*'s Paris correspondent reported that Hore-Belisha's speech had made a 'deep impression in political and military circles' in France, and had forcefully demonstrated Britain's 'manifest determination' not to fight on the basis of any policy of limited liability. *Le Temps* interpreted the new policy as a sign that the British people were willing to bear all the sacrifices necessary to enable Britain to fulfil its continental obligations. The London correspondent of *Jour-Echo de Paris* wrote that at last the British government was adopting a firm and realistic policy towards its military involvement on land which, taken with Chamberlain's declaration in February of Anglo-French unity, would have a 'real and incalculable significance in the practical and political spheres'.[27]

Certainly the psychological impact of the announcement of unlimited liability was considerable. In practical terms however there was little enough to reassure the French, who had consistently argued that only the introduction of peacetime conscription would enable Britain to send large land forces to the continent in the early — and critical — stages of a German offensive against the west.

[25] *Parl. Debs.* (Commons), 5th series, vol. 344, cols. 2161 – 84.
[26] *Daily Telegraph*, 9 March 1939; *The Times*, 10 March 1939; *Daily Mirror*, 14 March 1939.
[27] *Daily Telegraph*, 9 March 1939; *Le Temps*, 9 March 1939; *Jour-Echo de Paris*, quoted in the *Manchester Guardian*, 10 March 1939.

This view was rejected by officials in the Foreign Office and the War Office, who both argued that conscription would do nothing to improve Britain's military capabilities in the short term.[28] But it was common knowledge in France as well as Britain that the Territorial Army had been starved of modern equipment for years and would not be able to embark overseas and take the field until months after the outbreak of war. Yet without a stronger Regular contingent (which could not be increased) and in the absence of the numbers that peacetime conscription would bring, the Territorial Army remained the key to Hore-Belisha's assurance that Britain's contribution on land would not be 'half-hearted nor upon any theory of limited liability'.

Only a week after the announcement of Britain's new policy, German troops occupied Prague. The disintegration of Czechoslovakia came as a profound shock, and after an initially diffident response in the House of Commons, Chamberlain lashed out at Hitler's betrayal, and in a speech in Birmingham declared that Britain would take all steps necessary to defend her own security and the liberty of Europe. The Government, he said, would examine every aspect of national life and fairly distribute the collective responsibility for national defence. *The Times* reported (18 March) that the speech was greeted with a 'remarkable ovation'. It seemed as though the long policy of retreat before the demands of the dictators was finally over. The response in the country was immediate. After a decline in enlistment since the middle of February, National Service centres in London, Birmingham, Leeds, Manchester and Glasgow found that the day after Chamberlain's speech was one of the busiest they had experienced since the campaign opened in January.[29]

The French increased their pressure on Britain for a concrete demonstration of Britain's willingness, determination and ability to fulfil her new policy. In French eyes that meant the introduction of conscription, the first step to creating a continental army, and a visible sign that Britain would pledge her man-power to the common cause. When the Cabinet met to study specific measures to

[28] News Department, 'The French Government and Conscription in England', 4 February 1939, FO 371/22932, C 5575/682/17. The paper's conclusions were endorsed by the DMO at the War Office.

[29] *The Times*, 20 March 1939. Simon Newman argues in *March 1939: The British Guarantee to Poland* (Oxford, 1976) that Hitler's move into Czechoslovakia did not bring about a radical change in British policy towards Germany.

give effect to Chamberlain's speech, discussion centred on two courses of action: the introduction of conscription and the establishment of a Ministry of Supply. Halifax warned his colleagues that it was no longer enough to point to the National Service appeal. Something more had to be done to convince opinion both in Britain and in Europe of the Government's firmness in the face of German provocation. Conscription seemed an obvious choice. But as the Minister of Labour and Chamberlain pointed out, the introduction of any form of conscription (military, industrial or both) would infuriate Labour and bring about the resignation of all union representatives from National Service Committees. Furthermore — and much more dangerous — the alienation of Labour would seriously impair armament production, especially in the all-important aircraft industry.[30]

Within days of Chamberlain's speech the press began to demand conscription. 'Away with slackness', cried the Daily Mirror on 20 March. 'Our slack methods, our lack of discipline, are partly to blame . . . [for Europe thinking that] Britain is decadent and has lost her national spirit. Conscription will alter this false opinion. It will hearten our French ally.' Throughout the third week of March The Times carried many reports of growing support for conscription among Conservative MPs. Once again, however, opposition from Labour made Chamberlain hesitate. On 23 and 26 March, together with Lord Chatfield (who had succeeded Inskip in January as Minister for Co-ordination of Defence), Chamberlain met TUC representatives to discuss means of accelerating armament production in factories, but his proposals were rejected.[31] Also on 23 March, Halifax had met Bonnet, who had urged the Government to introduce some form of compulsory military service that would show that Britain 'meant business'.[32]

With conscription apparently ruled out for domestic reasons, some other way had to be found to demonstrate Britain's determination to stand by France. On the morning of 28 March, Sir Horace Wilson, Chamberlain's personal adviser, wrote to Hore-Belisha about the pressures on the Prime Minister. That night Chamberlain was to address the 1922 Committee, and would undoubtedly be expected to say something about the recent dramatic influx of recruits to the Territorial Army. So great had been the increase that many units were full and had to turn men away.

[30] Cabinet 12(39), 18 March 1939, CAB 23/98.
[31] Viscount Templewood, Nine Troubled Years (London, 1954), p. 337.
[32] DBFP, IV, pp. 487 – 90.

Wilson suggested the formation of new units or of 'Voluntary Training Units', even if the severe shortage of equipment meant that training could only be 'very basic'. Hore-Belisha was asked to have his proposals ready within several hours, so that Chamberlain could make an appropriate announcement that evening. When he met Wilson for lunch, Hore-Belisha advised him that the turn of events made the introduction of conscription absolutely necessary. Wilson rejected that approach, citing the attitude of the trade unions as the main stumbling block. Hore-Belisha got no further with Chamberlain, when he saw him later than afternoon. Instead Chamberlain fixed on the Territorial Army as the means by which Britain could make 'the most convincing gesture'. Hore-Belisha suggested doubling the size of the Territorial Army by over-recruiting in each unit and then splitting the units in two. Chamberlain immediately seized on this idea, and brushing aside Hore-Belisha's objections, told him to have the details ready to be announced within twenty-four hours.[33]

The Treasury was unhappy about the proposal which, it said, 'cannot be related to anything in particular', except that it would impose an enormous burden on industry and distort the already strained rearmament programme. Sir John Simon overruled these *caveats* on the grounds — unusual for him — that the proposal 'must necessarily be looked at from a wider point of view than that of the Exchequer'.[34] On 29 March Chamberlain admitted to the Cabinet that he personally favoured some sort of conscription, but dared not risk a break with Labour that would imperil industrial production.[35] Indeed, when he made the announcement the same afternoon in the House of Commons, he stressed that 'we have not by any means yet exhausted what can be done by voluntary service, and we shall demonstrate the possibilities of voluntary service to meet all our needs'.[36]

The press reaction on 30 March was mixed. Although *The Times* warmly approved of the Government's action, as did the *Daily Herald*, which saw it as proof of the Government's faith in the voluntary system, others were less impressed. Some thirty dissident Conservative MPs tabled a motion calling for the immediate

---

[33] Minney, *Private Papers of Hore-Belisha*, pp. 186 – 7.

[34] Unsigned memorandum, attributed by Wilson to the Treasury, 'Proposal to double the Territorial Army', 28 March 1939; memorandum by Wilson, 29 March 1939: PREM 1/296. See also Peden, *British Rearmament and the Treasury 1932 – 9*, pp. 1489.

[35] Cabinet 15(39), CAB 23/98.

[36] *Parl. Debs.* (Commons), 5th series, vol. 345, cols. 2048 – 50.

introduction of conscription. The *Daily Mail* deplored Chamberlain's 'tenacious respect' for the 'sacrosanct voluntary principle': 'By still letting every citizen choose whether or not to help, the Government conveys both to friends and to potential foes that Britain's leaders still have not reached the point of meaning business.' The French were not convinced. On 31 March *Le Temps* noted tersely that the British Government was trying to maintain the voluntary principle while building up its forces as much as possible.

Few, least of all the French, thought that the doubling of the Territorial Army was anything but a hastily devised scheme that would bear results in the distant, rather than the immediate, future. In the short term it meant that equipment would be in even shorter supply, while, perhaps more important, the available instruction would be spread so thinly as to be virtually useless. But those who equated numbers with military force paid little attention to these questions. For them the mere fact that men were in uniform was reassuring. Even before the announcement of the doubling of the Territorial Army, Liddell Hart had been taken to task for pointing out the drawbacks of conscription. One Territorial officer, Lord Hinchinbrooke, replied that the shortage of equipment was not a major obstacle to increasing the size of the Army — Regular or Territorial, even if individual soldiers might handle real weapons 'for perhaps only three minutes in every hour'. In times of crisis, he suggested, some training, no matter how elementary, was better than no training at all.[37]

Chamberlain's impulsive decision to double the size of the Territorial Army had been made in an attempt to allay public and parliamentary criticism in Britain and to give a 'convincing demonstration' abroad to Britain's allies and adversaries. It signally failed to do either. Only two days after his announcement, Chamberlain told the Commons that in the face of growing threats from Germany, Britain (and France) had pledged its support to Poland's efforts to maintain its independence. Even though on 1 April *The Times* tried to restrict the scope of the guarantee (and was widely abused for its pains), it was in fact a 'blank cheque'. By itself it did nothing to help Poland; on the contrary, on 3 April, Hitler, now convinced that the western powers were pursuing a policy of encirclement, ordered his military forces to be ready to attack Poland 'at any time, as from September 1, 1939'. Briefed by Liddell Hart, Lloyd George warned the House that without the aid

[37] Letter to *The Times*, 27 March 1939.

of the Soviet Union Britain was 'walking into a trap', but Chamberlain was not inclined to pursue an alliance with Russia: he distrusted the Soviet leadership and accepted the advice given to him by the military to the effect that the Red Army had little offensive power.[38]

The events of March 1939 and British reactions to them — the abandonment of limited liability, the doubling of the Territorial Army and the guarantee to Poland — again raised the question of whether the Territorial Army could fulfil the roles assigned to it. After the announcement in the Army Estimates debate of an expanded continental role for the British Army, it became essential to settle the matter of the pledge once and for all. Even though in June 1938 the great majority of Associations had shown that they would not oppose the abolition of the pledge, the War Office discovered that the vested rights of pledged men could not be done away with quite so easily. That at least was the more cautious view.

By the autumn, after the scares of September and the calling out of the anti-aircraft units of the Territorial Army, the War Office was less concerned about the reaction that abolition might arouse. Kirke told Derby that the War Office would go ahead and remove the pledge from Territorial Regulations and give anyone who objected the option of taking his discharge. It was far better, he said (and Derby agreed), to have a Territorial Army unencumbered by restrictive conditions of service, even if that resulted in numbers of men leaving the Territorials, than to have a large Army tied down by pledges that in all probability would have to be broken once war began. In any case, Kirke added, he did not think that many men would choose to leave. Nor did the Associations, who urged the War Office to get rid of the pledge while 'the lessons learnt during the recent crisis, and its after effects, are fresh in everyone's minds'. It was so much easier to act now, with public attention focused on matters of defence, than it had been when the Territorials were anxious for every recruit they could get. With men being turned away because establishments were full, there was no longer the fear of a decline in numbers if pledged men resigned rather than give up their privileges. The much more urgent atmosphere of March 1939

---

[38] For the immediate circumstances surrounding the guarantee to Poland, see Newman, *March 1939*, chapter 9. Bond, *British Military Policy*, pp. 307 – 8, points out Chatfield misled the Cabinet over the position of the Chiefs of Staff, and that Chamberlain demonstrated once again that he was prepared 'flagrantly to ignore unpalatable military advice'.

gave the War Office the chance it needed to face the issue squarely. A special meeting of the CCTA, attended by representatives of almost every Association, unanimously endorsed the War Office's proposals to abolish the pledge, and early in April Territorial Regulations were amended accordingly.[39]

The pledge was primarily the concern of units earmarked for the Field Force. A much more pressing question arose in March and April over the deployment of anti-aircraft units of the Territorial Army. At the special meeting on 29 March the Associations had agreed to recommend to their Territorial units that all men of the Field Force sign the undertaking already accepted by members of the anti-aircraft and coastal defence units, namely that they would be liable for service in an emergency when required by the War Office, even though the Territorial Army as a whole had not been formally called out. While that would enable the War Office to draw on Territorial troops at short notice, it did not solve the most urgent problem — how to provide anti-aircraft defence against a 'bolt from the blue'. Once the British guarantee to Poland had been given the fear grew that Germany might attack before the western powers could build a strong anti-German alliance. In particular the Chiefs of Staff pointed out that the approaching Easter weekend rendered Britain dangerously exposed to sudden air attacks. The Regular AA Brigades were due to go on practice camps, having just stood down from their war stations. By themselves they could provide only a very thin air defence, and that at the risk of unwanted publicity. It was likely that large numbers of Territorials would be taking holidays over Easter, which made the job of calling out the troops in case of an emergency that much more difficult.[40]

Chamberlain's answer to the problem of round-the-clock air defence was to have the Territorials keep their regular working hours and man their anti-aircraft posts at night for periods of between three and six months. Hore-Belisha told him that the idea was 'absolutely impracticable' and that the General Staff had advised him that it would 'completely dislocate' the Territorial Army. Instead the General Staff wanted a form of conscription so that when a state of emergency was declared the Territorial Army

[39] Kirke to Derby, 3 October; Derby to Kirke, 5 October, 1938: Derby Papers, Correspondence with Individuals: War Office 1938; Secretary, CCTA, to Under-Secretary of State, War Office, 3 November 1938, WO 32/4526; CCTA, 29 March 1939, Minutes, 1934–39.

[40] 'Note by the Chiefs of Staff Sub-Committee on Emergency Measures, 12 April 1939', annex to COS, 288th meeting, 5 April 1939, CAB 53/11.

could be called up to man the defences, while a nucleus of conscripts was being trained to take over if and when the emergency passed. But Chamberlain refused to take such a drastic step, and urged Hore-Belisha to think again about using the Territorials on an extended part-time basis. He agreed that Hore-Belisha should show the General Staff's paper to Chatfield and Simon, but would not allow him to circulate it to the rest of the Cabinet. Despite this Hore-Belisha did show it to Halifax, who told him that he thought conscription was 'the only course that would have any effect on Germany'. Shortly afterwards he met Simon who now admitted that conscription was necessary and unavoidable. Still Chamberlain resisted, rejecting Hore-Belisha's arguments that employers and representatives of the Territorial Associations had all spoken against using the Territorials on extended duty, and urging Hore-Belisha to think yet again.[41]

Several days later, on 19 April, Chamberlain relented and allowed Hore-Belisha to brief the Cabinet on the War Office proposals. Hore-Belisha told his colleagues that the only way to provide continuous anti-aircraft defence was to call out the Territorial AA units for extended duty, train Regular reservists for full-time AA work, and introduce a limited measure of conscription to flesh out AA units. That soon proved to be unacceptable, for on the same day the Territorial Advisory Committee rejected out of hand the proposal to use Territorial troops for extended periods on anti-aircraft duties. It would have a 'very disastrous effect' on recruiting, and would be regarded by both employers and men as a 'breach of faith'. Halifax too was unenthusiastic. He stressed to the Cabinet that foreign opinion, especially in France, would not be impressed if conscription were limited to providing men for anti-aircraft units stationed in Britain. The next day the British Ambassador in Paris forwarded an 'urgent and pressing appeal' from Daladier that Britain introduce conscription at once. Chamberlain capitulated and agreed that some form of conscription was needed.[42]

Considering that both Chamberlain and his predecessor, Stanley Baldwin, had several times given firm pledges that the Government

---

[41] Minney, *Private Papers of Hore-Belisha*, pp. 192–7.
[42] Cabinet 21(39), 19 April 1939, CAB 23/98; Territorial Army Advisory Committee, 12th meeting, 19 April 1939, WO 32/9700; Derby to Hore-Belisha, 19 April 1939, Derby Papers, Correspondence with Individuals: War Office 1939; *DBFP*, V, pp. 239–40; Minney, *Private Papers of Hore-Belisha*, p. 199.

would not introduce conscription in peacetime, the Cabinet discussions on how to do just that were remarkably brief. It was generally accepted that the situation in Europe had deteriorated to such a degree that a firm response was required. The Cabinet was faced with two problems. First, how to provide cover against a sudden air attack without imposing unduly on the Territorials and without having to add to international tensions by declaring a state of emergency. What was needed was the power to call out troops on a partial mobilisation, as could most countries in Europe, without creating among the Territorials (and other reservists) the feeling that their willingness to volunteer was being abused. Second, and quite distinct, how could they convincingly demonstrate to European opinion Britain's determination to resist German aggression? The possible solutions to the latter problem steadily narrowed down to one — the introduction of conscription. It was this that dictated how the Government dealt with air defence.

After discussing various alternatives, the Cabinet decided on 25 April to recommend a limited measure of compulsory military service. All men in the year of their twentieth birthday would become liable: after taking six months' full time training they would serve in Territorial units for a further three and a half years. The War Office estimated that each year about 250,000 men would be available, once allowances had been made for medical exemptions. Of these 80,000 would be sent to ADGB units, the rest going either to Field Force or to special units. A 'Reserve and Auxiliary Forces' Bill would enable the Government to call out the Territorials without declaring a state of emergency and to use a portion of the Army Reserve to complete the establishment of deficient Regular units, man the anti-aircraft defences after three months, and to help provide instructors for the new Territorial and militia (i.e. conscript) units. Thus in the short term the Territorials and the Army Reserve would be able to provide continuous air defence, while eventually the regular supply of large numbers of trained militia-men into Territorial units would put the system on a much sounder — and fairer — basis.[43]

The fact that pressure from France made the introduction of conscription unavoidable was almost incidental to the primary consideration of home defence, but it made the final scheme much more unwieldy. Opinion in France, warned Halifax, would not be reassured by a measure designed purely to strengthen Britain's defence system. The War Office wanted only 80,000 men for

[43] Cabinet 23(39), 25 April 1939, CAB 23/99.

ADGB units, but the final scheme envisaged an annual intake of 250,000. The additional 170,000 were the price of bolstering opinion in France, and of convincing opinion in Britain that the burden of conscription would be spread evenly throughout the youth of the country. The cost of that extra mass of conscripts was largely ignored for the moment, just as only three weeks before the enormous difficulties of doubling the size of the Territorial Army had been pushed aside in the rush to make a public display of strength and determination.

When he announced the decision to bring in conscription to the House of Commons on 26 April, Chamberlain explained that the Government had acted to put a stop to the gibe that Britain was 'ready to fight to the last French soldier' that had been 'bandied about from capital to capital'.[44] While that was true, it had been a less decisive consideration than the urgent need to provide both an immediate and a long-term solution to the problem of anti-aircraft defence. Chamberlain told the Commons that the usual system of voluntary recruitment would continue, but as with the doubling of the Territorials, little consideration was given to the impact of conscription on the Territorial Army. Since its reconstitution it had been promised that it would be the sole vehicle for the expansion of the country's Army in time of emergency. It continued to be a means of expansion, but the pressure of events since September 1938 had forced the Government, sometimes acting hastily in response to new threats, to adopt measures that undermined the Territorials' exclusive claim. The changes were unsettling, but so were the times. War had not yet broken out, but there was hardly peace in any normal sense of the word, as Chamberlain argued in defence of his decision to break his pledge.

[44] *Parl. Debs.* (Commons), 5th series, vol. 346, col. 1347.

12

Neither Peace Nor War

The introduction of compulsory military service and the establishment of a parallel second line of militia units could have dealt a serious blow to the Territorial Army; it had survived the lean years by holding on to the promise that in the event of war it alone would provide the vehicle for the expansion of the nation's forces. Since the Great War many Territorials felt that their services had simply been taken for granted, but that at least could have been interpreted as part of a deeper indifference to military affairs in general. By early 1939, however, a sense of urgency and impending crisis raised the public interest in defence matters to a level that would have been unthinkable only a year or so before. Yet the Territorials never quite captured the nation's attention and imagination in the way they would have wished. Recruiting figures, of course, increased enormously, encouraged by a strong and concerted publicity campaign in which *The Times* played a prominent part, but the Territorial Army was often swamped by the claims of other services and organizations, many of which — such as the ARP — seemed to be of more pressing importance and immediate concern. The National Service Appeal in January, many Territorials argued, had overlooked the needs of the Territorial Army in the rush to build up a civil defence system. Their complaint was supported by Sir Auckland Geddes (adviser to the Government on National Service), who was quoted by *The Times* on 28 March as saying that in some areas the Territorial Army had not been getting a 'fair show' from local National Service Committees, which had concentrated on enrolling ARP personnel to the exclusion of attracting recruits for Territorial Expeditionary Force units.

The announcement at the end of March that the Territorial Army would be doubled in size came as a welcome sign that the purely passive defence system, centreing on the ARP organization, was not to monopolize the Government's attention. The response to Chamberlain's appeal for Territorial recruits was immediate: by the end of April 88,000 men had enlisted in local Territorial units.[1] For the moment, at least, it seemed that the Territorial Army would retain its special place in the scheme for the expansion of the country's forces and that the nation would rise to the Government's challenge to affirm the effectiveness of the voluntary system. From the wording of Chamberlain's statement in the Commons the Territorial Army had every reason to believe that its exclusive position had been reaffirmed, but now unlike previous occasions when the Government had underlined the role of the Territorials in expanding the Army — in circumstances that perhaps for the first time gave weight to the undertaking. In contrast to the great influx of recruits in 1939, the vast majority of whom had gone to anti-aircraft units, the new recruits were encouraged to join active field units and to leave the doubling of anti-aircraft units to those over twenty-five years of age.

The euphoria that the Territorial Army experienced in the heady days of the doubling of establishments could have been destroyed by the adoption, barely a month later, of a policy of compulsory national service. For almost twenty years the Territorials had based their claim to public support on the assurance that they and they alone would provide the means for the expansion of the nation's military forces. Now, at the critical moment, it seemed that they had been bypassed or found wanting. There was no Kitchener at the War Office, as in 1914, but a study of current defence needs and an appreciation of the political pressures on Britain had convinced the Cabinet that the Territorials by themselves could not provide the margin of safety or the demonstration of will that was required. The decision to create a parallel second line of defence in the form of militia units could have dealt a devastating psychological and numerical blow to the Territorials. It did not, and for several reasons.

Just before conscription was announced there had been a sizeable rush of recruits to join the Territorial Army, in the hope of avoiding national service. Those who had joined the Territorials, or even submitted their names, were exempt from call-up. There was some resentment towards those who had foreseen the inevitable, but it quickly disappeared, and when the national service scheme was unveiled enlistment in the Territorials from the age group that was eligible for conscription continued unabated, especially once the Government had decided in early May that service with the Territorials would be counted towards the national

---

[1] *Parl. Debs.* (Commons), 5th series, vol. 346, col. 2230 (5 May 1939).

service requirement.[2] Henceforth a young man facing the probability of national service had every reason to join the Territorials, if
only to thereby reduce the time he would later have to spend with
the militia. Once the conscript had undertaken his six months' full-
time training he would then pass either to a special militia unit or to
the Territorials. It was this meshing of the Territorial system into the
hastily improvised national service proposal that gave the Territorial Army the reassurance that it needed in the face of the decision
to overthrow the system of expansion that it had always held as
essential to its survival. As Britain moved from the lethargy of peace
to the more urgent demands of the spring and summer of 1939 the
Territorial Army provided an element of stability and continuity in
the rush to expand the country's military forces.

The danger that the Territorial Army would be overshadowed by
the new conscripts was real enough. The decision to double the
strength of the Territorials had been taken without any reference to
the equipment and training requirements of the flood of recruits
who responded to the Government's appeal, and that problem was
simply exacerbated by the introduction of compulsory national
service. Shortly after Chamberlain announced the doubling of the
Territorial strength, *The Times* noted with satisfaction (11 April) that
the DGTA had assured prospective recruits that there was sufficient
equipment for all training purposes at headquarters and drill halls.
Additional accommodation, if required, was offered by the Board of
Education, which reversed its long-standing policy and made
school buildings available for units that found their normal
premises inadequate for their growing numbers. Not all offers were
as welcome. On 4 May *The Times* reported that the recruiting staff at
some Territorial units were embarrassed by the numbers of
applications they had received from 'middle-aged and elderly' men
to act as instructors, usually on the basis of their previous peacetime
experience in the Territorials, but sometimes on the strength of their
service in the Great War. They were advised to join National
Defence units, which had been established to guard vital installations and to take over less active responsibilities, thereby freeing
younger men for front-line roles.

The Territorials, and the community from which they drew their
strength, responded magnificently. Units that had struggled for
years to win a few recruits here and there were suddenly over-
whelmed. The London Rifle Brigade, which had taken twenty years
to reach full strength, raised a second unit within as many hours.

[2]   *Ibid.*, vol. 347, col. 493 (10 May 1939).

The London Irish decided that its second battalion would be made up exclusively of night workers, who had hitherto been unable to join because of the conflicting demands of their jobs and military training. In Seaford, where local employers had for years claimed that it was impossible to release workers for annual camp just at the height of the summer season, a Women's Volunteer Shop Assistants' Corps was formed to release Territorials from work so they could attend the full training period at camp. When the Football Association put its weight behind the Territorial appeal, all members of the Liverpool Football Club together with the manager and secretary agreed to form a club section of The King's Regiment and urged club supporters to follow suit. Norwich City Football Club did the same. Edinburgh was typical of many centres: *The Times* reported on 10 May that all recruiting records had been broken, and that since 1 May the daily intake had averaged two hundred.

Gratifying as this response was after so many barren years, it concealed the greatest weakness of the Territorial Army, and indeed of the country's forces as a whole. No influx of men could offset the grave shortages of equipment and instructors. Quite the contrary: the amazing surge in recruiting worsened an already difficult situation. Notwithstanding the assurances of the DGTA, it soon became clear that there was an embarrassing and alarming deficiency in equipment, and an even greater shortage of instructors. On 5 May *The Times* wrote of a 'grave shortage of instructors', especially in the artillery, which had prompted the Government to issue an appeal for ex-Regulars to join the Territorial Army with the promise of the immediate rank of sergeant. Once again the needs of the Regular Army quite properly came first, and the Territorials had to make do with what was left over. Nevertheless there was much closer cooperation between the two forces, especially at the summer camps of 1938 and 1939, when many Territorial units trained alongside their Regular counterparts. This was long overdue, for while there had been many contacts between the Regulars and the Territorials on the unit level, a sense of coolness and distrust had often marked their relations at the higher level, despite the repeated assertions that there was the utmost cordiality and friendly rivalry between the two armies.

The growing sense of urgency in 1938 and especially in 1939 brought the Regular and the Territorial Armies much closer together, but paradoxically it also kept them apart. After the announcement in March 1939 of the abandonment of the 'limited liability' policy, the emphasis in military planning swung to the needs of the Field Force. Even the introduction of conscription, which the Cabinet felt was made necessary by the requirements of the ADGB scheme for round-the-clock operation, was generally hailed by the press and public as proof that Britain would stand by France in a continental strategy. The emphasis in recruiting for the Territorial Army then swung from the needs of anti-aircraft defence to those of the Field Force. On 5 April *The Times* urged that men under twenty-five should be encouraged to join or transfer to the infantry. A month later, on 5 May, Liddell Hart stressed in *The Times* that young men had to be drawn into Territorial infantry units, which were still understrength in comparison with AA units, but that could not be achieved, he argued, until the infantry were regarded as a *'corps d'élite,* not as cannon fodder'. So long as the anti-aircraft role of the Territorial Army was stressed and its expeditionary role minimised — as had been the case for most of the 1930s — the Territorials had a strong claim on Government support that did not compete directly with the claims of the Regular Army. Once the public awoke to the very real dangers of air attack — and that came in 1938 — the Territorials also had an immediate and in some senses unrivalled claim on public support. By the spring of 1939, however, the Territorials were in a difficult position, notwithstanding the unprecedented numbers of recruits that flocked to join local units.

With the adoption of a policy of unlimited liability to underwrite Britain's potential military involvement on the continent, the Territorial Army was squeezed between the priority claims of the Regular Army, which was seen as the spearhead of Britain's continental capability, and the new conscript forces which — unfairly it must have seemed to the Territorials — were seen as evidence of the nation's willingness to shoulder the burdens of defence. The introduction of conscription was a sign that 'Britain meant business' in a way that the doubling of the Territorial Army, no matter how successful, could never have been. As part of the Field Force, the Territorials played a secondary role to that of the Regular Army; now their sole responsibility for anti-aircraft defence was undercut by the national service scheme.

So far as the deployment of the Field Force was concerned there had always been the clear assumption that before any Territorial units were despatched overseas they would have at least six months intensive training. Admirable as their training efforts throughout the year were, the Territorials simply could not hope to produce battle-ready troops, even from the best of the Territorial units, and the quality varied widely, as the War Office well knew. In 1938 when Liddell Hart pressed vigorously for a complete rethinking of the methods of training Territorial troops and urged a more realistic and demanding approach in place of the leisurely atmosphere that he observed at many Territorial camps, he was warmly supported by Major-General Sir John Kennedy, former GOC of the 44th Division (TA), who wrote to him:

> I . . . entirely agree and think it vitally important that it should be recognized that Territorial Troops at the beginning of a war can only be asked to perform very simple manoeuvres and if it is possible to give them purely (?) defensive role so much the better, but even defence must be on lines which are suitable to troops who may panic through ignorance or the shock of first casualties.
> Territorial training is largely a veneer — which the rough usage of war destroys almost at once — unless it is carefully preserved until war experience gradually produces the real fighting soldier, a man who reacts instinctively to any situation and is not dismayed by the unexpected.[3]

Notwithstanding this cautionary advice, when the new military policy of unlimited liability was announced in March, the time between the dispatch of the first (Regular) contingent of the Field Force and the dispatch of the first Territorial divisions that made up the second contingent was reduced to four months. Much more equipment was available than had been the case at any stage since reconstitution but now the size of the Territorial Army had increased enormously and placed strains on the training facilities — instructors and equipment — that could not be resolved by the good-natured improvisation that was such a feature of the spring and summer of 1939. Yet even under the reduced training period the Territorials could hardly make special claims on scarce resources: they were, after all, the second contingent of the Field Force, and clearly the needs of the Regular troops of the first contingent had to come first.

The Territorials also suffered at the hands of the national service troops. Not that their intake of recruits fell off. Far from it: *The Times* noted on 29 July that at the height of the summer camp period, when recruiting traditionally fell off as the chance of going to camp was lost until the following year, more than three thousand men had joined the Field Force units of the Territorial

---

[3] Kennedy to Liddell Hart, 28 August 1938, Liddell Hart Papers, 1/417.

Army. But where the Territorials did run second was in the competition for equipment and general training facilities. Even though in June Hore-Belisha strongly denied that the Territorials were being 'short-changed' to suit the national service troops, and promised that all units would have uniforms within a month,[4] there was evidence that the militia was favoured.

It was not surprising that this should have been so. The Government well understood that the adoption of peacetime conscription (a term they avoided using if at all possible) was a major departure from normal British practice, and a step it had pledged itself not to take. Its explanation for so abrupt a reversal of policy — that the conditions prevailing in Europe hardly constituted peace as it was usually understood — was accepted by most of the country, but the Government was acutely aware that acceptance would quickly turn to condemnation and bitter criticism if it were found that youth was being squandered by Government incompetence. The need for a general election in 1940 made the Government even more sensitive to the needs of the militia. So too with the Army, which had not been held in particularly high regard during the 1930s. The War Office realized that it would be folly to alienate the public by mishandling the intake of conscripts, and it therefore made every effort to make them feel welcome and satisfied.

It was a mammoth task. Lacking all plans the War Office had to create virtually overnight the machinery to train (and of course to feed, clothe and house) the first batch of conscripts. From the announcement of conscription at the end of April until the arrival of the first group of men in the middle of July the War Office had less than three months to adjust itself to the needs of the mass training of conscripts in peacetime. Chamberlain was right to argue in April that the times could hardly be called peaceful, but nor were they war, and the urgent sacrifices that could be readily demanded of the country in the midst of battle could not necessarily be expected before the battle had begun. In this sense it was perhaps fortunate that the war began when it did, for the War Office had barely faced two intakes of peacetime conscripts before the onset of hostilities cast the national service scheme in a very different light.

Even those two intakes, beginning on 15 July, strained the resources of the War Office almost to breaking point. There were simply not enough instructors to go around. Training in the Regular Army had been stepped up, and those instructors who could be spared were detailed to handle the new conscripts. Once

[4]   *Parl. Debs.* (Commons), 5th series, vol. 348, col. 194 (27 June 1939).

again the Territorials were left to manage as best they could: neither militarily nor politically were they in a position to demand preferential or even equal treatment. The summer camps of 1939, however, took on a new and more urgent atmosphere. There was a widespread feeling that it was no longer a matter of playing at soldiers or of having a pleasant and none-too-demanding holiday under canvas. A new sense of seriousness, an appreciation that war could not be far off, helped the Territorials concentrate on the essentials of training rather than on the inadequacies of their equipment or their grievances, real and imagined, at the War Office's favoured treatment of the militia.

Nevertheless willing spirit and hard work could not overcome the fact that the machinery and the resources for the enormous expansion of the Army that had taken place since the beginning of 1939 were simply not available. The problem was not in getting the men, for once the country was convinced that volunteers were really needed, they flocked to the recruiting stations by the thousands. Where the expansion threatened to break down under the weight of its own numerical success was in the Army's inability to provide the means by which young recruits could be turned into something akin to trained soldiers. For the swollen Territorial Army, the situation was perhaps even worse. Few if any of the first-line Territorial units had reached anything like proper efficiency by 1939, when they had to dilute their Regular training staffs and their own Territorial officers and NCOs to begin the training of the massive numbers of recruits who were to form the second-line units. The results were not surprising. In February 1940 Sir Auckland Geddes told Liddell Hart:

> This army business is worse than could have been believed. These second line T.F. divisions are more than a menace. The rubbish we have got here is appalling and the officers! My God! But the really frightening thing is the way the conscripts are being rotted. No discipline, no training, apparently no equipment.[5]

Notwithstanding those comments, the fact remains that by early 1940 three Territorial divisions — the 48th (South Midland), the 50th (Northumbrian), and the 51st (Highland) — had arrived in France and taken their places in the front line.

When war broke out in September 1939 the Government decided

---

[5] 'Notes', February 1940, Liddell Hart Papers, 1/311/11b.

to create one national army and as far as possible to get rid of the distinctions between the Regular Army, the Territorial Army, and the newly-created Militia. Under the Armed Forces (Conditions of Service) Act all land forces became part of the British Army for the duration of the war. For the Territorials this was signified by the order to discard the brass 'T' that had always been part of their uniform. For some Territorials this had been a mark of inferiority, especially in the penurious days between the wars. In 1937, when discussing proposals with Liddell Hart on how to raise the prestige and self-esteem of the Territorials, Hore-Belisha had thought of doing away with the 'T' and dropping the name 'Territorial' in favour of a 'new and more inspiring' title. Liddell Hart, obsessed with the need to avoid another continental involvement along the lines of the Great War, suggested 'Imperial Army' for the Regulars and 'National Army' for the Territorials.[6]

None of these ideas was implemented at the time, but the attempt to move the Territorial and Regular Armies closer together was one of the first war-time measures to be introduced by the War Office in September 1939. Yet for all those who welcomed the merging of the various forces into one Army, the old ways had their supporters. Rumours circulated that the Territorial Army had ceased to exist, and that the discarding of the 'T' was only the prelude to much wider changes that would wipe out the identities of Territorial units. The War Office denied any ulterior motive over the matter of the 'T',[7] but some Territorials were not mollified. Having argued for so long that they wanted to be treated on equal terms with their Regular counterparts, they now fought against the obvious policy of forging a single fighting force out of the disparate elements that had made up the peacetime Armies. Writing in 1943 of the Middlesex Association, Colonel E. J. King said bitterly:

The whole attitude of the Regular Army towards the TA in the first few months after mobilization was extremely disconcerting. The less intelligent type of staff officer, in the sacred name of discipline, lost no opportunity of shewing his contempt in the most offensive and provocative manner for the TA and all its ways. In at least one case a large body of Commanding Officers was informed that the TA had ceased to exist, and the sooner

[6] 'Notes of a talk with Hore-Belisha', 23 August 1937, Liddell Hart Papers, 11/HB 1937/176.
[7] *Parl. Debs.* (Commons), 5th series, vol. 355, col. 467 (5 December 1939).

they forgot its traditions, and the fact that they had ever belonged to it the better. It was impossible to protest against the insult, as the officers felt that if they did so, they would be reported upon by the staff officer concerned as unfit for their positions. The situation was not improved by the arbitrary and capricious order that TA officers must cease to wear the distinguishing letter 'T' on their shoulder-straps, which they had been so proud to wear all through the previous war.

The attitude of the Regular Army towards the Territorials, King charged, was far worse than it had been during the Great War. According to one (unnamed) 'distinguished and esteemed of their number' the only explanation for what seemed to be a deliberate policy was that 'the War Office had gone completely mad'.[8]

No doubt there were instances of condescending treatment of Territorials by Regulars, but the uncertainties of the first few months of the war put everyone under strain, and the reception that the overwhelming majority of Territorial units got was one of genuine welcome even if it was backed by a degree of puzzled reserve. How could it have been otherwise? Despite the claims of both Regular and Territorial spokesmen, relations between the two Armies had never been particularly close during the twenties and thirties. Resentment over the alleged war-time discrimination against Territorial units made many Associations very wary of taking the Regular Army's assurances of its good intentions towards the Territorials at face value. The successive cuts in spending during the twenties and early thirties, however much they were matched by proportionate reductions in the Regular Army, were taken by the Associations as a sign that the War Office, with its natural bias in favour of the Regular Army, did not or could not appreciate the special needs of the citizen-volunteer Territorial Army. For its part the Regular Army tended to look askance at the Territorial Army: the rate of turn-over, the elementary training at camp coming on top of a derisory number of drills during the year, the poor equipment and the all-too-apparent lack of real military enthusiasm and competence among many of the officers added up to a force that was truly little better than 'Saturday night soldiers'.

In fact, of course, neither side was completely right. The treatment of the Territorials during the Great War had not, on the whole, resulted from any hostility towards the Territorials as such,

[8] E. J. King, 'A History of the Territorial Army and Auxilliary Force Association of the County of Middlesex', pp. 65 – 6.

but from the view that for all their achievements they were ill-fitted to be the sole vehicle for the expansion of the country's military forces, especially on the scale that was envisaged. Given the general military priorities during the twenties and early thirties, it was only proper that the greater share of funds should be spent on the Regular Army, especially in the light of the Territorials' insistence on safeguards against their being called up for overseas service before conscription was introduced. In any case, though it might have been argued that the Territorials could least afford the cuts, the reductions in expenditure for the Territorial Army were no greater than for the Regular Army.

For its part, the Regular Army did tend to ignore the Territorials or — perhaps worse — not to take them seriously. Adjutantcies of Territorial battalions were considered professional backwaters and a sure end to any hopes of advancement that the officer might have had. Even though the duties of a Territorial adjutant were every bit as demanding of those of adjutants in Regular battalions, albeit of a very different order, Regular officers who were posted to such positions were paid less than their Regular Army counterparts, and they found it difficult to move from Territorial adjutantcies to Staff College, the key to promotion. The opening of the Imperial Defence College to Territorial (and Naval and Air Reserve) officers in 1937 was a hopeful sign that the War Office had begun to give more thought to the needs of the Territorial Army, but it was only a token, and the real acceptance of the second line by the Regular Army had to come on a much wider basis than that. It did come in 1938, when the March and particularly the September crises showed how dependent the country was on the Territorial Army, no matter how inadequate its performance had been. By the time war broke out, the bonds between the Regular and the Territorial Armies had necessarily grown stronger with the consciousness of the common task immediately before them.

Despite all the difficulties, shortcomings and confusion, the transition from peace to war for the Territorial Army was remarkably smooth. Once war was declared in September most of the old antagonisms and suspicions were forgotten under the pressure of preparing for battle. So too were some of the undertakings that the Territorials had thought so important. It had always been understood that before embarking for overseas service Territorial troops would receive considerable extra training as a supplement to that which they had already had and which of course varied widely from unit to unit and within individual units. That was dropped once war had been declared. In October Hore-Belisha was asked why mere 'boys', 'innocent lads, practically children', who had joined the Territorial Army in June at nineteen, had been sent to France in mid-September while twenty year old conscripts were kept back in England. He replied that these few units were indeed in France, but they were 'engaged in rearward positions' where they could perform useful duties, particularly in basic construction, while completing their training.[9] What he did not add was that just as the pledge presented the War Office with distinctions that it could not uphold, so it was not practicable to differentiate between various levels of training within individual units. In particular, units could not be broken up or withheld from active service simply because of the inadequate training of a few recent recruits.

All of these were, however, minor problems that were soon swept aside by the pressures of war. In peacetime the Territorials had been able to afford the luxury of endless arguments about their rights, though not without some long-term cost to their prestige, but these matters were disregarded in the rush to create a nation-in-arms. The Territorials were an essential part of that process.

[9] *Parl. Debs.* (Commons), 5th series, vol. 352, cols. 674 – 5, 702 (17 October 1939).

Conclusion

By the time of the German attack on western Europe in the spring of 1940 the integration of the Regular and Territorial Armies was well under way. There had already been an interchange of battalions between Regular and Territorial brigades, and Territorial troops had taken their place in the front line. Elsewhere, Territorial units were busy training, fortunately spared the immediate trial of battle. Four months after mobilisation on 1 September, for example, the Cheshire Yeomanry, part of the 6th Cavalry Brigade, arrived in Palestine and began a long overdue conversion from horses to mechanized vehicles. (In a Special Order of the Day for Christmas Eve 1940, the Brigade Commander admonished his troops that 'the change from "oats to oil" will make no difference'.[1]) It was a slow process, and most Yeomanry units did not see action until early 1943. Nevertheless there were Territorial units at El Alamein, in the wearying struggle up the Italian peninsula, and in the final assaults on north-west Europe beginning with the D-Day landings in Normandy. In every European theatre and in every way, Territorials distinguished themselves in battle and gave the lie to the gibe that they were merely 'Saturday night soldiers'.

Whether they completely vindicated the claims of the supporters of Haldane's original scheme is a more difficult question to answer. The Territorials who fought in the First World War were the wartime rump of Haldane's plan, for the great mass of his proposed 'nation-in-arms' had been drawn into Kitchener's 'New Armies'. There seems no reason why these armies could not equally well have been raised via the Territorial scheme, but we can get no further than that. In the Second World War the expansion of Britain's military power and the total mobilisation of her resources went far beyond what anyone could have anticipated. It is no criticism of the inter-war Territorials to say that while they made a valuable

[1] Cheshire Yeomanry War diary, 24 December 1940, WO 169/226.

contribution to the maintenance of a reservoir of military power in the twenties and thirties, though one that through little fault of their own was miserably inadequate, it needed the pressures of a life-and-death struggle to bring them to their full potential. And even this could be achieved only after a much longer period of intensive training than had originally been envisaged and as part of a much wider mobilisation scheme than had been foreseen.

The Territorial Army was never the framework for the British nation-in-arms that Haldane had hoped for. But it did help to make the transition from peace to war much easier than it might otherwise have been. (This transition was also assisted, paradoxically, by the very successes of the Germans in 1940. They established a stalemate in western Europe that gave the British, in their weakness, a breathing space of several years before they were able to re-enter the continent from Britain itself.) Haldane's ideas were the product of an earlier age and, in Michael Howard's words, were 'frankly militaristic'.[2] Such attitudes to military service in peacetime barely survived the battlefields of the western front, and then had to face the hostile environment of the twenties and thirties. When the opportunity to put the plan to the test did come after 1939 the scale of warfare was so enormous that a relatively small organisation like the Territorial Army was swept up in the rush to full mobilisation.

Amateurs who aspired to a degree of professional expertise in peacetime, citizens who chose to train as part-time soldiers in preparation for war, the Territorials were an important, if often overlooked and sadly neglected, part of Britain's military forces. Even if they were not as central as they might have wished, or indeed as essential as they thought themselves to be, they deserved better than the ungenerous comment of their latter-day midwife. Referring to Britain's position at the end of 1940, Churchill later wrote: 'I longed for more Regular troops with which to rebuild and expand the Army. Wars are not won by heroic militias.'[3] But then, as others have remarked, in war truth is the first casualty.

---

[2] Michael Howard, *Lord Haldane and the Territorial Army*, p. 92.
[3] Winston S. Churchill, *History of the Second World War*, vol. 2, *Their Finest Hour* (London, 1949), p. 163.

APPENDIX

Strength of the Territorial Army, by arms, all ranks, on 1 October 1908 – 38

Year	Yeomanry	Royal Artillery	Royal Engineers	Infantry	Royal Army Service Corps	Other Arms*	Total
1908	22,558	29,427	10,447	123,572	5,127	8,473	199,604
1909	25,610	39,923	13,395	173,148	7,686	12,739	272,501
1910	24,773	39,684	13,001	171,246	7,850	13,035	269,589
1911	24,423	39,607	13,102	168,457	7,850	13,262	266,701
1912	24,936	39,099	12,958	166,571	7,445	12,985	263,994
1913**	24,547	37,972	12,971	152,380	7,722	12,748	248,340
1920	2,384	15,018	2,701	37,683	2,081	2,334	62,201
1921	6,075	26,540	5,823	86,006	3,741	8,844	137,032
1922	4,514	29,026	6,734	87,273	1,162	7,891	136,600
1923	4,602	30,443	7,516	89,988	1,150	8,741	142,440
1924	4,670	31,067	8,101	90,188	1,273	9,313	144,612
1925	4,696	32,242	9,373	90,372	1,338	9,504	147,525
1926	4,756	32,893	9,339	90,522	1,403	9,829	148,742
1927	4,615	31,606	9,138	85,991	1,403	8,945	141,698
1928	4,726	31,666	9,066	85,647	1,402	8,963	141,470
1929	4,748	30,295	8,976	84,332	1,419	8,807	138,577
1930	4,823	28,685	9,077	84,146	1,426	8,807	137,141
1931	4,860	28,818	9,391	86,239	1,412	9,291	140,011
1932	4,642	26,423	8,662	79,276	1,291	8,463	128,757
1933	4,819	27,315	9,298	84,316	1,412	8,984	136,134
1934	4,752	27,492	9,474	81,736	1,505	8,776	133,735
1935	4,831	27,751	9,442	79,096	1,555	8,942	131,617
1936	4,964	30,902	11,863	81,220	2,521	9,929	141,399
1937	5,610	38,366	23,256	75,323	3,399	10,811	156,765
1938	5,650	45,018	36,862	81,735	4,652	12,504	186,421

* 'Other Arms' includes Signals, Royal Army Ordnance Corps, Royal Army Medical Corps, and Royal Army Veterinary Corps.

** Separate details are not available for the years 1914 to 1919, when the Territorial Force was mobilized serving with the British Forces in the Field.

Source: Annual 'Statistical Abstract for the United Kingdom'.

Bibliography

Primary Sources

Public Record Office, London

The following classes of papers were used in this study:

Cabinet
CAB 2   Committee of Imperial Defence, minutes of meetings
CAB 16 CID Sub-Committees, including the Defence Requirements Committee
CAB 21 Registered files
CAB 23 Conclusions of Cabinet meetings
CAB 24 Cabinet Papers
CAB 53 Meetings and memoranda of the Chiefs of Staff
Foreign Office
FO 371 General Correspondence
Premier's Office
PREM 1 Prime Minister's Office: correspondence and papers
War Office
WO32   Miscellaneous
WO163   Minutes and précis of the Army Council
WO169   War Diaries

Private papers

Derby papers, Liverpool Record Office
Haldane papers, National Library of Scotland
Kitchener papers, Public Record Office
Liddell Hart papers, Liddell Hart Centre for Military Archives, King's College London
Scarbrough papers, in the possession of the Earl of Scarbrough
Wilson papers, Imperial War Museum, London

County Association records

There were more than eighty County Territorial Associations that raised and administered the Territorial Army. When the 'old' Territorial Army was wound up in 1965 the Associations were directed by the War Office to deposit their records in the appropriate County Record Office. Most did so, but a few have retained their records: the latter, for the most part, are uncatalogued, hence the lack of any detailed references in the notes. Some records have apparently been lost (e.g. Merionethshire) or destroyed (e.g. Glamorganshire, as the result of a flood during the Second World War).

1968 ?

Those Associations' records consulted were:

Bedfordshire Territorial Association, Bedfordshire Record Office

Berkshire Territorial Association, Berkshire Record Office

Buckinghamshire Territorial Association, Buckinghamshire Record Office

Caernarvonshire Territorial Association, Caernarvonshire Record Office

Cambridge and Isle of Ely Territorial Association, Cambridgeshire Record Office

City of Aberdeen Territorial Association, Scottish Record Office

City of Dundee Territorial Association, Scottish Record Office

City of Edinburgh Territorial Association, Lowland TA&VR Association, Edinburgh Office

City of Glasgow Territorial Association, Lowland TA&VR Association, Glasgow Office

City of London Territorial Association, Guildhall Library, London

Cornwall Territorial Association, Cornwall Record Office

Council of County Territorial Associations, Council of TA&VR Associations, Duke of York's Headquarters, London

County of Aberdeen Territorial Association, Scottish Record Office

County of London Territorial Association, Greater London Record Office

Cumberland Territorial Association, Cumbria Record Office

Denbighshire Territorial Association, Flintshire Record Office

Derbyshire Territorial Association, Derbyshire Record Office

Devon Territorial Association, Devon Record Office

Dumbarton Territorial Association, Scottish Record Office

Dumfriesshire Territorial Association, Scottish Record Office

Durham Territorial Association, North of England TA&VR Association, Durham

East Lancashire Territorial Association, Manchester Public Library, Archives Department
East Lothian Territorial Association, Lowland TA&VR Association, Edinburgh Office
Essex Territorial Association, East Anglia TA&VR Association, Chelmsford
Fife Territorial Association, Scottish Record Office
Flintshire Territorial Association, Flintshire Record Office
Gloucestershire Territorial Association, Gloucestershire Record Office
Hampshire and the Isle of Wight Territorial Association, Hampshire Record Office
Hertfordshire Territorial Association, Hertfordshire Record Office
Inverness Territorial Association, Scottish Record Office
Kent Territorial Association, Kent Record Office
Kirkudbrightshire Territorial Association, Scottish Record Office
Lanarkshire Territorial Association, Scottish Record Office
Leicestershire and Rutland Territorial Associations, Leicestershire Record Office
Lincolnshire Territorial Association, Lincolnshire Archives Office
Middlesex Territorial Association, Greater London Record Office
Monmouthshire Territorial Association, Gwent Record Office
Northumberland Territorial Association, Northumberland Record Office
Nottinghamshire Territorial Association, Nottinghamshire Record Office
Oxfordshire Territorial Association, Oxfordshire Record Office
Peebles Territorial Association, Lowland TA&VR Association, Edinburgh Office
Perth Territorial Association, Scottish Record Office
Staffordshire Territorial Association, Staffordshire Record Office
Stirling Territorial Association, Scottish Record Office
Suffolk Territorial Association, Suffolk Record Office
Surrey Territorial Association, Surrey Record Office
Sussex Territorial Association, Sussex Record Office
Warwickshire Territorial Association, Warwickshire Record Office
West Lancashire Territorial Association, Liverpool Record Office
Westmorland Territorial Association, Cumbria Record Office
West Riding, Yorkshire, Territorial Association, City of Leeds Archives Department

Secondary Sources

Biographies and memoirs

Brett, M.V. (ed.). *Journals and Letters of Reginald Viscount Esher.* London, 1934.

Bond, Brian (ed.). *Chief of Staff: The Diaries of Lieutenant-General Sir Henry Pownall*, vol. 1. London, 1972.

Calwell, C.E. *Field Marshal Sir Henry Wilson: His Life and Diaries.* London, 1927.

Cassar, George H. *Kitchener, Architect of Victory.* London, 1977.

Churchill, Randolph. *Lord Derby, King of Lancashire.* London, 1959.

Feiling, Keith. *The Life of Neville Chamberlain.* London, 1946.

Fraser, Peter. *Lord Esher: A Political Biography.* London, 1973.

French, Viscount. *1914.* London, 1919.

Gilbert, Martin. *Winston S. Churchill*, vols. 4 and 5. London, 1975, 1976.

—— *Winston S. Churchill*, vol. 5. *Companion Volumes.* London, 1977.

Grey, Viscount, of Fallodon, *Twenty-five Years, 1892 – 1916.* London, 1925.

Haldane, Richard Burdon. *Before the War.* London, 1920.

—— *Richard Burdon Haldane: an Autobiography.* London, 1929.

Koss, Stephen. *Haldane: Scapegoat for Liberalism.* New York, 1969.

Liddell Hart, B.H. *Memoirs*, vol. 1. London, 1965.

MacLeod, Roderick and Kelly, Denis (eds.). *Time Unguarded: The Ironside Diaries, 1937 – 1940.* New York, 1962.

Magnus, Philip. *Kitchener: Portrait of an Imperialist.* London, 1958.

Maurice, Frederick. *Haldane, 1856 – 1915.* London, 1937.

Minney, R.J. *The Private Papers of Hore-Belisha.* London, 1960.

Pile, F.A. *Ack-Ack: Britain's Defence Against Air Attack during the Second World War.* London, 1949.

Sommer, D. *Haldane of Cloan: His Life and Times, 1856 – 1928.* London, 1968.

Spiers, Edward M. *Haldane: an Army Reformer.* Edinburgh, 1980.

Verney, John. *Going to the Wars: A Journey in Various Directions.* London, 1955.

Newspapers and periodicals

Army Quarterly, Daily Herald, Daily Telegraph, Daily Mail, Daily Mirror, Fortnightly Review, Journal of the Royal United Service

Institution, The Nineteenth Century and After, The Times.
  Several Associations (e.g. West Lancashire, Suffolk, Berkshire) kept extensive collections of clippings from the local press, which are now kept with the Associations' papers. These proved valuable in providing a local perspective on Territorial affairs.

Official publications
Parliamentary Debates (Lords and Commons)
Parliamentary Papers

Other Secondary works
Barrett, J. *Falling In: Australians and 'Boy Conscription' 1911 – 1915.* Sydney, 1979.
Bewsher, F.W. *The History of the 51st (Highland) Division, 1914 – 1918.* Edinburgh, 1921.
Bond, Brian. *British Military Policy between the Two World Wars.* Oxford, 1980.
Clive, Lewis. *The People's Army,* London, 1938.
Codrington, G.R. *What is the Territorial Army?* London, 1933.
Cousins, Geoffrey. *The Defenders.* London, 1968.
Cunningham, Hugh. *The Volunteers: A social and political history.* London, 1975.
Dennis, Peter. *Decision by Default: Peacetime Conscription and British Defence, 1919 – 1939.* London, 1972.
D'Ombrain, N. *War machinery and high policy: defence administration in peacetime Britain, 1902 – 1914.* Oxford, 1973.
Dudley Ward, C.H. *History of the 53rd (Welsh) Division (T.F.) 1914 – 1918.* Cardiff, 1927.
Dunlop. John K. *The Problems and Responsibilities of the Territorial Army.* London, 1935.
——*The Development of the British Army, 1899 – 1914.* London, 1938.
Durand, A.T.M. and Hastings, R.H.W.S. *The London Rifle Brigade, 1919 – 1950.* Aldershot, 1952.
Edmonds, J.E. *Military Operations, France and Belgium, 1914 – 18.* London, 1925 – 48.
Ellis, L.F. *The War in France and Flanders, 1939 – 1940.* London, 1953.
French, David. *British Economic and Strategic Planning 1905 – 1915.* London, 1982.
Germains, Victor Wallace. *The Kitchener Armies.* London, 1930.
Gibbs, N.H. *Grand Strategy,* vol. 1, *Rearmament.* London, 1976.

Gooch, John. *The Plans of War: The General Staff and British Military Strategy c. 1900 – 1916*. London, 1974.

Gooch, John and Beckett, I.F.W. (eds.). *Politicians and Defence*. Manchester, 1981.

Green, W.E. *The Territorials in the Next War*. London, 1938.

Hamilton, Ian. *Compulsory Service: A Study of the Question in the Light of Experience*. London, 1910.

Hayes, Denis. *Conscription Conflict: The Conflict of Ideas in the Struggle For and Against Military Conscription in Britain between 1901 and 1939*. London, 1949.

Howard, Michael. *Lord Haldane and the Territorial Army*. London, 1967.

—— *The Continental Commitment*. London, 1972.

Newman, S. *March 1939: The British Guarantee to Poland*. Oxford, 1976.

Peden, G.C. *British Rearmament and the Treasury 1932 – 9*. Edinburgh, 1979.

Roberts, Earl. *Fallacies and Facts: An Answer to 'Compulsory Service'*. London, 1911.

Sellwood, A.V. *The Saturday Night Soldiers*. London, 1966.

Shay Jr., Robert Paul. *British Rearmament in the Thirties. Politics and Profits*. Princeton, 1977.

Spiers, Edward M. *The Army and Society, 1815 – 1914*. London, 1980.

Templewood, Viscount. *Nine Troubled Years*. London, 1954.

Woodward, E.L. and Butler, Rohan (eds.). *Documents on British Foreign Policy, 1919 – 1945*, Third Series, 1938 – 9. London, 1949 – 55.

Index

Acland, Sir Francis, 22, 60
Air Defence of Great Britain, 101,
102, 213 – 14, 246
Anti-aircraft defence (AA): General
Staff on TA role in, 95 – 6, greater
TA role in, 98, 101 – 2; raising TA
troops for, 102, 108-9; and
London TA divisions, 111; TA
recruiting for, 127, 164, 181, 189,
190, 205 – 6, 224 – 5; DRC on,
185, 192; TA central to, 196;
greater priority to, 208 – 9;
conversion of TA infantry to, 209,
211; priority of questioned,
213 – 14; in September 1938 crisis,
228 – 30; TA divisions for
increased, 237; provision for in
emergencies, 244 – 5; conscription
for, 246
Arnold-Forster, H.O., 6
Asquith, H.H., 30, 35 – 6

Backhouse, Admiral Sir Roger, 233
Baldwin, Stanley, 199, 201
Balfour, Arthur, 7
Barnes, George, 177
Belcher, Sgt. D.W., vc, 34
Bethune, Lt. Gen. Sir Edward, 28,
35
Birch, Gen. Sir Noel, 76, 90, 94,
96, 102
Bonar Law, Andrew, 53, 69
Bonham-Carter, Gen. Sir Charles,
193 – 4, 237
Bonnet, Georges, 240
bounty: requested, 27 – 8; granted,
29 – 30; questioned, 60, 87, 90;
reduced, 98; abolition discussed,
110, 111 – 15; abolished, 115;

reaction to abolition, 115 – 19;
partial restoration ('proficiency
grant'), 119 – 21 *passim*
Brodrick, W. St John, 6
Bromley-Davenport, Brig. Gen. Sir
William, 104, 112, 113 – 4, 116,
117, 134 – 5, 175
Brown, Col. (Brig. Sir) John, 105,
136, 207

Cabinet: and ten year rule, 46, 123;
on TA reconstitution, 57, 58 – 9;
on aid to civil power, 71, 72 – 3,
81 – 2; on TA cuts, 101; on
rearmament, 182 – 3, 184, 189; on
DRC 1st report, 186; on TA role,
196, 199, 201; accepts limited
liability, 209, 211, 213 – 15;
accepts continental role, 234;
accepts conscription, 246
cadets, 103, 129
Campbell-Bannerman, Sir Henry, 4
Camrose, Lord, 140
Cavan, Field Marshal Lord, 97, 99
Chamberlain, Neville: on defence
spending, 183, 204, 209, 212; on
contintental strategy, 193,
199 – 201, 211, 234; advises Hore-
Belisha, 202, 206; on Anschluss,
213; in Czechoslovak crisis, 227,
228; talks with French, 231;
opposes Ministry of Supply, 235;
launches National Service
Appeal, 235; reaction to Prague
crisis, 239 – 40; doubles TA, 241;
gives pledge to Poland, 242; on
TA and AA defence, 244 – 5; on
conscription 245, 247
Chatfield, Admiral Lord, 211, 240

122, 128, 195 – 6, 222
Czechoslovak crisis, 227 – 8, 239

Daily Herald, 241
Daily Mail, 235, 242
Daily Mirror, 236, 238, 240
Daily Telegraph, 236 – 7, 238
Daladier, Edouard, 228, 232, 245
Defence Force: created, 73; size of, 74 – 5, 76; relationship to TA, 75; effect on TA, 76 – 80, 81, 153, 163
Defence Requirements Sub-Committee (DRC), 184, 210, 211; first report, 184 – 6; discussed, 186 – 8; third report, 191 – 2
Derby, Earl of: on compulsion, 23; on 'pledge', 36, 126, 134 – 8, 139 – 40, 141; on financial cuts, 103, 105, 106, 127 – 8; warns War Office, 120, 121; on Hore-Belisha, 203; on National Service Appeal, 236
Deverell, Field Marshal Sir Cyril, 207
'Duma', 11
du Maurier, Maj. Guy, 17
Dunlop, Lt. Col. J.K., 207

Eden, Anthony, 209
Edward VII, 11, 14 – 15, 17, 26, 27
Elles, Gen. Sir Hugh, 195
Ellison, Col. G.F., 6
Esher, Lord, 11, 12 – 13, 23, 26, 50, 165
Ewart, Maj. Gen. J. Spencer, 12
Expeditionary Force: Haldane considers, 6; establishes, 7 – 8; Haldane on TA role in, 13 – 14; compulsion urged, 21; COS press expansion of, 183 – 4; DRC urges increase in, 185, 191 – 2; War Office priority for, 190; Cabinet discusses, 199 – 201; financial limits on, 204; and AA claims, 205; given fourth priority, 210 – 14; French urge increase in, 231 – 2; increase discussed, 232 – 4; and 'unlimited liability', 237 – 8; and TA 'pledge', 243 – 4; and TA recruiting (1939), 248 – 9, 251 – 2; TA training for, 252 – 3

Fascists, British Union of, 153 – 4
Fisher, Admiral Sir John, 5

Fisher, Sir Warren, 210 – 11
Foreign service obligation: Volunteer objections to, 13; low acceptance rate of, 29; and the 'pledge', 35; General Staff insists on, 42; Churchill on, 49, 55, 57, 58 – 9, 118; Cabinet discusses, 55 – 7, 58 – 9; TA Associations on, 57, 61 – 2
France: and Haldane's plans, 6 – 7; in British planning, 186 – 7; and Maginot Line strength, 206; reliance on British aid, 208 – 10, 212 – 13; and Munich settlement, 231; urges more British divisions, 231 – 2; and 'unlimited liability', 238 – 9; and doubling of TA, 242; urges conscription, 246 – 7
French, Gen. Sir John, 34

Geddes, Sir Auckland, 57, 58, 248, 255
Geddes, Sir Eric, 69
Geddes Committee, 89, 93, 155; reactions to, 94 – 5; Cabinet decision on, 97 – 8
General Staff: created, 5; on TA reconstitution, 42; on aid to civil power, 67 – 8; on value of TA, 94 – 5, 96 – 7, 101, 196; urges selective TA reductions, 96 – 7; insists on AA role for TA, 101; and expeditionary force reinforcements, 125; on conscription for AA defence, 244 – 5
George, David Lloyd, 69, 73, 242 – 3
Golightly, Col. R.E., 112
Gort, General Viscount, 207, 212 – 13, 214
Grey, Sir Edward, 4, 6

Haig, Field Marshal Earl, 26, 49 – 50, 67
Haldane, Richard Burdon: appointed to War Office, 4 – 5; reform plans, 5 – 7, 10 – 11, 25 – 6; first Estimates, 7 – 8; on role of TA, 13 – 14, 19; enlists royal support, 14 – 15; optimism, 15; rejects compulsion, 20, 21; appeals to Kitchener, 31; scheme of, 260 – 1

271

limits lifted, 228
marriage allowance: partially
  established, 27, 197; and camp
  attendance, 28; full application
  urged, 155 – 9, 193, 194;
  rejected, 188; extended, 197
officers: difficulty in recruiting,
  25, 154 – 5; in reconstitution
  scheme, 44; camp allowances,
  98, 129 – 30, 197
other ranks: payment of, 27 – 8,
  189, 197; marriage allowance,
  155 – 9
pledge, the: in Great War, 35 – 6;
  and reconstitution, 45 – 6, 59,
  131 – 2; reaffirmed, 125 – 6;
  abolition discussed, 131 – 9
  passim, 198 – 9, 221 – 3; abolition
  accepted, 146, 243 – 4
reconstitution of TA, 41 – 59
  passim, 63 – 4
reductions in TA, 96 – 8, 101 – 2,
  109
relations with Regular Army, 251,
  256 – 8, 260
role of: Haldane on, 13 – 14, 19,
  20, 260; in Great War, 31 – 7; in
  reconstitution scheme, 45, 59,
  86, 131; aid to civil power, 67,
  70, 71 – 2, 73, 74, 79, 85; and
  ten year rule, 89, 123; and AA
  defence, 95, 109, 201, 205 – 6,
  237, 244 – 5; and expeditionary
  force, 190 – 2, 195, 196,
  199 – 201, 205 – 6, 207 – 9,
  211 – 12, 213 – 15, 234, 237 – 8,
  252 – 3; 'general purposes',
  220 – 1, 226, 231
staff, 25, 32 – 3, 75, 90 – 1, 93,
  251, 254 – 5
training: duration criticised, 26;
  nature criticised, 149, 216 – 19,
  252 – 3; and equipment, 151 – 2,
  215; and conscription, 254 – 5,

258 – 9
  see also Anti-aircraft defence,
  bounty, recruiting
Thwaites, Gen. Sir William, 141
Times, The, reports in, 9, 50, 57, 63,
  75, 76, 142, 152, 166, 218, 239,
  240, 248, 250, 251, 252, 253;
  leaders: critical of War Office, 63,
  118; on unlimited liability, 238;
  approved doubling of TA, 241;
  letters to, 22, 24, 50, 143, 218, 232
Trade Unions, hostile to TA, 16,
  197
Trenchard, Lord, Marshal of the
  RAF, 127
Troup, Sir Edward, 69

Vansittart, Sir Robert, 191, 210
Verney, John, 180, 181
Volunteers, 8 – 10, 12 – 13, 14, 15

Wilson, Field Marshal Sir Henry:
  on lack of role for postwar TA,
  46 – 7, 88; on reconstitution
  terms, 48, 49, 57, 58; on aid to
  civil power, 68 – 9, 72
Wilson, Sir Horace, 240 – 1
Wodley, 2nd Lt. G.H., vc, 34
Wood, Col. Evelyn, 136, 138
Worthington-Evans, Sir Laming:
  appeals for Supplementary
  Reserve, 79; rejects abolition of
  TA divisions, 91; and financial
  cuts, 97 – 8, 103, 110, 112 – 3, 122;
  abolition of bounty, 112, 119 – 21;
  rejects Associations' compromise,
  114, 119

Yeomanry: origins, 9; and creation
  of TA, 11, 12, 14; and
  reconstitution, 59; reductions of,
  92, 110; appeal of, 180; in Second
  World War, 260